CULTS, WORLD RELIGIONS and the OCCULT

CULTS, WORLD RELIGIONS and the OCCULT

Kenneth Boa

VICTOR BOOKS®

A DIVISION OF SCRIPTURE PRESS PUBLICATIONS INC.
USA CANADA ENGLAND

All Scripture quotations are from *New American Standard Bible*
© the Lockman Foundation 1960, 1962, 1963, 1968, 1971, 1972, 1973,
1975, 1977. Used by permission.

Library of Congress Cataloging-in-Publication Data

Boa, Kenneth.
  Cults, world religions, and the occult / by Kenneth Boa.
      p.   cm.
  ISBN 0-89693-823-9
      1. Includes bibliographical references. 2. Religions.
  3. Christian sects—United States. 4. Occultism—United States.
  5. Cults—United States. 6. United States—Religion—1960-
  I. Title.
  BL80.2.B62 1990
  291–dc20

5   6   7   8   9   10   Printing/Year   98   97   96   95

CONTENTS

INTRODUCTION   7
PART ONE:
Major Non-Christian Religions of the East   15
   1 Hinduism   17
   2 Jainism   25
   3 Buddhism   30
   4 Sikhism   40
   5 Zoroastrianism   44
   6 Confucianism   51
   7 Taoism   56
   8 Shintoism   61
   9 Islam   66
   10 Judaism   76
PART TWO:
Major Pseudo-Christian Religions of the West   83
   11 Mormonism   85
   12 Jehovah's Witnesses   96
   13 Christian Science   106
   14 Seventh-Day Adventism   116
   15 Unity School of Christianity   125
   16 Theosophy   131
PART THREE:
Occult Religions and Systems   139
   17 Witchcraft and Satanism   141
   18 Astrology   152
   19 Spiritualism   165
   20 The Kabbalah   173
   21 The I Ching   182
   22 The Tarot   189
PART FOUR:
New Religions and Cults   195
   23 Transcendental Meditation   197
   24 The Unification Church   210
   25 The Hare Krishna Movement   223
   26 The Way International   236
   27 The New Age Movement   246
Comparison of Cults, World Religions, and the Occult   264
BIBLIOGRAPHY   279

89516

DEDICATION

---◆---

To my mother,
Ruthelaine Boa,
with love and
gratitude.

---◆---

INTRODUCTION

The Purpose

This is the day of new religious cults and occult groups. Strange concepts that till recently were known only to a few in the West are now proliferating. Eastern mysticism and occult practices are gaining more adherents, especially among teenagers and young adults. More than ever, ours is a pluralistic society in which Christianity is no longer a consensus but just another option in a whole cafeteria of religious choices.

There are several reasons for this dramatic growth of non-Christian religions, cults, and the occult. One is the bankruptcy of the materialistic values our society has promoted. Materialism and empty humanism do not satisfy the spiritual needs that are a part of every human being, and many people are searching for some kind of personal and spiritual fulfillment. Along with this is an increasing experiential rather than factual orientation. People are trying to find meaning through emotional and mystical experiences, which are precisely the kinds of experiences offered by many religious and occult movements today.

Others turn to these movements because of loneliness, lack of personal identity, and alienation. By submitting to the teachings and requirements of the cult, they hope to find the love, acceptance, and fellowship they long for. Still others are attracted by the charisma of the authority figures in these religions or by the promise of power over one's circumstances and destiny. Some are drawn in by the exotic ideas and lifestyles represented by the various religions and cults.

While it is unfortunate that so many have turned to non-Christian sources for the fulfillment of their spiritual needs, this should not be so surprising if we remember that a large number of Christian churches have lost their spiritual vitality. They have exchanged a life-giving relationship for an external religiosity. Thus, instead of attracting those who are on a spiritual quest, some Christian churches and enterprises repel them. The current religious alternatives should be seen as a *challenge* to the Christian community to get serious about the progress of the Gospel, the good news of new life in Christ.

This book is primarily directed to Christians, particularly those who find themselves uninformed and bewildered by these religious movements. Many such Christians are either afraid to share their faith with these people or think that it would be futile to do so. However, if you are a follower of Christ who is solidly rooted in the Scriptures, you need not be afraid to present Him to anyone. This does not mean that God will call you to become a missionary to the cults, but He may give you some opportunities in this area. As these movements continue to spread, we should expect to encounter their members with increasing frequency.

Even if you do not have these opportunities, it is hoped that this presentation of some of the religious ideologies to which people are committing themselves will give you new perspectives on the needs people have and what they will do in their quest for truth. Some are willing to sacrifice their possessions, their rationality, and their volition in order to attain promised enlightenment or salvation.

There are four sections in this book. "Major Non-Christian Religions of the East" deals with world religions such as Hinduism, Buddhism, and Islam. Sikhism, Jainism, Confucianism, and Shintoism were included for completeness, even though they seem to be disappearing. The Rabbinic Judaism of today is so different from Judeo-Christianity that it is included as a separate chapter. This section is designed to give an overview of the primary religions of man still in existence.

The second section, "Major Pseudo-Christian Religions of the West," is concerned with some of the more important religious movements developed in the Western Hemisphere. Mormonism, Jehovah's Witnesses, Christian Science, and the Unity School of Christianity are all pseudo-Christian cults which originated in the United States. Though Seventh-Day Adventism is included in this section, it is not considered a cult because its current standpoint is harmonious with many of the primary doctrines of orthodox Christianity. Theosophy was created in America and England, but it does not claim to be "Christian" per se.

The third section is called "Occult Religions and Systems." This includes six of the more prevalent occultic movements, including Satanism, witchcraft, astrology, and the Tarot. These and other occult practices are often thrown together in various combinations by those who use them.

The fourth section deals with "New Religions and Cults." In America alone there are literally hundreds of new religious movements which are actively seeking converts. They come from the East and the West, and many are variations and hybrids of older religions. Dozens of these groups are popping up each year, and it would be impossible to survey more than a tiny fraction in a book of this size. Four of the most influential movements are described in this section: Transcendental Meditation, The Unification Church, The International Society for Krishna Consciousness, and the Way International. In addition, a chapter on the growing New Age movement has been included.

Each movement considered in this book is handled in three ways. First, its background and teachings are described. This is followed by a brief biblical evaluation. Points of special interest to Christians who may encounter members of the movement are also listed.

This book is designed to provide *simple and organized* information about these non-Christian and pseudo-Christian religions. It attempts to give the reader a clear understanding of the movements in a *minimum* number of pages. The assumption is that most readers will want a brief but adequate overview. The few who may wish to become experts in a particular religion or cult could begin with the appropriate chapter in this book, turn to the bibliography at the end, and go on from there.

The Principles

Each religion and cult has its own distinctives. But there are a number of general biblical principles which Christians ought to apply no matter whom they encounter. The following presentation of some of these principles is based on a crucial New Testament verse: "But sanctify Christ as Lord in your hearts, always being ready to make a defense to everyone who asks you to give an account for the hope that is in you, yet with gentleness and reverence" (1 Peter 3:15).

"But sanctify Christ as Lord in your hearts."

(1) Before you witness to another, be sure you have submitted your life to Jesus as Lord. He must be free to rule in your heart. This submission-commitment should be reinforced daily.

(2) Expect that God will work through you. Be confident in Him, not in yourself, realizing that the results must be left to Him. If you are praying for opportunities, expect God to work through you when one comes along. You may be planting a seed or watering one which has already been planted. "I planted, Apollos watered, but God was causing the growth" (1 Cor. 3:6).

(3) This is a spiritual battle, not just a battle of knowledge or cleverness. Ephesians 6:10-18 describes the kind of armor believers should wear in this warfare. Our two offensive weapons are the Word of God and prayer. Use both during any encounter with a cultist.

(4) Search for any unloving attitudes you may have and confess them so you can be used more effectively. Prepare yourself spiritually so that you will be able to personally share God's love with others. Knowledge without love will profit little (see 1 Cor. 13:1-2).

(5) Be patient—it may take hours of discussion and many encounters before the claims and credentials of Christ break through to the other person. Decide at the outset whether you are willing to invest the time it takes.

(6) Check your motivations. Are you sharing Christ out of real concern for the person or because you feel it is your duty? One can do a good thing for the wrong reasons.

"Always being ready"

(1) Part of being ready is developing a good knowledge of the Bible. This requires reading and studying the Scriptures on a regular basis. You should try to read the Bible through once a year if possible. However, avoid the extreme of thinking that you must have an exhaustive understanding of its contents before you can be an effective witness.

(2) Know how to use specific passages from the Scriptures. You won't have time to run to a concordance or a reference book when you are sharing Christ. You should always be able to present a clear biblical case for the deity and exclusive claims of Jesus Christ. Be ready to share the way of salvation from the Bible. Emphasize the problem of man's sinfulness and God's loving provision. Know how to defend the historical resurrection of Christ. It would also help to be familiar with some Old Testament messianic prophecies that were fulfilled in the life of Jesus.

(3) Be able to defend the authority of the Bible as the revealed Word of God. There are good books which can help you in this kind of defense.

(4) Be ready to straighten out misconceptions about the meaning of Christianity. Many who are in the cults have rejected a caricature of Christianity, which they find unappealing because of their distorted perception about its teaching and the person and work of Jesus. It is often necessary to explain what Christianity is *not* before you can effectively explain what it *is*.

(5) It helps to have some understanding of the teaching

of a particular religion or cult, especially if you have regular contact with a representative. You may want to obtain some of the official materials published by the cult.

"To make a defense"

(1) Don't allow yourself to get sidetracked into minor issues. Always focus on the cardinal doctrines about Christ and His work of salvation. Stress the uniqueness of Jesus Christ. Do not waste time on peripheral doctrines or strange customs and dress.

(2) Never let a cultist use biblical proof texts out of context to support his cult's doctrines. Make him look at passages in both the immediate and broad contexts. Scripture is its own best interpreter, and clear passages should always be used to illuminate unclear passages.

(3) Remember your need for reliance on the convicting and regenerating ministry of the Holy Spirit. Pray that He works in this way through you during your conversation. If your witnessing is not done in His power, you are wasting your time.

(4) Clearly distinguish between salvation by works and salvation by grace through faith. Every non-Christian religion and cult teaches some kind of works-approach to salvation or enlightenment. It may be meditation, devotional service, or moral living, but it demands human works. Because of this, no one but a biblical Christian can really be sure of his condition after death. No form of works will be sufficient to please the Holy God. A sinner cannot atone for his own sins, or anyone else's, even if he is reincarnated a million times.

(5) Some cultists may claim that their position is not essentially different from Christianity; the problem is just one of semantics. But you must not let them minimize the radical differences, particularly when it comes to the question of who God is, who man is, and who Jesus Christ is. You must be ready to use the Scriptures lovingly but firmly. Read clear passages and let the Bible speak for itself.

(6) Many cultists appeal to a superior experience.

When this happens, emphasize that experience alone can be quite misleading, no matter how intense. Satanists have powerful experiences but this does not mean that God is working through them. The truth of God's Word must be primary, and experience secondary. Experience should always be based on truth; truth is not determined by one's experiences.

(7) If you give a cultist any books or other material to read, be sure you have read it first. Make sure it is not written in an offensive or harsh tone. If you use literature, don't let it become a substitute for your use of the Bible itself.

"To every one who asks you"

(1) Pray for opportunities in which people will ask you about your faith in Christ.

(2) It is wise to ask good questions and listen carefully to the answers. This will help you understand the basic position of the religion or cult being represented. Ask penetrating questions of information and clarification. Your interest will not only increase their respect for you and your position, but it will also give you the understanding you need. Miscommunication can be a two-way street, and because of it Christians sometimes overlook the crucial issues and concentrate on the minor ones.

"To give an account for the hope that is in you"

(1) Though you are not building the case for Christianity on your own testimony, it is often appropriate to use your personal experience to illustrate the power of Jesus' claims.

(2) The hope that is in you should be evident from your love and concern which springs from your vital personal relationship with God.

"Yet with gentleness and reverence"

(1) The word "gentleness" tells us to be loving and patient when we defend the hope that is within us. Even if we bear witness to Christ, it is dishonoring to Him if we do it in an unloving manner. Do not quarrel when witnessing. "Reverence" tells us to treat the other person

with respect. He is a person created in the image of God and one for whom Christ died. According to 2 Corinthians 4:4, "The god of this world has blinded the minds of the unbelieving, that they might not see the light of the Gospel of the glory of Christ, who is the image of God." Christ's love working through you is the light which can dispel this satanic blindness.

(2) Look for areas of common ground to establish personal points of contact. There is some truth in any religion or cult, otherwise no one would be attracted to it. Try to identify points of commonality and move from there. One common area is that of human needs. Try to find out why the person joined the cult and tell how Christ can better meet that need.

(3) Whenever possible, it is desirable to witness on a one-to-one basis. Cultists usually like to work in teams of two or more, however, and this seriously hampers the chances of getting through to them.

P A R T   O N E

Major Non-Christian Religions of the East

People who do not revere the Creator-God are nevertheless bound to worship some object of their ultimate concern. It is as much a part of our created nature to worship as to eat and sleep. But an abnormality called sin has invaded God's noble creation. The first and most serious sin anyone commits is to worship and serve the creation rather than the Creator (see Rom. 1:25).

We may pity the aboriginal man who worships his carved bit of stone. However, when unenlightened by the Holy Spirit, we all do the same thing in principle. We may practice a highly sophisticated religion, or we may worship the material work of our hands, but such worship is like the skyrocket we shoot up into the sky. It explodes and we marvel at its glory. In the same way we applaud our self-made objects of ultimate concern (worship).

One of the dominant principles that Eastern man has accepted for millennia is the absolute unity of all reality. In its various refinements we call this principle *monism:* "all is one." Particulars and distinctions within the universe are perceived as illusory, including the distinctiveness of deity. The result is that *pantheism* ("all is God") pervades the life of many in the East. Indeed we shall notice later in this book that monism and pantheism emerge vigorously in Western forms of nontheistic religion as well as in the religions of Asia.

A form of monotheism exists in some Eastern religions (e.g., Zoroastrianism, Islam, and Amidism). We observe that the founders of these religions came directly or indirectly under the outside influence of ideas contained in the previous biblical monotheism of the Hebrews, or of ideas contained in the Christian Gospel. Anthropologists have recently noted that variant religions do not "evolve" within a culture. Monotheism does not grow out of polytheism, as once thought, but such a change is imported from the outside.

Sometimes monists inconsistently worship a variety of lesser deities, as in Hinduism. Others refine the monistic idea into either a spiritualized or secularized humanism in which all truth and values are effectively reduced to a system of relativity. Buddha was outspokenly monistic and humanistic. Though Confucius was not manifestly "religious," his philosophy is based on the humanist folk religions and nature cults of China. Ironically, the Chinese elevated Confucius himself to godhood.

1

HINDUISM

Background and Teachings

Hinduism is difficult to describe because it has absorbed innumerable customs and concepts and has branched off into many other religions, some radically different from their source. There are so many schools of Hindu thought today that almost anything we say about this vast religion must be qualified.

The earliest stage of Hinduism is usually called the pre-Vedic period, beginning about 3,000 years ago. Little is known about the pre-Vedic Indians who lived in the Indus Valley of northern India and the Dravidians who populated the Indian peninsula. By the time of Abraham, they had developed a civilization similar to that of the early Mesopotamians. Their polytheistic religion, a sort of proto-Hinduism, was in some ways like early witchcraft.

The pre-Vedic Hindus especially worshiped a Mother Goddess and a horned god in the posture of a yogi. They also offered sacrifices to the various gods, but they did not have temples.

The Vedic period began around 1500 B.C., when a central Asian people called Aryans invaded northern India and progressively pressed toward the south. These light-skinned conquerors imposed their Vedic civilization and religion on the Indians. Vedic religion differed greatly from the Dravidian religion—the Aryans worshiped the powers of nature rather than images. The most important of their gods were Indra, a god of the atmosphere and stars; Varuna, a sky god; and Agni, the fire god. There were many other gods, one of which was Soma, the god of the soma plant.

The Aryans developed an elaborate system of sacrifices which later led to the formation of a priesthood (the Brahmans). They also absorbed the Dravidian gods and concepts into their religion, and this assimilation resulted in a complicated array of gods and goddesses.

The Vedic period was followed by the Upanishadic period, about 600 B.C. During this time Hinduism began dividing into the popular religion of the masses and a more philosophical religion. The Upanishads were sacred books which reinterpreted the Vedic religion and boiled all the gods down into a single principle or absolute universal soul. This monistic or pantheistic viewpoint held that the universe is God, and God is the universe. The impersonal universal soul was called Brahman, and this form of Hinduism was called Brahmanism.

During the Upanishadic period, the Hindu concept of salvation shifted from an emphasis on fulfillment and on life to an emphasis on release and escape from life. Life on earth began to be viewed quite pessimistically as the doctrines of *karma* and *samsara* grew.

The law of karma was a moral law of cause and effect which could not be violated. It was called the "the law of the deed," and one could build either good or evil karma.

The doctrine of samsara—transmigration—taught that all life goes through an endless succession of rebirths. *Every* living thing is on the wheel of life, and each new rebirth depends on the karma built up in its past lives. Salvation—breaking away from this wheel—could be achieved by philosophical speculation on the words of the sages and by meditation. Release and liberation from the wheel of life *(moksha* or *mukti)* would finally come when one realized his individual soul *(the Atman)* was identical with the universal soul (Brahman).

Hinduism was now so philosophical in theory and so corrupt and legalistic in practice that reform movements arose within it. Two of the most prominent were Buddhism and Jainism. Another reform was a movement back to the worship of a supreme personal God. Not that Hinduism became monotheistic; polytheism was never really eliminated. Instead, a triad of Hindu gods was often used to represent the impersonal and absolute Brahman (neuter). Brahma (the masculine form of the word *Brahman)* was regarded as the Creator, Vishnu as the Preserver, and Shiva as the Destroyer.

Many Hindus (called Vishnuites) chose to worship the god Vishnu and his 10 incarnations. These incarnations, called *avatars,* or descents of God to earth to save the world from grave perils, were a fish, an amphibian, a boar, a man-lion, a dwarf, Parasurama, Rama, Krishna, Buddha, and Kalkin, who is yet to come. The seventh and eighth incarnations of Vishnu—Rama and Krishna—are the most important and are worshiped more than Vishnu himself.

Other Hindus (called Shivaites) worship the god Shiva and his wife, who is variously represented as Durga, Kali, Sati, Parvati, Deva, and others. Many of these representations, especially Kali, are quite sinister and bloodthirsty. Among the Kali worshipers is a cult known as the Shakti, which encourages such immoral practices as temple prostitution.

After the time of Christ, philosophical Hinduism was

dominated by Vedantic thought. The *Vedanta,* a philo-sophical Hindu book based on the earlier Upanishads, teaches that man needs liberation. Individuals go through stages of wanting pleasure and worldly success. If they mature, their desires may turn to self-renunciation and moral duty *(dharma).* But the deepest need, whether people recognize it or not, is for liberation *(moksha).*

Moksha occurs when a person extends his being *(sat),* awareness *(chit),* and bliss *(ananda)* to an infinite level. Since Brahman, the impersonal absolute, is infinite being, awareness, and bliss, the only way a man can attain *moksha* is to come to the realization that his hidden self *(atman)* is actually the same as Brahman. A common phrase used to describe this is "Thou art that" *(tat twam asi).* Salvation is therefore achieved by detachment from the finite self and attachment to reality as a whole. This is when a person reaches *nirvana,* a state of passionless peace.

Three basic approaches are used to achieve this salva-tion. (1) Salvation by knowledge *(Jnana Yoga)* is acquired by listening to the sages and the scriptures, practicing meditation by turning awareness inward, and realizing the Atman-Brahman identity. (2) Salvation by devotion *(Bhakti Yoga)* is less philosophical and more popular. In this technique, God is thought of in a more personal way. The devotee chooses a particular manifestation of God, and hopes to break through to a union with God. (3) To gain salvation by correct works *(Karma Yoga),* one must perform ceremonies, sacrifices, pilgrimages, and other good actions without attachment or desire for their rewards. All of these methods may in varying degrees also involve *Raja Yoga,* an involved technique of medita-tion which includes control over the body, breathing, and the thoughts. The main goal of Yoga is *samadhi,* a union between the devotee and the Absolute.

Hindu philosophy regards this world as an intermedi-ate place, a training ground for the soul. There are innu-merable galaxies and other worlds like our own, and the moral law of karma pervades all. The universe goes through endless temporal cycles during which it is repeatedly created and destroyed.

In an ultimate sense, however, this world with its pleasures and pains, its rights and wrongs, is all deceptive. It is all *maya* or illusion, because all things are really one. Why does the universe exist at all? It is *lila*, a great game played by God, the cosmic dance of the divine.

In the 19th century, some reform movements again sprang up within Hinduism. One of these was the Brahma Samaj, founded by Ram Mohan Ray, which was influenced to some extent by Christianity. Another reform movement, the Arya Samaj, also promoted social reform but was much more militant in its adherence to Hinduism.

Hinduism also went through a sort of renaissance, which began in the last half of the 19th century and continued into the 20th. Ramakrishna and his disciple Vivekenanda began a movement now known as the Ramakrishna Mission (also called the Vedanta Society). This movement stresses the unity of all religions, but emphasizes Vedantic Hinduism above all others, with a missionary zeal.

Other modern names of importance in Hinduism are Rabindranath Tagore, Mahatma Ghandhi, Sri Aurobindo, and Radhakrishnan.

Most of what we have been describing is *philosophical Hinduism*. We should keep in mind that the Hinduism of the masses is very different. Popular Hinduism emphasizes the observance of the caste system. The four original castes or stations of life were the Brahmans (priests), the Kshatriyas (warriors and rulers), the Vaisyas (craftsmen, farmers, artisans), and the Sudras (laborers, servants). Below these were the outcastes, or "untouchables." These social and occupational groups have now been further divided into about 3,000 subcastes.

Another strong element in popular Hinduism is worship of the images of many gods. There are several levels of gods and goddesses ranging from the supreme triad of Brahma, Vishnu, and Shiva, to such lesser vedic gods as Indra and Agni, down to a host of village gods, demigods, demons, and genii. Hinduism of the masses is an extremely idolatrous and polytheistic religion, as evidenced by the millions of gods and innumerable temples and cults. Religious practices include pilgrimages, food restrictions, special postures and gestures, possession by the gods, sacred places, recitation of sacred formulas, phallic emblems, and geometrical patterns. India abounds with spiritual teachers *(gurus)* and wandering holy men *(sadhus* and *swamis)*. Indians are immersed in folklore and legends about the exploits of the various gods and goddesses.

As we shall see in part four of this book, the growing contemporary influence of Hinduism in the West has been accelerated by movements such as Transcendental Meditation, Hare Krishna, and the New Age movement.

Here are some of the important scriptures of Hinduism. There are many books and they often contradict one another:

	Vedas (Rig-Veda, Sama-Veda, Yajur-Veda, Atharva-Veda)
Sruti	Brahmanas
revealed scripture (canonical)	Aranyakas
	Upanishads
	Bhagavad Gita (the last part of the Mahabharata)
	Sutras
	Codes of Law
Smriti	Agamas
tradition (semicanonical)	Mahabharata
	Ramayana
	Darshanas
	Puranas

Biblical Evaluation

(1) In philosophical Hinduism, God is generally an It, not a Person as in the Bible.

(2) In popular Hinduism, there are great multitudes of gods and goddesses. This is polytheistic and idolatrous in practice.

(3) Popular Hinduism also abounds in immoral practices, superstition, fear, and occultism. Demon worship and possession by the gods can also be found.

(4) The caste system is rigid, unjust, and cruel. There were very few attempts to reform this system before the time when Hinduism was influenced by Christian ideas.

(5) There is no recognition of sin and moral guilt. Sin is an illusion. In an ultimate sense, man is God. He is therefore not separated from God by his sin, as the Bible teaches.

(6) Hinduism is a works system. Forgiveness of sin does not fit into the picture of karma (the law of cause and effect). Each person has many lives in which to achieve salvation. There is a slow, evolving process toward the highest.

(7) Hinduism denies the exclusive claims of Christ and despises the Christian teaching that Christ is the only way to God.

Things to Keep in Mind

(1) Various forms of Hinduism (particularly vedantic ideas) have become popular with young people in America. The most important issue that must be handled is the Hindu argument that all religions are the same. Many Hindus feel their religion is vastly superior to Christianity because it is more tolerant. Christians should point out that the vedantic view of God also represents a particular religion and that it cannot include the unique claims of Christ. Hinduism can no more "tolerate" biblical Christianity than biblical Christianity can tolerate Hinduism.

(2) Christians should not only emphasize the unique claims of Christ, but should connect these with the fact

that no other religion offers a real solution to the problem of *sin*. Only the substitutionary work of Christ adequately copes with man's sinfulness. Hinduism only covers up the problem by calling sin an illusion.

(3) We must be careful to explain all our terms, because many "religious" words have a different meaning to the Hindu.

(4) Another important approach to take is that of authority. The Hindu must be asked what group or teaching within Hinduism he represents. He may respond by referring to the many different groups within Christianity, but the essential issue is still *authority*. All the books of the Bible present a harmonious picture of God's plan of redemption; most of the Hindu scriptures contradict one another. A Hindu cannot consistently accept all of the Hindu scriptures because of their many contradictions.

2

JAINISM

Background and Teaching

Jainism is almost nonexistent outside of India, and even in India it has relatively few followers (about 1½ million). But it exerts an influence disproportionate to its size.

Jainism is regarded by some as a sect within Hinduism and by others as a separate religion. It was founded about 32 years before Buddhism, and both religions began as reformation movements within Hinduism.

Mahavira (great hero), also called Jina (conqueror), lived in the sixth century B.C. He is credited with founding Jainism. Mahavira was born into the ruling caste (the Kshatriya) and lived a life of luxury until he renounced it when he was about 30. For 12 years he went to such extremes in self-mortification and meditation that he allegedly reached nirvana. He spent his remaining 30 years as an omniscient being *(kevali)*, teaching his followers.

By the time of his death, Mahavira had established large monastic groups, and one of these orders survived to carry on this religion. As time went on, Jainism divided into three sects. The Digambara (sky-clad) sect forsook *all* clothing, but the Shvetambara (white-clad) sect allowed the wearing of white clothes. The Sthanakavasi sect later rose as a reformation against idol worship in Jainism. Each of these three sects has a different list of canonical scriptures. The general name for the body of sacred books in Jainism is *Agamas* (precepts). The list of books varies from 33 to 84 depending on the sect.

The Jains believe that their religion is older than even Hinduism because Mahavira was the 24th and last Thirthankara (a saint; one who knows virtue). The religion is supposed to have begun in the remote past with the first Thirthankara, named Rishabha. The idea is that Mahavira was the organizer, systematizer, and reformer, but not the originator.

The goal of all Jains is to become Jinas (victors) as Mahavira did, for only then can they be delivered from the cycle of rebirth. Jainism is an atheistic religion in the sense that it denies the existence of a Supreme Being or Creator, along with all supernatural powers. Jains think of the Hindu gods as only a little greater than man.

Because of their antisupernaturalism, the Jains' view of salvation is humanistic. Man must rely on his own resources. It is foolish to look to any outside forces for help. Relief from suffering and escape from rebirth can only be achieved by severe self-discipline and asceticism.

According to Jainism, the universe is uncreated and eternal. It consists of two independent and eternal categories: the living *(jiva)* and the nonliving *(ajiva)*. The living is soul and the nonliving is matter. Jains believe that everything possesses a living soul.

Though they never explain how this happened, Jains assert that each *jiva* (living soul) is constantly bound to *ajiva* (nonliving matter) by karma, the subtle material that keeps the soul in bondage to matter. Salvation *(kaivalya)* consists of releasing the soul from matter, which can be accomplished only by stopping new karma and by ridding the soul of existing karma. Jainism's monastic system is designed to stop new karma by the practice of activities which prevent its inflow.

The "three jewels" of Jainism are right knowledge, right faith, and right conduct. Right knowledge means an understanding of Jain philosophy. Right faith means belief in the Jain scriptures. Right conduct involves several things, of which the most important are noninjury *(ahimsa)* and asceticism *(tapas)*.

Jainism has carried *ahimsa* so far that it has become the best-known characteristic of the religion. Jain monks sweep the paths in front of them as they walk in order to avoid killing insects. They strain all the water they drink and examine all their food before they eat it. They are strict vegetarians, but admit that even the vegetables, fruits, and nuts they eat have life. So they must confess their sins daily and minimize them by eating nonsentient living forms. Since most work involves the inadvertent killing of small forms of life, serious Jains are limited to few occupations (for example, banking and insurance).

Though it contradicts the Jain doctrine of noninjury, the ultimate act of asceticism is to starve oneself to death, thus assuring sainthood or liberation.

Other rules of right conduct are the practice of austerities, truthfulness, nonstealing, chastity, and nonattachment of this world or matter.

Biblical Evaluation
(1) Jainism is an egocentric rather than a God-centered religion. It completely rejects the supernatural in favor of an uncreated, eternal, dualistic universe of matter and soul. There is no place in Jainism for a personal God.

(2) There is no mercy or grace in Jainism, only works. It has developed one of the most severe systems of legalism the world has ever known.

(3) Jainism is ritualism rather than relationship, legalism rather than liberty. Even love is rooted out because it produces attachments. Each person is ultimately concerned about his own efforts, not the struggles of other climbers.

(4) This religion is characterized by pessimism, not hope.

(5) It has no place for the weak, the lame, or the young. Only the strong can obtain salvation.

(6) It is a social and spiritual failure. It has not been able to eliminate castes, and it has never purged itself of its temples or the idolatry and polytheism it denounces. Jains actually worship and pray to the 24 Thirthankaras, and their temples are full of their idols.

Things to Keep in Mind

Few of us will ever meet Jains since almost all of them live in India. However, they have established the World Jain Mission, an organization which seeks to spread Jainism to other countries by means of literature. Much of this literature is in English, and it particularly stresses the principle of right conduct.

The practical Western mind may find this emphasis on right conduct appealing and it is therefore conceivable that Jainist literature could win some acceptance here. Should you encounter someone who is being influenced by Jainism, keep the following points in mind:

(1) The *ahimsa* concept is not really workable since there is no way a human being can avoid killing living organisms by the millions. Even though some Jains strain their drinking water to save small insects, they nevertheless kill millions of microscopic organisms with every cupful. Therefore it is humanly impossible to avoid the influx of new karma; if the system is logically consistent, no one can attain liberation short of dying by starvation or thirst. Some Jains see this problem and hope to get around it by daily confession. But to whom or to what do they confess?

(2) Jains have no clear and consistent authority for their doctrines. The three sects do not agree on what books are canonical. None of their books was put in permanent written form much before A.D. 500, about 1,000 years after Mahavira's death.

(3) It is interesting that Jains now claim *ahimsa* is a positive precept of universal love. This concept is not to be found in their scriptures, and it can be directly traced to a Christian influence in the modern writing of Jains. In actual practice, the injunctions of Jainism are negative, and they can be followed only by ascetics.

(4) The problem of sin is important in this religion, and even though it is defined differently in Jainism, Christians can still use this as a point of contact to build on. The issue is whether a sinner can atone for his own sins by works of noninjury and asceticism.

3

---◆---

BUDDHISM

---◆---

Background and Teachings

Buddhism, like Jainism, began as a reformation movement within Hinduism. Its founder was Siddhartha Gautama, who was born about 560 B.C. in the Kshatriya (ruler, warrior) caste of Hinduism. His father, Suddhodana, was a feudal lord, and his mother's name was Maya. When Gautama was 16 or 19, he married the princess Yasodharma and later had a son named Rahula. Gautama's life was one of luxury, but he grew dissatisfied in his 20s.

The legend of the Four Passing Sights tells how he became aware of the world's suffering in spite of his parents' efforts to keep him away from the rest of the world. He saw an old man, a person suffering from a disease, a dead man, and a shaven monk. He saw for the first time that great suffering exists, and chose a path of renunciation.

When Gautama was 29, he abandoned his family and began his "great going forth" in search of enlightenment. He first subjected himself to Hindu masters and then decided to become a complete ascetic. For about six years he practiced self-mortification and finally came close to the point of death.

When Gautama realized the futility of asceticism, he developed the principle of the Middle Path. He kept himself away from the two extremes of asceticism and indulgence and practiced deep meditation. During one of these periods of meditation, while sitting under a fig tree, he reached a state of enlightenment. He had entered nirvana while still alive. At that time (525 B.C.) he became the Buddha, the Enlightened One, and the tree under which he sat came to be known as the Bo or Bodhi (Wisdom) Tree.

For the next 45 years, Gautama built a large core of disciples and proclaimed his message in northern India. His disciples knew him not only as the Buddha, but also as Sakayamuni (the sage of the Sakyas), Tathagata (the one who comes thus), the Truth-Winner, and Bhagara (Lord).

He died of food poisoning when he was about 80 (ca. 480 B.C.).

Gautama's approach to religion was quite different from the Hinduism out of which he had come. Hinduism had degenerated on the one hand to empty philosophical speculations and disputes, and on the other hand to a crass form of polytheism, rituals, magic, and superstition. Authority for truth was the special possession of the highest caste. Gautama attacked the caste system and rejected all forms of speculation, ritual, and occultism.

Buddhism is built on the Four Noble Truths: (1) Life is full of pain and suffering *(dukkha)*. This is especially evident in birth, sickness, decay, death, the presence of hated things, and separation from loved things. Even the forces which hold life together *(skandas)* are full of suffering. These include the body, the senses, thoughts, feelings, and consciousness. (2) Suffering is caused by *tanha,* the desire or thirst for pleasure, existence, and prosperity. (3) Suffering can be overcome by eliminating these cravings. (4) This is done by following the Eightfold Path.

The Eightfold Path is a system of therapy designed to develop habits which will release people from the restrictions caused by ignorance and craving. Each follower must join an order *(the Sangha)* and associate with other disciples of Buddha. The Eightfold Path consists of: (1) right knowledge (the Four Noble Truths), (2) right aspirations (intentions), (3) right speech (overcoming falsehood and promoting truth), (4) right conduct, (5) right livelihood (certain occupations must not be followed, such as slave trader, tax collector, or butcher), (6) right effort, (7) right mindfulness (self-analysis), and (8) right meditation (the techniques of Raja Yoga).

Right conduct (number 4) includes the five precepts forbidding killing, stealing, lying, adultery, and drinking intoxicants. Five additional precepts are followed during some holy seasons and by some monasteries: do not eat at forbidden times; do not dance, listen to music, or attend theatrical plays; do not indulge in personal adornment (cosmetics or jewelry); do not use a broad or high bed; do not receive gold or silver.

Each member of a Sangha must also have a shaven head, wear a yellow robe, practice meditation, and affirm the Three Refuges: (1) I take refuge in the Buddha, (2) the Dharma (doctrine), and (3) the Sangha (the order).

The goal of each Buddhist is the attainment of the state of nirvana. Though this word means "to extinguish" or "to blow out," it does not imply annihilation but means a release from suffering, desire, and the finite self. Gautama's original teaching was that nirvana is not God or heaven, for his system has no place for deity. The Absolute is completely impersonal, and salvation is attained solely by self-effort.

Gautama carried over the twin Hindu teachings of transmigration *(samsara)* and karma into his doctrines. However, he modified the meaning of transmigration by claiming that men have no souls *(anatta)*. There is no enduring self or no actual substance *(anicca)* which goes through rebirth, but only a set of feelings, impressions, and present moments. All external reality is illusion *(maya)*. The goal of the Buddhist saint *(arhat)* is to become independent of the causal realm of nature, to have total awareness and total being. This is enlightenment.

Gautama listed 5 mental hazards and 10 fetters which must be overcome before the saint can reach his goal. Some of these fetters are: belief in a self, belief in efficacy of good works, desire for a future life in heaven, pride, and ignorance. When a person finally attains nirvana he is freed from further rebirth and from the law of karma.

After Gautama's death, Buddhism developed slowly in northwest India until about 265 B.C., when it was received by Asoka, the emperor of India. Asoka was responsible for dramatically accelerating the growth of Buddhism in India and for spreading it to other countries. Buddhism became a missionary religion and it quickly advanced throughout Asia.

Even before Buddhism reached other countries, however, it had divided into conservative and liberal schools of thought. The conservative form of Buddhism is known as Theravada (The Way of the Elders), or Hinayana (The Lesser Vehicle) Buddhism. It is also known as Southern Buddhism because it was strongest in Sri Lanka, Burma, Thailand, and Cambodia. Theravada Buddhism follows the original canon of scripture which is written in the Pali language and is called the Tripitaka, or Three Baskets. It consists of the Vinaya (the law and rules of monastic Buddhism), the Sutra (the sermons and teachings of Buddha), and the Adhidharma (philosophical interpretations of Buddha's teachings). First transmitted orally, the Tripitaka was not reduced to written form until about four centuries after Gautama's death.

The liberal school of Buddhism is called Mahayana (The Greater Vehicle) Buddhism, or Northern Buddhism. It was strongest in Nepal, China, Korea, Japan, Tibet, and Indonesia. There are so many clear contrasts between Theravada (Hinayana) and Mahayana Buddhism that they are more like two separate religions than two branches of the same faith. Here are a few contrasts:

Theravada conservatively holds to the Pali canon and the early accounts of Gautama's teachings; Mahayana is more liberal and simply emphasizes Buddha's life.

Theravada is concerned with insight and wisdom *(bodhi)*; Mahayana is concerned with feelings and compassion *(karuna)*.

Theravada teaches that each man is on his own and salvation must be reached by self-effort; Mahayana teaches that the salvation of one person is dependent on the grace of others.

Theravada is the path of the few because it centers on renunciation and the monastic system. This is why it is called The Lesser Vehicle; only a few can hope to achieve nirvana. Mahayana is the path of the many (The Greater Vehicle) because it can be followed by laymen.

The ideal of Theravada is the saint *(arhat)*, and Buddha is seen as an *arhat*. The ideal of Mahayana is Buddhahood (Buddha is seen as a savior, not just a saint) or the Bodhisattva. A Bodhisattva is one who comes to the verge of nirvana but renounces it in order to become a helper or a savior of mankind.

In Mahayana, salvation is achieved by placing faith in Gautama (who has been elevated to a deity) and the many Bodhisattvas. This is done partly by repeating and calling on their names. (Incidentally, Mahayana has developed a whole line of Buddhas, all of whom go back to Dharmakaya, the eternal Buddha. The next Buddha to come is Maitreya.)

Note that Buddha himself was a professed non-theist and humanist. The emergence of the doctrine of his deity 700 years later is therefore a betrayal of Buddha's own convictions. Just as European art and sculpture were now being accepted in northwest India, so also elements of the Christian Gospel were being "borrowed" even by those who did not convert to Christianity. Cross-indoctrination has been a common phenomenon throughout the history of world religions. The invasion of early Christianity by Gnostic ideas is an example.

Theravada tries to avoid cosmological speculations; Mahayana has introduced graphic portrayals of heavens and hells.

Theravada is essentially atheistic; Mahayana is polytheistic and idolatrous.

Theravada uses only the Three Baskets (the original Buddhist scriptures); Mahayana Buddhism has added many books to the canon.

Unfortunately, most of these foregoing descriptions of Mahayana can be only general, for Mahayanism has many forms, sects, and subsects. The difference between some of the sects is sometimes as great as the difference between Theravada and Mahayana Buddhism. We can touch on only a few of the most important sects of Mahayana Buddhism.

(1) *Pure Land Buddhism.* Buddhism reached China shortly after the time of Christ, but it did not grow much until the fourth century, when Buddhism spread to Korea. Korea introduced it to Japan in the 6th century. Interestingly, as Buddhism spread to other countries, it began to decline in its native India. By the 13th century it had practically disappeared there. Most of it was reabsorbed into Hinduism since Mahayanism lost many of its distinctives as it moved away from Gautama's original teachings.

Pure Land Buddhism, which became popular in China

and Japan, focuses on a Buddha called Amitabha in India, Omito Fu in China, and Amida in Japan. Salvation consists of placing faith in Amida Buddha and chanting his name, whereby one can reach the Pure Land, a paradise created in the West by Amida. This form of Mahayanism appeals to the masses because of its approach to salvation and its vivid descriptions of heaven and hell.

The later development of Amida Buddhism by Honen in the 12th and 13th Christian centuries bears some similarity in form to Christianity. It does not seem likely that Buddhism took on these revisions as a matter of chance, but rather that primitive Buddhism had by now borrowed these new elements from the Christian Gospel which was then spreading eastward.

(2) *Zen Buddhism.* This is almost the exact opposite of Pure Land Buddhism, and is in fact much closer to Theravada Buddhism. In Zen, salvation can only be achieved through the self. Its adherents seek to go beyond the limitations of language and reason, and look for a supernatural experience or flash of intuition known as *satori.*

The word *zen* is the Japanese equivalent of the Chinese word *ch'an*, which in turn is a translation of the Sanskrit word *dhyana. Dhyana* refers to meditation that leads to insight. Zen Buddhists practice seated meditation *(zazen)* using the lotus posture. They also use a number of irrational problems *(koans)* to baffle the mind of the meditator. These eventually exhaust reason and open the way for the intuitive flash *(satori).* Though Zen is very individualistic, the serious student must follow a Zen master, with whom he consults concerning his meditation (this is called *sanzen*).

Zen has had a profound influence on Japanese culture, including landscape painting and gardening, flower arrangement, and the tea ceremony. It has also become popular in America in recent years.

(3) *Nichiren Buddhism.* Nichiren (1222–1282) based this form of Buddhism on the Sutra of the Lotus of Truth. He

attacked every other form of Buddhism in Japan, claiming that salvation could be found only in the Lotus Sutra. This continues to be a nationalistic, militant, and emotional sect of Buddhism.

(4) *Tibetan Buddhism (Lamaism)*. Buddhism reached Tibet around the seventh century. There it combined with the occult and magical religion of Tibet to form a special sect of Buddhism known as Lamaism—the priests of this religion are called lamas. At the head of this hierarchical system is the Dali Lama, a man who is worshiped as an incarnation of a Bodhisattva. Lamaism also involves the worship of many Buddhas, Bodhisattvas, and demons. Its adherents use prayer wheels, mills, rituals, and secret formulas.

The rise of Communism has seriously affected Buddhism in most Asian countries. In China, for example, the Buddhist influence on culture has diminished greatly because of Communism. World Buddhism continues to grow, however.

Biblical Evaluation
(1) As we have noted, there are many different forms of Buddhism in the world today. In Japan alone there are about 200 sects and subsects. Therefore, anything said about Buddhism as a whole must be very general in view of all the opposing schools of thought and practice.

(2) No form of Buddhism has a place for the biblical doctrines of God, man, sin, salvation, or resurrection. Most Buddhist sects are either polytheistic, pantheistic, or atheistic.

(3) Some sects have abandoned rationality altogether (Zen Buddhism), while others have developed superficial similarities to Christianity. Amida Buddhism, for example, speaks about salvation by faith, not works. It uses such terms as the new birth and changed lives. Satan has developed many counterfeits of Christianity, but none of them really confronts and overcomes the problem of sin.

Things to Keep in Mind

(1) The Christian must overcome many barriers as he attempts to share the Gospel with Buddhists, no matter what sect or subsect of Buddhism he encounters. Therefore, the believer must rely on the guidance and power of the Holy Spirit. Because the issue of sin is dulled in Buddhism, Christians who witness to Buddhists should pray for the effectual ministry of the Holy Spirit in convicting unbelievers of sin, righteousness, and judgment.

(2) If a Christian has the opportunity to work regularly with Buddhists in America or abroad, he has the corresponding responsibility to study and understand the form(s) of Buddhism he is confronting. He should ask honest, friendly questions for information and clarification. In this way a Christian can determine the exact beliefs of the other person and demonstrate his genuine interest in him at the same time. He can determine the Buddhist's view of God and salvation (that is, whether it is through self-effort or the help of another).

(3) The believer should look for common ground and build on it as much as possible. A positive and clear presentation of the claims of Christ and His victory over sin and death is far more effective than a critique of the weaknesses of Buddhism. This does not mean that the believer should be unaware of these weaknesses, for there are times when they must be brought up. Here are three:

(a) Buddhist scriptures and sayings attributed to Gautama were written about four centuries after Buddha's death. There is no way to be sure these are really Gautama's words. By the time they were written Buddhism was split into opposing sects.

(b) What form of Buddhism does one adhere to? The differences among the sects of Buddhism are greater than those found among many religions. The question of authority is very important here.

(c) Christ offers the genuine, original salvation of the eternal God. Though some Buddhists (e.g., Amida) have more recently deified a figure they call "Lord Buddha," remember that Buddha himself said at the end of his life, "Buddhas do but point the way— work out your salvation with diligence."

(4) One real difficulty the Christian must be prepared to handle is the exclusiveness of the claims of Christ.

(5) Another difficulty which must be faced in such countries as Japan is the way Buddhism has become embedded in the culture. It is often more a way of life than a religion.

4

S I K H I S M

Background and Teachings

Sikhism began as a late reform movement in Hinduism about the same time as the Protestant Reformation. It was founded by Nanak (1469–1538), who was born a Hindu of the Kshatriya (ruler, warrior) caste in northern India.

Nanak was strongly influenced in his youth by itinerant holy men who taught and proselytized in the villages of India. Some of these men represented the Bhakti school of Hinduism and others were spreading the Sufi form of Islam.

When Nanak was 36, he abandoned his family so that he could fully absorb himself in prayer, fasting, and meditation. When he concluded that all religions were using different names for the one true God, he began to spread this message during several missionary journeys. He proclaimed, "There is no Hindu and no Muslim!" Nanak's name for God was Sat Nam (True Name). Sikhs ("disciples") believe that sins are removed by repeating and meditating on this name.

Nanak wanted to rid religion of ritualism, ceremonies, self-mortification, and pilgrimages. For him, salvation consisted of a combination of grace and works. Because the ideas of karma and transmigration were carried into Sikhism, righteous living is required, in addition to the grace of Sat Nam, to achieve salvation.

Sikhism developed an abstract and mystical monotheism which in some ways borders on pantheism. God is regarded as formless, sovereign, unknowable, and absolute, yet a righteous person can call on the grace of Sat Nam. If a person reaches salvation, he is absorbed into God. This concept of absorption into the Absolute is Hinduistic, but the ideas of submission to God and action as a means of salvation are Islamic.

Nanak denounced many Hindu practices such as idol worship, caste, sacrifices, and infanticide, but he never officially broke with Hinduism. He replaced Hindu ritualism with a need for obedience to the divine guru (teacher), Sat Nam. But the will of the divine guru is made known through special human gurus, and Nanak was the first of these. He was followed by nine other gurus.

Under the leadership of the gurus, Sikhism separated itself from Hinduism and developed into a religion led by devout laymen. Guru Arjun (1581–1606), the fifth guru, was especially important because he compiled a Sikh bible out of the poems, prayers, and sayings of the first four gurus and a number of other writers. This book came to be known as the *Adi Granth* (The Original Book), and one of the things it contains is a short book of psalms called *Japi* (Praise), written by Nanak. Arjun was also responsible for turning Sikhism into a social and political organization as well as a religious movement.

The Sikh faith now centers around the temple. Most

prominent among Sikh temples is the Golden Temple of Armritsar, where the Adi Granth is kept.

The last five gurus shaped Sikhism into a military theocracy. Guru Gobind Singh (1675–1708), the 10th and final guru, organized the militant Sikhs into the order of the Khalsa. Those initiated into the Khalsa were called Singhs (lions) and were required to display five distinctive marks: long hair *(kes)*, a comb *(kangha)*, short pants *(kach)*, an iron bracelet *(kartha)*, and a sword *(kirpan)*. The militant Sikhs overthrew the Moghul Empire in India in 1849. Now they are a part of the Republic of India.

Gobind Singh was the last of the gurus because he declared that after him the *Granth* (the book) would be the guru of Sikhism. These scriptures came to be known as *Guru Granth Sahib,* were given absolute authority, and were treated as though they were a person. Despite the early Sikh prohibition of idolatry, the Granth has come to be worshiped as an idol. This religion has produced the ultimate form of bibliolatry. The original *Granth* was supplemented by a second *Granth* written by Gobind Singh known as the *Desam Granth.*

The *Granth* is the most difficult sacred book to read because it was written with a special script in six languages in poetic form. Very few Sikhs can read it at all. Most of them simply worship it. The Granth is often celebrated by processions in which the book is carried around the city accompanied by singers and musicians.

Most Sikhs today are only nominal adherents of their faith. The five distinctive marks are beginning to fade, and the average Sikh simply observes certain special days and ceremonies (initiation, baptism, marriage, and funerals). There are between 6 and 8 million Sikhs in India today, but it is difficult to tell whether this religion will remain distinct or be absorbed into Hinduism.

Biblical Evaluation
(1) The Sikh concept of God is monotheistic in form, but it is so mystical and abstract that it is ultimately pantheis-

tic. This is especially true of Sikhism's description of salvation as absorption of the soul into God.

(2) This religion teaches salvation by works as well as grace. It does not really deal with the problem of sin. It also includes the Hindu ideas of karma and transmigration.

(3) Sikhs claim to spurn idolatry, but in practice they worship their sacred book as an idol.

(4) Sikhism claims that all religions worship the same God under different names. The God of the Bible, however, has revealed that there is only one way a man can enter into a right relationship with Him, and that is through the redemptive work of Jesus Christ.

Things to Keep in Mind

(1) As with Jainism, Sikhism has few adherents outside of India. Christians who minister to Sikhs are most effective when they capitalize on the good features of this religion and build on common ground. Sadhu Sundar Singh and Bhakt Singh are two examples of Christian nationals who have made significant inroads with the Gospel among the Sikhs because of their creative and original approaches to these people.

(2) Christians who work with Sikhs must emphasize the personality and work of Jesus Christ, and especially His substitutionary death on behalf of sinful men. Stress should be placed on the vitality of a personal relationship with Christ in the life of the Christian.

5

ZOROASTRIANISM

Background and Teachings

Zoroastrianism was once a widespread religion, but now it has few adherents (about 150,000). It connects more closely with the Bible than any other religion, excepting, of course, Judaism and Christianity. For example, the Bible mentions some of the Zoroastrian kings who ruled the Persian Empire. These kings (Cyrus, Ahasuerus, and Darius) are named in Isaiah, Daniel, Ezra, Nehemiah, Esther, Haggai, Zechariah, and 2 Chronicles.

Some of the teachings of Zoroastrianism are surprisingly similar to those of the Bible. Zoroaster spoke of monotheism, the coming of a savior, the resurrection of the body, judgment, and eternal life. Some Bible critics have alleged that the similar biblical doctrines were borrowed from the Zoroastrians. What the critics neglect to say is that Israel had held these doctrines for centuries before Zoroaster was born (just at the time of the Babylonian Captivity, when the Jews were bringing their religion from Palestine to Babylon). It therefore makes more sense to perceive that Zoroaster got his ideas from the already monotheistic Jews.

This religion is the product of one man, Spitoma Zoroaster, who lived about the seventh century B.C. (his dates are sometimes given as 628–551 B.C.). Zoroaster is the Greek form of his name; he is also known by his Avestan name, Zarathustra.

What little we know about Zoroaster comes from the *Gathas*, a set of hymns included in the Zoroastrian scriptures (the *Avesta*). Zoroaster was born in Persia at a time when the popular religion was the worship of the Aryan nature gods.

When Zoroaster received a series of visions at the age of 30, he brought one of these gods, Ahura Mazda, to the place of complete supremacy. He was convinced that truth had been revealed to him, so he began to preach the message about Ahura Mazda, the God of light. Ten years passed before Zoroaster won a convert, his cousin. But when Zoroaster was 42, he achieved success. He converted the Persian King Kavi Vishtaspa. When the king became a Zoroastrian, many other Persians naturally followed suit.

At this time Zoroaster and his followers turned to force for the spread of the new religion. A series of "holy wars" eventually brought Zoroastrianism to a position of firm international strength. The entire Persian Empire was brought into the fold.

Almost nothing is known of Zoroaster's last 20 years, but an extracanonical book says that he was assassinated by a priest of the old religion as he was performing a ceremony before the altar fire of Ahura Mazda. Zoroaster had no prophetic successor, and Zoroastrianism eventually degenerated into a polytheistic form of angel worship. Zoroaster himself was elevated to a supernatural level and worshiped by his followers as a miraculously born wonder-worker.

In the third century A.D., a reformation movement within Zoroastrianism began, which helped restore its original monotheistic purity. However, the spread of Christianity and especially the spread of Islam all but eliminated Zoroastrianism in Persia.

The Muslims defeated Persia (A.D. 651), and the Zoroastrians who would not renounce their religion had to flee. They eventually found refuge not far from Bombay, India (A.D. 717). The priests reorganized the people and the religious worship ceremonies in the new land. These Zoroastrians who moved to India came to be known as Parsis (Persians). Today there are only about 120,000 Parsis in India and another 30,000 in Iran. The Parsis are well-educated, moral people, and many of them are financially successful. They have kept themselves aloof from Hinduism, almost like a separate caste.

The Zoroastrian scriptures, the *Avesta* (knowledge) are written in Avestan, a language similar to Sanskrit. A commentary *(Zend)* was added in the third century A.D., and the combined scriptures and commentary are called the *Zend-Avesta*. The Avesta is divided into two parts: (1) The Great Avesta contains the Yasna (which includes the Gathas, songs written by Zoroaster), the Visparad, and the Verridad. (2) The Small Avesta is a ritual and prayer book.

The most distinctive feature of Zoroastrian teaching is its dualism. It paints a picture of a constant struggle between two primal spirits, one good and one bad. Ahura Mazda (or Ormazd) is considered the supreme deity who will eventually triumph over Angra Mainyu (Ahriman), the devil. While Ahura Mazda is one god, he is depicted as having seven diverse attributes, called the Amesha-Spentas. Later Zoroastrianism turned these attributes into lesser gods or archangels. Angra Mainyu also has seven attributes, the corresponding opposites of those of Ahura Mazda:

Ahura Mazda	*Angra Mainyu*
The Seven Attributes (The Amesha-Spentas)	The Seven Attributes
1. Ahura Mazda (God of Light, Wisdom)	1. Angra Mainyu (Prince of Darkness)
2. Asha (Right, Justice)	2. Druj (Falsehood)
3. Vohu Monah (Good Mind, Thought)	3. Akem (Evil Mind)
4. Kshathra (Power, Strength)	4. Dush-Kshathra (Cowardice)
5. Armaiti (Piety, Love, Faith)	5. Taromaiti (False Pretense)
6. Haurvatat (Health and Perfection)	6. Avetat (Misery)
7. Ameretat (Immortality)	7. Merethyn (Annihilation)

Zoroastrianism presents a works salvation which emphasizes high moral standards. The three great virtues are good thoughts, good words, and good deeds. Each person must freely choose truth over falsehood. Salvation is achieved only if a person has a moral credit balance, that is, if his good deeds outweigh his bad deeds.

The bodies of all the dead will be resurrected, and there is a final judgment. Each soul comes to the Sifting Bridge or Deciding Bridge which leads to heaven (the House of Songs). Those who fall off this bridge descend into hell. At the end of time all who are evil are finally destroyed by a fiery stream of molten metal. Angra Mainyu and his demons will also be annihilated. Before these judgments occur, the Avesta teaches, a savior or deliverer *(Soshyant)* will appear.

Zoroastrianism has developed an extreme ritualism centering around the fire-temple. The sacred fire plays such an important role in this religion that Zoroastrians are sometimes called fire worshipers. Zoroastrians strongly deny this, claiming that the fire is only a symbol of the light and purity of God. In practice, however, the

Parsis treat the fire as much more than a symbol.

Each temple also houses a special white bull. Zoroastrians say that this bull is another symbol (of creation and procreation), but again, practice seems to differ from theory.

Rituals and formulas have become so much a part of this religion that Zoroastrians seem to be concerned more with ceremonial purity than with ethical purity. There is an emphasis on avoiding defilement by certain things, especially dead bodies. When a Parsi dies, he is not buried or burned because Zoroastrians do not want to defile the earth, water, or the sacred fire. Therefore they place the body in a Tower of Silence where the bones are picked clean by vultures.

The stifling effect of excess ceremonialism and mechanical worship has deadened Zoroastrianism. The Parsis regularly recite prayers in the ancient Avestan language even though few of them know what the prayers mean. Many crude and meaningless practices have crept into Zoroastrianism, causing a division between the more orthodox Parsis and the reforming Parsis. The majority, however, have simply become materialistic and apathetic.

Biblical Evaluation
(1) The Zoroastrian view of God is closer to that of Christianity than any other major Eastern religion. It is monotheistic, and Ahura Mazda has many of the attributes of Jehovah. However, the god of Zoroastrianism falls short in at least two ways:

(a) Angra Mainyu, the spirit of evil, appears to be as powerful as Ahura Mazda. This dualism indicates that Ahura Mazda is not really sovereign and omnipotent. He does not actually have the power to defeat Angra Mainyu even though the Avesta says he will at last.

(b) Ahura Mazda is not a personal god like the God of the Bible. Worship is centered around ritual forms, not a personal relationship.

(2) Salvation is achieved by works, not by faith. If a man's good works outweigh his bad works, he is allowed into heaven. The problem of man's sinfulness is not resolved, and heaven will be populated by sinners. Because of this, Ahura Mazda does not possess the burning righteousness of the God of the Bible.

(3) In this religion the good has become the enemy of the best. There are a number of parallels with Christianity, but these similarities often obscure the critical differences.

(4) In actual practice, Zoroastrianism involves superstition and occultism. This is especially true of the near worship of the sacred fire and the white bull in the temples.

(5) Modern Zoroastrianism is characterized by empty ritual, ceremonial forms, and by legalism.

Things to Keep in Mind

(1) Except in rare instances, the only Christians who have regular contact with Zoroastrians are missionaries. Christian missionaries who work with Parsis must be familiar with this religion so that they can find common ground on which to build. Christians should build on the best this religion has to offer. This can be done because Zoroastrianism is similar to Judeo-Christianity.

(2) Not until the fourth century after Christ did Zoroastrians begin claiming a supernatural birth for Zoroaster (and his mother as well). His coming, they now began to say, was foretold 3,000 years beforehand. Zoroaster was now even viewed by his adherents as a god-man. Who would believe that these tenets, so imitative of the Christian Gospel, are mere coincidences? Remember that Jesus and the Gospels affirmed these christological doctrines from the very beginning—not several centuries after Christ!

(3) We can emphasize the problem of sin and the futility of works. With a credit-balance kind of salvation, few people can really be certain that their good deeds out-

weigh their evil deeds. This is especially true if the thought life is taken into account.

(4) There is a deadness to this religion, and Christ's gift of eternal and abundant life stands in great contrast. Zoroastrianism offers ritual and teaching, but Christ offers a relationship.

(5) Zoroastrianism teaches that a savior will come. Christians can carry this a step further by showing that the Saviour has come. But there is an offense of the Cross, particularly to people in whom a works-oriented religion has fostered pride of heart. Such people therefore reject salvation as a free and undeserved gift.

6

---◆---

CONFUCIANISM

---◆---

Background and Teachings

Confucianism seems to go back to the beginnings of Chinese civilization. Confucius served as its most important organizer, editing and refining the ethical and cultural heritage of the Chinese.

The big question usually asked about Confucianism is whether it is a religion or an ethical philosophy of life. This question is raised because Confucius' writings and teachings clearly emphasize earthly rather than heavenly affairs. Nevertheless, Confucius did not deny the existence of the Chinese spirit-beings and deities. He simply was not interested in them.

Thus, a religious base centering on a combination of animism and ancestor worship underlies the ethical system of Confucianism. The most important deity is Shang

Ti, who is the supreme ancestor and is identified with heaven. From early times, the emperor made a yearly ceremonial sacrifice to Shang Ti, on the altar of heaven near Peking, on behalf of all the people. This practice continued until the Republican period (1912).

In addition to Shan Ti, the Chinese offered sacrifices to and worshiped other nature deities. The uneducated masses were concerned with placating the innumerable spirits through religious and magical ceremonies.

Even more widespread than nature worship was the worship of family ancestors (ti). This continues today in spite of Communism's efforts to eliminate it. Departed ancestors are considered to be a part of family life, and it is the responsibility of their descendants to respect them. Rites practiced for the benefit of the ancestors involve the use of ancestral tablets and daily offerings. Family solidarity and a strong respect for parents has resulted from these practices.

Chinese culture and religion were firmly established when Confucius (551–479 B.C.) came on the scene. He was named Chiu Kung when he was born in the principality of Lu, reportedly the youngest of 11 children. A precocious youth with a lust for learning, he became a philosopher and teacher, and soon built a core of disciples around him. His disciples called him Kung Fu-tzu (Kung the Master). Later this was latinized into Confucius.

At length Confucius decided to implement his political and ethical ideas in a practical way by going into public office. Tradition says that he did well in the post he held but because of his integrity, he was unable to secure any position of power.

Confucius went through a period of discouragement and denial, but many of his disciples remained with him. He continued to teach, and in his last years he edited the books which are now known as the *Classics*. These include the Books of History, Poetry, Changes, and Rites.

After Confucius' death at age 73, his disciples collected

his sayings, which became known as the *Analects* of Confucius. In the decades that followed, his disciples wrote other books which helped spread and popularize Confucius' teachings. Confucius never wanted to produce a religion. He did not even want people to rely on the gods for salvation. But, ironically, he was eventually deified in the eyes of the Chinese people.

In Confucius' day, most of the social systems of China were crumbling. Anarchy was beginning to prevail, and some were advocating the use of force to restore order in China. Confucius believed that force was external and clumsy, yet he was realistic enough to know that people would not spontaneously begin to love one another and live in harmony.

Confucius' solution to the problem was *deliberate* tradition. The old spontaneous traditions were losing strength as people became more aware of themselves. The only way the adhesive strength of the past could be preserved was to consciously guide and inculcate old and new traditions. These ethical ideas had to be spread by means of schools, temples, entertainment, homes, stories, festivals, and every other way possible.

Confucius' ethical system included the ideas that men have freedom to make their own choices, and that human nature is basically good. Confucius sought to demonstrate in his life and teachings the principles of *chun-tzu*, the superior man. He taught that the ultimate virtue is *jen*, a combination of self-respect and humanitarian feeling toward others. He expressed this in the so-called Silver Rule: "What you do not want others to do to you, do not do to them."

He also taught the principle of *li* for governing the details of life. This idea, the concept of propriety, involved the doctrine of the mean (*chung yung*), the middle path that must be followed to avoid extremes. It also involved respect for age, and the five relationships: father and son, ruler and subject, elder brother and younger brother, friend and friend, and husband and wife. Confucius emphasized the need for close family bonds. Every aspect of life was to be so controlled by definite patterns that life would become a great ritual.

Confucius said the government should rule by power (te) of virtue and moral example. This would instill an attitude of trust in the subjects. He also urged the development of the arts (wen). The state that developed the highest culture and the finest arts would achieve the ultimate victory.

It is clear from Confucius' teachings that he was much more concerned about earth than he was about heaven. He had only a vague idea of the future life. But his preoccupation with ethical matters does not mean that he had no regard for religious affairs. Instead, he simply tried to shift the popular emphasis from heaven to earth without completely dropping heaven from the picture. Confucius did not deny the supernatural, yet he did not say much about it.

Confucianism became the state religion of China during the Han Dynasty (206 B.C.–A.D. 220) and remained so for over 2,000 years, until the Republic was established in 1912. During this time the *Analects* was the most important book in the Chinese schools, and Confucius' teachings dramatically shaped Chinese thought and civilization. He ultimately affected every aspect of Chinese life, especially the high respect for age, family relationships, social sensitivity, poetry, and the arts.

The rise of Communism in China has seriously hurt Confucianism. The Communists have attempted to systematically suppress all aspects of Confucianism including the *Classics* and the *Analects*. The same has been true for Chinese Buddhism and Taoism.

Biblical Evaluation

(1) Confucianism is a self-effort system. Confucius taught that man needs no help beyond himself. The Bible, on the other hand, stresses man's need of God's grace.

(2) A savior is not needed because people are really not

sinful, according to Confucius. Human nature is good. Contrast this with Jeremiah 17:9 and Romans 3:23.

(3) This is a religion of ethics which begins and ends with the wisdom of man. There is no emphasis on the supernatural. There is only a hint of God and heaven.

(4) Confucius originally taught an ethical philosophy. This must be distinguished from the popular religion of the Chinese which simply absorbed Confucius' teachings and is now known as Confucianism. This popular religion is a combination of ancestor worship, animism, and involved social traditions.

Things to Keep in Mind
(1) Confucianism offers many good ethical guidelines, but it falls short of satisfying man's real needs. Confucianism's lack of a solution must be stressed. Because of Christ's resurrection, a solution leading to new life is available in Christ.

(2) One problem which should be recognized is that religion, education, and culture are practically one and the same in the Chinese mind. It is difficult to separate them when presenting the claims of Christ.

(3) Many Confucians are also adherents of Taoism and Buddhism, strange as this may seem to Western thinking. They are inclusivists, and the exclusive claims of the Gospel must be presented with wisdom.

(4) Communism has captured the thinking of the Chinese. This atheistic system has developed into the new "religion" of China, and Confucianism has largely lost its hold on the people.

7

TAOISM

Background and Teachings

The founder of Taoism (pronounced *dowism*), a mystical Chinese religion, is a legendary figure, and many scholars doubt that he ever existed. His name was Lao-tzu (also spelled Lao-tse), and his traditional dates are given as 604–517 B.C. *Lao-tzu* means the "Old Master," a name relating to one legend that he was born a wise old man with white hair. Legend also says he was a keeper of the royal archives until he decided to abandon society and travel west.

As Lao-tzu was leaving the civilized world, a gatekeeper convinced him to stop and write down his philosophy. He took a few days to do this, and then continued his journey. The book of 5,000 characters he wrote has become the central scripture of Taoism, and it is called the

Tao Te Ching (The Classic of the Way and its Power). Some writers suggest, however, that the *Tao Te Ching* was written anonymously in the fourth or third century B.C. It contains 81 short chapters describing the meaning of Tao and how one should live according to the Tao.

Though *Tao* is an indefinable and incomprehensible concept, the word is variously translated "way," "path," and "eternal principle" to give the idea of a creative force which orders the cosmos, life, and reason. Tao is said to be the mother of 10,000 visible things, an ultimate and transcendent reality which is beyond the senses. However, Tao is also used to speak of the way of the universe and the driving principle in nature.

The greatest Taoist philosopher was Chuang-tzu, who lived in the late fourth and early third centuries B.C. He did much to develop and spread the teachings of Lao-tzu, writing commentaries which Taoists regard as scripture. Now the Taoist canon, known as the *Tao Tsang*, consists of about 1,120 volumes.

Lao-tzu and Chuang-tzu taught that the wise man should do everything according to the Tao. He should live passively, in tune with the universe. This concept is expressed in the term *wu wei*, which means something like "not doing" or "actionless activity." One must not alter nature. Instead he should lead a life of reflection and quiet passiveness. He must avoid violence of all forms. The wise man will go with Tao and live in complete simplicity and quiet. In these respects Taoism is similar to the Greek Epicureans' philosophy that the Apostle Paul debated (Acts 17:18).

The best symbol of the Tao is water. Water moves gently forward, it seeks its level and adapts itself to its surroundings. When it is still it becomes clear. It also has tremendous power and is able to wear away the hardest stone.

Taosim in its original form taught that men should avoid aggressiveness and competition. It is a monistic philosophy which asserts that all things are an expression of the Tao. All is *one*. This includes even those things which are contrary to one another such as good and evil, light and dark. All these things are relative, not absolute, and they all go back to the Tao. This concept is expressed in the *Tai chi* diagram:

Nature is full of conflict between *Yang* and *Yin*, but as the diagram shows, they perfectly balance one another and invade each other's hemisphere. When this diagram is rotated all things become one at the center.

Here are some of the contraries represented by *Yang* and *Yin:*

Yang	*Yin*
Male	Female
Good	Evil
Active	Passive
Light	Darkness
Heaven	Earth
Sun	Moon
Summer	Winter
Positive	Negative
Life	Death

The only ultimate in philosophical Taoism is the Tao itself. There is no personal Creator-God.

After a few centuries Taoism degenerated into a crude

popular religious system very different from original Taoist philosophy. Lao-tzu, if he did actually exist, would have been quite unhappy with what became of his teachings. The Chinese turned Taoism into a folk religion and used it to control the good and evil spirits. It became a religion of magic, superstition, witchcraft, and occultism, involving the worship of many gods, the fear of evil spirits, and demonic possession. Innumerable Taoist temples and shrines appeared because of the efforts to placate the evil spirtis of the dead and to worhsip all kinds of deities. Even today Taoist priests brew magical potions and are paid to drive away evil spirits.

There is also a mystical and esoteric form of Taoism practiced by secret societies. Members of these societies often engage in ascetic practices.

The popular form of Taoism became so decadent that even before the rise of Chinese Communism it was losing its hold. Now many Taoist practices are suppressed by the Communists, and it has been even more seriously weakened. There is a Chinese Taoist Association, but it is strictly controlled by the government. Many scholars think that Taoism as a religion will virtually disappear from China.

As with Confucianism, so also with Taoism: we must be careful to distinguish the original philosophy from the religion that developed out of it. It is significant that the original philosophical form of Taoism is growing in popularity in the West. This is partly due to the similarities between philosophical Taoism and Zen Buddhism. Japanese Zen was produced by a combination of Indian Buddhism and Chinese Taoism.

Biblical Evaluation

(1) In contrast to the Bible, there is no personal Creator-God in any form of Taoism. Taoism is instead involved with nature, mysticism, and an impersonal principle.

(2) The issue of sin and morality is minimized in Taoism. Salvation is achieved by following the Tao (the way).

A person must commit himself to the Tao and live a life of simplicity and quiet.

(3) Popular Taoism has degenerated into a system of magical practices and incantations. Its priests sell charms against demons and evil spirits of the dead. It is both polytheistic and animistic. There are many heavens and hells.

Things to Keep in Mind

(1) The future of Taoism in China is not bright, but the original philosophical form of Taoism, as represented in the *Tao Te Ching* and in writings of Chuang-tzu, has been gaining a good deal of interest in America. But it is really only an attractive system of speculation. It is not a revelation from a personal Creator and its only authority is human conjecture.

(2) As in the case of Buddhism (especially Zen Buddhism), the Holy Spirit's ministry of convicting men of their sinfulness is a critical matter when working with those enmeshed in Taoist philosophy. The Christian must emphasize that people think and practice evil things, and that this is borne out by the evidence of our senses and thoughts.

(3) Even though personality is on a higher level than impersonality, philosophical Taoism teaches that all things ultimately come from the impersonal. The problem here is that the effect appears to be greater than the cause.

(4) Missionaries who work with Taoists are quick to sense the intense spiritual warfare that is taking place to win souls of men. People involved in the popular forms of this religion are often plagued with demonic possession and fear.

SHINTOISM

Background and Teachings

Shinto, the indigenous religion of Japan, has been influenced by Buddhism, Confucianism, and more recently, Christianity. It is a combination of many things, and within it are wide differences of thought and practice. Because of this, an isolated portrait of Shintoism is somewhat misleading.

Shintoism is an undeveloped primitive religion which centers on the worship of nature deities and deified people. It has no founder, no prophet, no savior, and little formal doctrine. Its main emphasis is the worship of the *Kami*, a concept which involves the gods, all aspects of nature, supernatural power, and certain people. Kami is everywhere and the world is Kami. It is the divine consciousness which flows through all. It is the vital force of the universe. This concept is pantheistic because there is no real distinction between the creator and the created.

The origins of the ancient Shinto religion are obscure. Two Chinese words, *shen* (spirit) and *tao* (way), were combined to produce the word Shinto. The equivalent in Japanese is *kami no michi*, which essentially means "the way of the gods." Only after Buddhism began to threaten Shintoism did the Japanese try to preserve their religion by recording the old myths and oral traditions.

Buddhism entered Japan in A.D. 522 by way of China and Korea. About two centuries later the two books of Shinto scriptures were produced as a response. The *Kojiki* (Records of Ancient Matters) appeared in A.D. 712, and the *Nihongi* (Chronicles of Japan) appeared in A.D. 720.

These books say that after the formation of heaven and earth, two of the gods, Izanagi and Izanami, stood on the floating bridge of heaven. Izanagi was leisurely stirring the ocean brine with his spear, and when he lifted it out, the drops which fell from it coagulated to form Awaji, one of the Japanese islands. Izanagi and Izanami descended to this island, mated, and produced the rest of the Japanese islands. They also produced other deities and the Japanese people.

One of the chief deities formed was the sun goddess, Amaterasu Omikami. Amaterasu had a grandson named Jimmu Tenno, who descended to the sacred Japanese islands to become the first historical Mikado (emperor) of Japan in 660 B.C. Japanese tradition claims an unbroken line of succession from Jimmu Tenno, and this has led to a strong emphasis on emperor worship. Since the emperors were thought to be gods, they had to be obeyed unquestioningly by all Japanese.

Shintoism emphasizes loyalty to Japan and to the Mikado. Because of its intense nationalistic spirit, it is very exclusive. Most of its forms teach that one must be Japanese to be a Shintoist.

In Shintoism, salvation is achieved by observing the many social and physical taboos which have become a part of Japanese life. Ritualistic purity (ceremonial washing and sweeping) is very important since this is how evil is thought to be banished.

In addition, the ancestors and gods must be propitiated by worship offerings of food and rice wine *(saki)*. For this purpose, about 100,000 shrines in Japan are run by a Shinto priesthood. Each shrine houses a *shintai* (a sacred Kami symbol or image) which can be seen only by the priests. The shrine area is always marked off by a *torii* (an arch). Each Shinto home also has its miniature shrine, known as the *Kami-dana*, where offerings are made. This is the god shelf, and it contains symbols and names of the sun goddess and other gods.

The Shinto concept of salvation is deliverance from the troubles and evils of the world. There is no real concept of sin or depravity. The gods made man and therefore man is good. Thus, if a man appeases the gods and ancestors, follows the correct taboos, and expresses his Kami nature, he will find his place of immortality among the ancestral Kami beings.

Shintoism has been strongly affected by Confucianism and Buddhism. Pure Shinto, for example, has no ethical system of its own. Ethical teachings were introduced into Shintoism from Confucianism (filial piety and the five relationships) and from Buddhism.

The Mahayana form of Buddhism that came to Japan in the sixth century was very tolerant, and many of the Shinto deities were identified with various Buddhas and Bodhisattvas. From about A.D. 800 to 1700, many regarded the two religions as simply two aspects of one religion. This was called Ryobu (mixed or dual) Shinto.

However, a rise in the Japanese nationalistic spirit led to a revival of pure Shinto at the expense of Buddhism. Emperor Meiji in 1882 officially made Shinto the state religion. State Shinto became a political force used to promote the superiority of the Japanese people and to prove that the Japanese Empire was a divine mission. National shrines were established. Before and during World War

II, all students were indoctrinated in the Shinto myths and taught to worship the emperor and the state. State Shinto was used as the basis for a total war effort. Thus, when Emperor Hirohito on January 1, 1946 denied that he was divine, Shinto suffered a severe blow. State Shinto was eliminated, but popular and sect Shinto managed to survive the downfall of a divine emperor.

In popular Shinto, local and family shrines are still being used. In sect Shinto almost 150 sects have appeared, some with a missionary zeal for converts in non-Japanese countries. Those involved in sect Shinto are generally more fervent than those in popular Shinto. The latter are Shintoists by custom and decree, but the former are Shintoists by conviction. Most of the sects have founders, doctrines, and programs in contrast to popular Shinto.

State Shinto is gone, but its nationalistic emphasis on a sacred soil and race has been perpetuated in other forms of Shinto. However, it is likely that Japan's increasing emphasis on urbanization, industrialization, and scientific education will weaken the impact of Shinto with its nature and ancestor worship and its mythology.

Biblical Evaluation

(1) The Shinto concept of Kami is far removed from the infinite, personal Creator God of the Bible. It involves polytheism and nature worship. Many of the gods are depicted as immoral.

(2) Pure Shinto minimizes the value of all who are not of Japanese descent. It teaches the supremacy and celestial origin of the Japanese race and promotes an intensely nationalistic spirit. Even the Kami are of Japanese origin.

(3) Shinto minimizes the idea of sin and moral guilt. Since the Japanese have a divine origin, they are naturally good. Instead of a system of ethics, Shinto has developed a set of social rules and taboos.

(4) Unlike the Bible, Shinto is based on nebulous stories devoid of any historical facts. The eighth-century *Kojiki* and *Nihongi* are entirely unverifiable.

Things to Keep in Mind

(1) Because of some of the new sects in Shinto, a number of Shinto "churches" are beginning to appear in countries outside of Japan. For instance, the Tenrikyo sect alone has established more than 500 churches overseas. Christians are therefore encountering Shintoism in many places. One of the most important issues the Christian can use in a discussion with a Shintoist is the problem of sin. The cruelty and moral guilt of man must be acknowledged before a person will seek a solution. Christ is the only one who can solve the problem of sin.

(2) The Bible offers its solution in the context of space-time historical events. The reliability of the books of the Bible is affirmed by archeology, history, and fulfilled prophecy. In contrast, the myths of the *Kojiki* and *Nihongi* are removed from the realm of history. They have no more factual basis than the legends of Egypt, Greece, and Rome.

(3) Nationalism is a difficult force to overcome in Shinto. The lordship of Jesus Christ is often a stumbling block in the minds of those who have always been taught to revere the emperor, the state, and the family over all else.

(4) Emphasis must be placed on the resurrection of Jesus as a victorious alternative to the centuries of ancestor worship found in Shinto. The customs of the Japanese run deep, and they can only be overcome by the power and convicting ministry of the Holy Spirit.

9

ISLAM

Background and Teachings

Today Islam claims over 400 million followers around the world. Though Mohammed is its founder, it is not correct to call it Mohammedanism. The word *Islam* essentially means "surrender" or "submission" to the will of Allah. *Muslim* (or *Moslem*) is related to this word, and it means "one who submits."

Islam is an intensely monotheistic religion whose primary name for God is Allah. This word probably came from *al illah*, which means "*the* God."

So extreme is the monotheism of Islam that the greatest and unpardonable sin is *shirk*—associating Allah with anything created. The only true way to define Allah is by the *via negativa* (negative way), i.e., by eliminating all the things that Allah is *not*. Also, metaphor or analogy may be used sparingly in describing Allah, e.g., "the merciful" or "the compassionate."

Islam combines elements from the Old Testament and Christianity and accepts Noah, Abraham, Moses, David, Jesus, John, and others as prophets of Allah. It claims, however, that Mohammed is the last and greatest of the prophets and that Islam is the true continuation of the Old Testament faith.

Mohammed, whose original name was Ubu'l Kassim, was born in A.D. 570 in Mecca (near the southwest coast of the Arabian Peninsula). His father Abdullah, a member of the powerful Quraish tribe, died shortly before his birth, and his mother, Amina, died when he was six years old. His grandfather cared for him for a short time, and then he was brought up by Abu Talib, his uncle. He became a camel driver and his uncle often took him on lengthy caravan journeys, sometimes as far as Syria and possibly Egypt. Because of this, Mohammed had extensive contacts with people of different religions and nationalities, and this later influenced his thinking.

When Mohammed was 25, he was employed by Khadijah, a wealthy widow in the caravan trade. He served her so well that she decided to marry him even though she was 15 years his senior. None of their children survived to maturity except a daughter named Fatima. As Khadijah's husband, Mohammed no longer had to work. Instead, he began to occupy himself with meditation and reflection on the meaning of life.

The Arabian people were polytheistic idolaters who had a pantheon of deities (including Allah), as well as angels and demons *(djinn)*. Mecca was a religious center with 360 shrines and a small temple known as the Kaaba, which housed the Black Stone. This stone (probably a meteorite) was thought to have been given to Abraham by Gabriel.

Mohammed was disturbed by the idolatrous practices of his countrymen and came to the conclusion that Allah was the one true God. He spent many hours of thought in a cave in Mount Hira, a few miles from Mecca. In A.D. 610, when he was 40, he began to receive frightening revelations which were accompanied by violent seizures. He was not sure whether the visions were divine or demonic, but his wife encouraged him to submit to the revelations which were supposed to be coming from the angel Gabriel. He was told to recite the revelation he received, and his followers recorded these after his death in the Koran (Qur'an, or Recitation). As a prophet of Allah, Mohammed received visions for 22 years until his death in A.D. 632.

Mohammed's first convert was Khadijah, and his second was Ali, a young cousin. Probably the most important early convert was a merchant named Abu Bakr. For several years Mohammed had little success in gaining followers. When he began to openly proclaim his message about Allah, he ran into immediate opposition. Meccan businessmen depended on pilgrimages to the shrines, and Mohammed was denouncing all forms of idol worship. Everything he taught was against the moral and social order of Mecca.

Mohammed's followers were persecuted, and the prophet himself was protected only because of his influential wife and his uncle, Abu Talib. Both of them, however, died in A.D. 620. A number of Muslims moved to the nearby city of Yathrib because of the pressure in Mecca. Later, the Meccan opposition became so intense that Mohammed also decided to leave, and accepted an offer to become the leader of the city of Yathrib. He just managed to escape a plot to assassinate him as he secretly fled Mecca on July 16, 622 with his disciple Abu Bakr. The two of them had to hide in a cave for three days before they could set out for Yathrib.

Mohammed's escape to Yathrib was called the Hegira (Hijrah, or "flight"). This is the most important date in Islam since it marks the official beginning of Islam as a religion. Muslims reckon their calendars from this day using the designation A.H. ("in the year of the Hegira").

The year of Mohammed's death (632), for example, is 10 A.H.

After Mohammed became the magistrate of Yathrib, its name was changed to Medina, the "City of the Prophet." Mohammed was successful in his leadership of Medina, and most of the people there became Muslims. He set up a theocracy, combining politics with the new religion. Mohammed was both king and prophet. At this stage it seems he used his "divine revelations" to establish new laws and policies which aided his career of conquest. In Medina he also started a harem, with 10 to 12 wives.

For a time, Mohammed tried to win over the Jewish population of Medina. But when he was rejected by the Jews, he stopped praying toward Jerusalem and began to face Mecca instead. He also persecuted the Jews because of their rejection.

Mohammed replenished the treasury of Medina by plundering the caravans of pilgrims to Mecca. This led to war with the Meccans, and Mohammed's years in Medina were marked by almost constant warfare. There were military reverses, and the prophet himself was wounded in one of the battles. But the Medinese were eventually victorious and a number of tribes submitted to Mohammed. He finally took Mecca, tore down the idols, and rebuilt the Kaaba with its Black Stone. By continuing the ancient pilgrimage ritual to the Kaaba, Mohammed made Mecca the most holy city of Islam. Mohammed died not long after his return to Mecca, but by time of his death he was ruler of all Arabia.

Soon after the prophet's death it was agreed that his successor (caliph) would be Abu Bakr. He died in A.D. 634 after a reign of only 2 years. The second caliph, Omar, reigned 10 years (A.D. 634–644). He was quite aggressive, and his armies spread Islam by means of the conquering sword. They defeated Syria, Jerusalem, Egypt, Persia, and Mesopotamia.

Othman was the third caliph and Ali was the fourth. During their reigns, Islam continued to spread until it took parts of India, all of north Africa, and a part of Europe. It might have conquered Europe except for Charles Martel's victory over the Islamic armies at the Battle of Tours in A.D. 732.

Though the Islamic nations are no longer directed by the caliphate, Islam as a religion continues to be a powerful binding force among the Arabs. It is enjoying a new surge of power due to the increasing Arab oil revenues. A great deal of this money is being poured into Islamic missions with special emphasis on the African continent.

The Koran is the authoritative scripture of Islam. About four-fifths the length of the New Testament, it is divided into 114 surahs (chapters). Parts were written by Mohammed, and the rest, based on his oral teaching, was written from memory by his disciples after Mohammed's death.

Over the years a number of additional sayings of Mohammed and his early disciples were compiled. These comprise the *Hadith* ("tradition"), the sayings of which are called *sunna* ("custom"). The Hadith supplements the Koran much as the Talmud supplements the Law in Judaism.

The basic beliefs and practices of Islam are usually summarized by *the five doctrines* and *the five pillars*. The five doctrines are:

(1) Allah is the one true God. Muslims believe that since God is one, the Christian doctrine of the Trinity is polytheistic. Allah is omnipotent, omniscient, and so transcendent that he is practically unknowable.

(2) Allah has sent many prophets (some place the number at over 100,000) to guide men. The Koran mentions 28 of these, most of whom are found in the Old and New Testaments. Jesus is said to be a sinless prophet, but Mohammed is the last and greatest of the prophets.

(3) Of the four inspired books, the Koran is the most important. The other three are the Tauret (the Pentateuch) of Moses, the Zabur (Psalms) of David, and the Injil (Evangel) of Jesus. Because Islam recognizes these

three, Jews and Christians are regarded as "people of a book." Nevertheless, Muslims believe that the earlier revelations are in corrupted form and the Koran supersedes them. The Koran is held to be as eternal as Allah. It was simply dictated to Mohammed by Gabriel over a period of years.

(4) There are many intermediary beings (angels). There are also fallen angels (djinn or demons) and a ruler of the djinn known as Iblis or Shaitan (Satan).

(5) There will be a day of judgment, a resurrection, and a heaven and hell. Each man's deeds will be weighed on a pair of balances to determine his destiny. Heaven is a place of sensuous delight and gratification.

Along with these doctrines there is a commonly held sixth doctrine of *Kismet* ("fate"). Those who hold to this view of foreordination often think of reality in a fatalistic way.

The five pillars of Islam relate to the main religious practices of the Muslims. They are:

(1) Recitation of Islam's creed (the *Shahadah)* or word (*Kalima): "There is no God but Allah, and Mohammed is his prophet." This creed must be said aloud, publicly, and with conviction in order for one to be a believer. It is repeated several times a day.

(2) The practice of prayer (*salat)* five times a day (upon rising, at noon, in midafternoon, after sunset, and before retiring). The worshiper must recite the prescribed prayers (the first surah and other selections from the Koran) in Arabic while facing the Kaaba in Mecca. The Hadith (book of tradition) has turned these prayers into a mechanical procedure of standing, kneeling, hands and face on the ground, and so forth. The call to prayer is sounded by the *muezzin* (a Muslim crier) from a tower called a *minaret* which is part of the *mosque* (the place of public worship).

(3) The practice of almsgiving (*zakat).* This was once a voluntary practice, but it has become a tax usually based on one-fortieth of one's income and holdings. In Moslem

countries there is always a vagrant class which is supported by the giving of alms.

(4) The month of fasting (the month of Ramadan). During this month (which occurs at different times of the year since the Muslims use a lunar calendar), Muslims are not allowed to eat or drink anything during the daylight hours. Many of them rise before dawn to eat breakfast, and as soon as it gets dark they eat another meal.

(5) The pilgrimage to Mecca (the *Hajj*). Muslims are required to make this pilgrimage at least once in their lifetimes if at all possible. This trip, which helps them attain salvation, is usually expensive and dangerous to the health if one is not strong. A complex and arduous set of ceremonies must be performed, many of which center around the Kaaba shrine.

In addition to these five pillars, a sixth is often added—the Holy War (*Jihad*), a religious war in which force is used to overcome infidels and spread Islam. The use of force is sanctioned in the Koran (Surah 2:163-64; 9:5, 29). Soldiers who die in such a war are assured of entrance into heaven.

Other practices in addition to these pillars are circumcision, the veiling of women with a *purdah*, polygyny (a man is limited to four wives at a time), and abstention from alcohol, gambling, and certain foods (especially pork). There are also a number of festivals and feasts, depending on the sect or branch of Islam to which one belongs.

In Islam everything has been codified into rigid practices. This has led to much externalism. Religion becomes a matter of custom, national heritage, and ritual rather than a relationship with God.

The two major sects of Islam are divided over the question of who was the rightful successor to Mohammed. The Sunnites, by far the majority of Muslims, assert that the four caliphs (Abu Bakr, Omar, Othman, and Ali) were the rightful successors. The Shiites are opposed to this view, believing that only those in the family of Mohammed should be recognized. They begin the line of succession with Ali, Mohammed's cousin and son-in-law (he married Fatima, Mohammed's daughter). These successors are known as the Imams, and Shiites claim that they were sinless men who performed miracles, died as martyrs, and are on an equal plane with Mohammed. The Shiites are divided over whether there were 7 or 12 Imams. Those who believe there were 12 say that the 12th Imam disappeared about A.D. 882 and that he will appear again as the Madhi ("the guided one") or Messiah and set up his kingdom on the earth. Some subsects (such as the Ismailis) believe that there is always an Imam on the earth.

There are many other small sects of Islam, one of the most important being the Ahmadiya, founded in the 19th century by a man who claimed to be the Madhi Imam. This sect is very active in Europe and America in its attempts to win converts.

In addition to the sects there are also different orders to which a Muslim can belong, regardless of his sect. The most important order is that of the Sufis. The Sufis are the mystics of Islam who engage in esoteric practices and beliefs. Many Sufis emphasize the immanence of Allah to such an extent that they are actually pantheists. They have organized several fraternal orders for the practice of their secret rites. The best known of these fraternities is the Dervish fraternity (sometimes called the "whirling dervishes" because of their exercises and dances which lead to trancelike states). The Wahhabi order, by contrast, is a fanatically orthodox movement in Islam which emphasizes the transcendence of Allah.

Biblical Evaluation
(1) Islam combines elements of the Old Testament, Christianity, and the native Arabian religion. Mohammed, writing in the Koran, refers to the Old and New Testaments as the truth, but his doctrines often contradict their teachings. Whenever there is a conflict between the

Koran and the Bible, Muslims say that the Bible is not accurate at that point because it has been changed by men. They claim the Koran is uncreated and eternal (this creates a problem because it implies that the Koran has an independent existence apart from Allah).

(2) Though Islam's doctrine of God is monotheistic, it is deficient in many ways. Allah is so transcendent that he is practically unknowable (the Sufis, however, would say otherwise). He is all-powerful, but little is said about the attributes of holiness and love. Muslims have a distorted picture of the Trinity (they think Christians teach that it consists of God, Mary, and Jesus). They hate this doctrine, as a form of *shirk*, because they believe it destroys the divine unity. For them it is an unpardonable sin to associate a "partner" with God.

(3) Unlike the God of the Bible, Allah has done nothing for man that cost him anything. Islam makes no real provision for sin. One's salvation is never certain since it is based on a works system and on complete surrender ("Islam") to the will of Allah. This religion rejects the biblical teaching of the crucifixion and resurrection of Jesus, though it concedes that He was a sinless prophet. Mohammed did not rise from the dead, and there is no basis for a resurrection in Islam.

(4) Islam has an elaborate system of angels and demons *(djinn)* that lends itself to a practical polytheism among the masses, who tend to treat these beings as deities.

(5) Islam is pervaded by a great sense of fatalism *(Kismet)*, in spite of efforts to overcome it.

(6) Mohammed's revelations were accompanied by violent fits and foaming at the mouth. From a New Testament perspective, they appear to have been demonic in origin.

Things to Keep in Mind
(1) Christians must focus on the problem of sin, contrasting what the God of the Bible has done about it with what Allah has *not* done.

(2) Islam is marked by sectarian differences and differing concepts of God (for instance, the difference between the Sufis and the Wahhabis). Questions must be asked to determine what particular views a Muslim holds.

(3) Islam is a rapidly spreading religion for several reasons. It is the state religion of Moslem countries and this gives it a strong cultural and political base. It has the appeal of a universal message because of its simple creed and tenets. Anyone can enter the *Ummah*, the community of faithful Muslims. There are no racial barriers. Thus it spreads quickly among the black communities of Africa, and more recently, of America. Its five doctrines and five pillars can be easily communicated. In the West it is making appeals to the universal brotherhood of man, world peace, temperance, and the uplifting of women.

(4) Islam is externalistic. A Muslim has no vital personal relationship with God. Prayers and worship lack spontaneity or individuality because everything is codified.

(5) Mohammed's life contrasts greatly with the life of Christ. Mohammed spent his last 10 years in almost constant warfare. He treated the Jews in Medina cruelly. He violated the law of the desert by plundering caravans to Mecca even during the months of pilgrimages. Because of his many wives (which exceeded the accepted limit of four), his household was filled with conflict and strife.

(6) In Moslem countries women have few rights. A man can easily secure a divorce, but a woman cannot. Though Islam condemns such things as stealing, lying, gambling, and drinking, these things have reached epidemic proportions in Moslem countries.

10

JUDAISM

Background and Teachings

The origin and development of modern Judaism is traced in the Old Testament. Moses was not the founder of Judaism since Yahweh, the God of Abraham, Isaac, and Jacob, was revered by the Hebrews before Moses' birth. The infinite-personal God of the Old Testament revealed Himself to man from the very beginning, but in a progressive way.

One of the central features around which current Judaism is built is the covenant relationship God established with Abraham (about 2085 B.C.). The Lord singled out this man and covenanted that his descendants would be a holy nation, set apart from the rest of the world to God.

The chosen line ran from Abraham through Isaac to Jacob. Then it continued through Jacob's 12 sons and their descendants, the 12 tribes of Israel. During their time of bondage in Egypt, the people of Israel grew from a small band to a full nation. At the end of this time Yahweh revealed Himself to Israel in action (the Exodus) and in words (the giving of the Law at Mount Sinai).

The Pentateuch (or Torah), which was written by Moses, remains the primary document of Judaism.

The Old Testament outlines the early history of Israel in detail. It describes the Conquest of Canaan under Joshua, the Period of the Judges, the United Monarchy under Saul, David, and Solomon, and the Divided Kingdoms of Israel (the Northern Kingdom, 10 tribes) and Judah (the Southern Kingdom, 2 tribes). The Northern Kingdom was overthrown by the Assyrians in 722 B.C.; the Southern Kingdom was destroyed by Babylon in 586 B.C. The Babylonian Captivity (or Exile) lasted for 70 years, and many Jews returned to Palestine afterward. Yahweh revealed much to the Israelites before, during, and after the Exile through a number of prophets (Judaism generally accepts the 39 books of the Old Testament as Scripture).

Many writers have speculated that early Jewish religion was polytheistic, idolatrous, and primitive. There is no evidence to support this view. It is built on an antisupernatural evolutionary presupposition rather than on solid data. Actually, the earliest books of the Old Testament reveal an advanced ethical monotheism without parallel in ancient literature. From the very beginning the God of the Old Testament is seen as a God of unlimited power, love, goodness, and justice. He is the infinite and personal Creator of all.

In God's covenant relationship with Israel, He made high moral demands, saying that blessing was dependent on social and moral justice. Yahweh constantly used the prophets to bring reform in the political and personal lives of His people.

The sacrificial system was given to show that sin required atonement. Israel had to be a redeemed people in order to enjoy fellowship with the holy God. In contrast, the gods of the other nations were immoral and indifferent. The Old Testament teaching is that ultimately God will bless all the nations of the earth through Israel. A Messiah, who is a descendant of King David, will come to redeem mankind and to reign as King over all the nations of the earth.

However, the Judaism of today is very different from the Old Testament religion. In the centuries following the Babylonian Exile, a number of important changes began to appear. Meeting places known as synagogues were instituted during the Exile. Even when the temple was rebuilt in Ezra's time, the synagogues continued to be the worship centers for most of the Jews. When the temple was finally destroyed by the Romans in A.D. 70, the synagogues became the official rallying points for Judaism.

With the end of the temple came the end of the sacrificial system. The synagogues substituted ritual, prayer, and the study of the Law for the sacrifices. The levitical priesthood was replaced by teachers of the Law, many of whom were Pharisees who had developed an elaborate oral tradition based on the Mosaic Law. The Law was applied in a complex way to every detail of life. External things like Sabbath observance, food preparation, dietary rules, and holy days were stressed. These Pharisees came to be known as rabbis (teachers).

About A.D. 200, the oral rabbinic traditions were finally written down. The result is known as the *Mishnah* (repetition). The Mishnah is placed almost on a par with the Mosaic Law. It is so important that lengthy commentaries on the Mishnah, known as the Gemaras, were also written. The Babylonian Gemara (A.D. 500) is longer and more popular than the Palestinian Gemara (A.D. 200). The combination of the Mishnah and the Babylonian Gemara is called the Babylonian Talmud. Similarly, the combination of Mishnah and the Palestinian Gemara is known as the Palestinian Talmud. The Talmud fills many volumes and contains Jewish folklore, traditions, and scholarly teachings.

The Romans drove the Jews out of Palestine in A.D. 135. Judaism survived because Jewish communities had been established. Each such community had at least one synagogue, and each synagogue was directed by a rabbi. Any Jew could become a rabbi if he acquired a good knowledge of the Law and was accepted as such by the congregation. The rabbis applied the Law and the talmudic teachings to the changing conditions of daily life.

With the temple, the priesthood, and the sacrificial system gone, synagogue teachers stressed the idea that every Jew had immediate access to God. As a Jew he needed no conversion or redemption. Instead, he could reach salvation by obedience to the Torah (the Law and the rabbinic interpretations of the Law). The rabbis broke the Law down into 613 precepts—365 negative precepts and 248 positive precepts. Each of these precepts has been elaborated in rabbinic teachings down to the finest details. The result is that Jewish life can become a carefully controlled ritual from cradle to grave.

In the 12th century, a Jewish philosopher named Maimonides produced a creed which is generally regarded as the basis of Orthodoxy. This creed emphasizes the omnipotence, omniscience, eternality, and oneness of God. God is an invisible spirit Being. As the only Creator and Source of Life, He alone should be worshiped.

Maimonides held Moses to be the greatest of the prophets and the Law to be the highest revelation. He also taught rewards and punishments, the coming of the Messiah, and the resurrection of the dead.

Judaism rejects the doctrine of original sin, saying that sin is an act, not a state. Thus, man has the ability to live according to the Law. If he fails, he only needs to come to God in repentance. With this view of sin, Judaism has eliminated the need for a Saviour. Many Jews do not anticipate the coming of a personal Messiah at all, but a Messianic Age. Those Jews who do expect a Messiah usually think of Him as a political and social deliverer, not a Saviour from sins.

One of the most important facets of Judaism is the series of festivals and holy days in every year. Rosh Hashanah is the new year festival marked by 10 days of penitence and solemnity. The 10th day of penitence is the Day of Atonement, when Jews acknowledge their sins and pray for forgiveness. Also important are the Festivals of Tabernacles (Succoth or Booths), Passover (commemoration of the Exodus), the Feast of Weeks (Shabuoth or Pentecost), Hanukkah (the Festival of Light), and Purim. These special days commemorate the joys and sorrows of Jewish history and serve as the main link with the past. They illustrate Judaism's concept of history as the meaningful product of God's activity.

Today Judaism is divided into three main branches: Orthodox, Reform, and Conservative. Within orthodoxy, there is also an ultraorthodox form of Judaism known as the Hasidic Movement. Orthodox Judaism has changed little in the last 20 centuries. It follows the talmudic teachings and precepts about Sabbath observance, kosher dietary rules, and marriage.

One reason for the absence of change over the centuries is the introspective tendency in Judaism. Atrocities and oppression have dogged the Jews in many countries, and this has forced them to maintain a cultural and religious isolation.

In the last century, however, Jewish people have shown increasing desire to adapt themselves to modern society. This is especially true in America, where they have been given more freedom and respect than in most countries. This has led to the rise of Reform Judaism. In this liberal form of Judaism, the talmudic practices and precepts have been put aside. Reform synagogues are usually called temples, and the Sabbath observance in many cases has been changed to Sunday. Reform Judaism has spiritualized doctrines such as the coming of the Messiah and the resurrection of the body. All that remains is an ethical system based on a monotheistic philosophy.

The third branch of Judaism is Conservative. This is an intermediate position between the Orthodox and Reform extremes. Conservative Judaism retains the feasts and many of the Jewish traditions in an attempt to hold to the essentials of Judaism. At the same time it cautiously reinterprets the Law in order to make it relevant for modern thought and culture. Conservative Jews are very progressive and active in the intellectual community.

Judaism also has its mystical and esoteric school of thought known as the Kabbalah (sometimes spelled Cabbala, Cabbalah, or Cabala). Practitioners of this pantheistic system seek a mystical experience of oneness with the cosmic whole. We will consider the Kabbalah in chapter 20.

Judaism, then, covers a wide range of beliefs and practices. There is nothing one must believe in order to be a Jew. In fact, there is a rapidly increasing secularization of Jews today. More and more of the Jewish population is moving away from all forms of Jewish religious practice. This has led to confusion in defining what makes a person Jewish. The biblical teaching is that the Jews are a race of people, descendants of Abraham through Jacob.

Biblical Evaluation
(1) Judaism essentially denies the sin nature and minimizes man's need of redemption. Repentance (turning back to God) is all that is needed when one fails to live according to the Law.

(2) Most expressions of Judaism are built on culture and tradition. Practice is usually emphasized more than belief. It is an ethical system and a way of life with a transcendent God in the background.

Things to Keep in Mind
(1) The real issue, of course, is the person and work of Jesus of Nazareth, who claimed to be the Messiah and whose life fulfilled many messianic prophecies. Christians can use the many Old Testament messianic texts to

support the New Testament claims about Christ. The Old Testament tells where Messiah would be born, when He would be cut off, and how and why He would die. Concentrate on Isaiah 53.

(2) It is important to note that the first Christians were Jews. Jesus was also a Jew. Most of the New Testament was written by Jews. Christianity has erroneously been pictured as a Gentile religion. Jews often think that to be "converted" to Christianity they must give up their Jewishness and become Gentiles. The New Testament, however, teaches that the great divide is between non-Christian and Christian, not between Jew and Gentile. There are Gentile Christians and there are Hebrew Christians. A Jew does not have to abandon his heritage in order to become a Christian.

(3) When dealing with Jews, focus on the meaning of Christ's sacrificial death and the fact of His resurrection. The Old Testament makes it clear that God has chosen blood to be the means for the forgiveness of sins (see Lev. 16–17). Isaiah 53 tells us that the Messiah had to die to provide a once-for-all blood sacrifice for sin.

(4) Rabbinic teaching has traditionally held that there must be two Messiahs: Messiah, the Son of Joseph (a suffering Saviour who would die), and Messiah, the Son of David (a victorious King who would establish the messianic kingdom on earth). The New Testament resolves this Old Testament paradox by combining the two Messiahs into one Person who comes two times.

PART TWO

Major Pseudo-Christian
Religions of the West

One or both of two characteristics are common to this group of religious societies: eclecticism and deception. Though Mormonism, Jehovah's Witnesses, and Seventh-Day Adventism could not be defined as eclectic movements, they do indulge in varying measures of deception. Christian Science, Unity, and Theosophy engage in both kinds of behavior rather freely.

By eclectic behavior we mean that the last three groups select, cafeteria style, what in their opinions are the most desirable features of several world religions. Then they combine and peddle them as though they were new products. They also deceptively promote these opinions by using biblical language while at the same time rejecting the biblical meaning of the language they use.

Seventh-Day Adventism has repositioned itself in recent times to reflect a more orthodox stance in regard to historic Christianity. However, there are some in the Seventh-Day Adventist Movement who still stumble over the continued recognition of Ellen G. White's divine authority and a salvation conditioned on keeping the Saturday Sabbath and dietary laws. To the extent that these Seventh-Day Adventists insist on these requirements, they are espousing the "other gospel" which the Apostle Paul sharply condemned (Gal. 1:6-9).

11

MORMONISM

Background and Teachings

Mormonism is one of the most effective counterfeits of biblical Christianity ever devised. It is a rapidly growing church whose influence far exceeds its numbers. Today there are over 6 million adherents of Mormonism, and it continues to multiply because of its zealous missionary program. Many of its young people spend two years as full-time missionaries. As a result, the church has about 18,000 missionaries who spend all their time promoting Mormonism. These missionaries are well trained, and they quote the Bible extensively. They work anywhere, but often concentrate on college towns.

Mormonism claims many influential and distinguished scientists, businessmen, and politicians. It exalts education (e.g., Brigham Young University and many seminaries) and has a strong literature campaign. The church, which is run like a giant corporation, has a huge annual income because of its many holdings and business investments. The church owns a great deal of land and is constantly erecting new buildings. All Mormons are required to tithe their incomes to the church and to give special offerings as well (for instance, "fast offerings").

Mormons have a good reputation with the general public because of their emphasis on high moral standards and on the family. They take care of their bodies, avoiding such indulgences as tea, coffee, Coca-Cola, alcohol, and tobacco.

The church has not always enjoyed good public relations, however, and has tried to cover up its questionable early history.

The founder of Mormonism, Joseph Smith, Jr., was born on December 23, 1805 in Sharon, Vermont. His father spent much time in Vermont and New York digging for buried treasure (he was looking especially for Captain Kidd's plunder). He also got into trouble for trying to mint his own money. A poorly educated and superstitious youth, Joseph Smith accompanied his father on digging expeditions and made extensive use of divining rods and peek stones in his attempt to find buried treasure. Smith's habits earned him a bad reputation among those who knew him as he was growing up in Palmyra, New York.

In 1820 Smith claimed he had received a vision in which both God the Father and God the Son appeared to him. He was told in this vision that all churches were abominations to God and that he was being charged as a prophet to restore the true gospel to the world.

In 1823 the angel Moroni allegedly appeared to Smith and told him about a number of golden plates which he would later uncover and translate. (In one account, however, Smith contradicted himself by calling this visitor Nephi rather than Moroni. This error, like many other grammatical and factual errors in Smith's writings, was "corrected" in later editions of his work.) Smith said that he finally uncovered the golden plates in 1827 in the hill Cumorah near Palmyra. These plates were inscribed with "reformed Egyptian hieroglyphics," which Smith was able to translate by means of a huge pair of spectacles called the "Urim and Thummim." From 1827 to 1829 he "translated" these plates, and in 1830 he published the result as *The Book of Mormon.*

After receiving the Aaronic priesthood from John the Baptist in a vision in 1829, Smith moved to Fayette, New York and founded the "Church of Jesus Christ of Latter-Day Saints." He built a core of followers and moved again in 1831 because of a "revelation" that the Mormons should settle in Ohio and Missouri.

Kirtland, Ohio and Zion, Missouri became the Mormon headquarters for several years. Mormons were accused of a number of crimes in those places and were required to leave Missouri by order of Governor Boggs in 1839.

Smith led the Mormons to Illinois, where they built a city named Nauvoo. There he instituted the practice of polygamy. Criticism began to mount in Illinois because of Smith's excesses, and when he tried to destroy a local newspaper office because of its stand against the Mormons, he and his brother Hyrum were placed in jail in Carthage, Illinois to await trial. Unfortunately, an angry mob stormed the jail on June 27, 1844 and shot Smith and his brother, thus making them martyrs for the cause of Mormonism.

Most of the Mormons soon submitted to the leadership of Brigham Young as the new "First President" and prophet of the church. He led thousands of Mormons on a strenuous journey toward the Southwest until they arrived in the Salt Lake Valley of Utah in July 1847. There Young announced, "This is the place!"

He guided the church in the office of First President until his death in 1877. He encouraged the practice of polygamy and took 25 wives for himself. He literally ruled the church and also had considerable influence on

Mormon theology. One of the lowest points in Mormon history occurred when Young ordered Bishop John D. Lee in 1857 to destroy a group of 150 non-Mormon immigrants (this incident was called the Mountain Meadow Massacre).

The Mormons vehemently resisted the U.S. government's efforts to make Utah a state and later resisted the laws forbidding polygamy. They officially repudiated this practice only when the United States government threatened them with the loss of their property.

Today the Church of Jesus Christ of Latter-Day Saints (headquarters in Salt Lake City, Utah) is divided into a series of "wards" and "stakes," and led by a First President, a Council of Twelve Apostles, and a Council of Seventy. There are also bishops, counselors, and teachers. In addition, most Mormon males serve as deacons or elders. Males over 12 years old are also members of the Mormon priesthood of Aaron or Melchizedek. The idea is that the Mormon Church restored both priesthoods. (Heb. 7–9 clearly refutes this doctrine by teaching that the Aaronic priesthood has been replaced by the new priesthood of Melchizedek. This is the priesthood of Christ and it is untransferable. All Christians today are priests by virtue of their belief in Christ.)

Mormons view all non-Mormons as "Gentiles," charging that for many centuries there was no church at all until the restoration of the true church by Joseph Smith. It is interesting that during the time when Smith said all the churches were apostate they were actually going through one of the greatest periods of revival in church history.

Mormons emphasize the many Protestant denominations in existence and charge that the Bible is not an adequate revelation because it has not produced unity. They fail to realize, however, that real Christians cross denominational barriers. Most denominations accept the Apostles' Creed. The many strong transdenominational organizations (for instance, Campus Crusade for Christ, the Navigators, Search Ministries, Inter-Varsity Christian Fellowship, and numerous missionary societies) prove that these barriers are overemphasized.

Moreover, the Mormons have undergone splits of their own—there are at least six different Mormon sects. By far the largest is the Utah "Brighamite" Mormon church which accepts Brigham Young as the true successor of Joseph Smith. The second largest group is the Reorganized Church of Jesus Christ of Latter-Day Saints with headquarters in Independence, Missouri. This sect, also known as the "Josephite" church, claims that the President of the church must be a descendant of Joseph Smith. (However, they had no descendant of Smith to be their president until 16 years after his death.) They also repudiate polygamy and some of the doctrines of Brigham Young. They accept Smith's "Inspired Version" of the Bible, while most "Brighamites" do not.

Other Mormon sects include the "Hendrickites," the "Bickertonites," the "Cutlerites," and the "Strangites."

The scriptures of Mormonism include the Bible, *The Book of Mormon, Doctrines and Covenants,* and *The Pearl of Great Price. The Book of Mormon,* which supposedly was written by several people from about 600 B.C. to A.D. 428, tells of the migration of an ancient people from the Tower of Babel to Central America. These people, known as the Jaredites, perished because of apostasy. A later migration occurred in 600 B.C., when a group of Jews were supposedly told by God to flee Jerusalem before the Babylonian Capitivity. These Jews, led by Lehi and his son Nephi, crossed the Pacific Ocean and landed in South America. There they divided into two opposing nations, the Nephites and the Lamanites. The Lamanites, cursed with dark skin because of their iniquity, were the ancestors of the American Indians. Similarly, the black people are said to have been cursed with dark skin because they are descendants of Cain, the first murderer. Until recently, Mormons have not allowed blacks to enter their priesthood.

The Nephites recorded prophecies about the coming of Christ, and after His resurrection Christ visited them there in South America. He instituted communion, baptism, and the priesthood for the Nephites. They were annihilated in a battle with the Lamanites in A.D. 428. Before they were killed in this battle, Mormon, the compiler of the divinely revealed *Book of Mormon*, and his son Moroni took the golden plates on which the "revelation" was recorded and buried them. These plates were uncovered 1,400 years later by Joseph Smith.

Here are just a few of the problems with *The Book of Mormon:*

(1) Joseph Smith allowed only a few "witnesses" to see the alleged golden plates, which were then taken into heaven by the angel Moroni. There were two sets of witnesses, a group of three (Oliver Cowdry, David Whitmer, and Martin Harris), and a group of eight. The people in the first group were later denounced by Smith as men of low character. Furthermore, their stories did not agree, and Harris admitted that he only saw the plates "by the eye of faith." Of the second set of witnesses, four were Whitmers, the fifth was married to a Whitmer, and the remaining three were Smith's father and two brothers. The Whitmers were later expelled from the church as apostates and repudiated by Smith. This leaves no reliable witnesses of the plates.

(2) Though *The Book of Mormon* was buried in A.D. 428, it contains about 25,000 words *verbatim* from the A.D. 1611 *King James Version* of the Bible! This is a 1,200 to 2,200 year anachronism (depending on what book within *The Book of Mormon* is being considered). The words of Christ, Peter, Paul, John, and other New Testament writers are indiscriminately placed in the mouths of people who lived centuries before Christ, and all copied from the *King James Version*. This is especially interesting since these plates were allegedly translated by Smith from "reformed Egyptian hieroglyphics." In addition to these obvious plagiarisms, *The Book of Mormon* is written in a wordy

imitation of the biblical style of the early 17th century.

(3) The book is full of historical and factual errors. For instance, the American Indians are of Mongoloid extraction, not Semitic, as *The Book of Mormon* claims. There is no archeological evidence to support the existence of the huge civilizations described in *The Book of Mormon*. Everything known about pre-Columbian archeology of the Americas contradicts Mormon claims.

(4) Over 2,000 corrections have been made in *The Book of Mormon* since the 1830 edition. Many of these changed the meaning of the text. This is strange, since Smith claims his translation was divinely given. In spite of all these corrections, the book still abounds with factual and grammatical errors, anachronisms, contradictions, and false prophecies. Smith even copied translation errors of the *King James Version* as he was plagiarizing verses.

(5) There is no such thing as "reformed Egyptian hieroglyphics," and certainly this was not the language spoken by the early inhabitants of the Americas.

(6) Most researchers on the subject agree that *The Book of Mormon* is actually Smith's expansion of a romance called *Manuscript Found,* written by a retired minister named Solomon Spaulding. The story behind Smith's "translation" of the *Pearl of Great Price* is even more bizarre. Smith purportedly bought from a traveling showman some mummies which were wrapped in papyrus sheets containing the writings of Abraham!

Yet the Mormon attitude toward the Bible is that it is not very reliable since it supposedly contains many translational errors. Mormons accept the *King James Version* only "insofar as it is correctly translated." What determines when it is correctly translated? Mormon doctrine. Whenever Mormon doctrine is contrary to biblical passages, those passages are said to be improperly translated. However, it is interesting that the thousands of verses plagiarized from the *King James Version* in *The Book of Mormon* were adopted unchanged. Those verses at least were not corrupted!

Mormon theology is definitely not a form of Christianity. Smith's earlier writings were monotheistic, but his view of God degenerated in his later work. He said that "God was once as we are now, and is an exalted man." God was not always God, but developed into His present state. God has a body of flesh and blood.

Smith, Young, and other Mormon authorities teach that men have the potential to become gods themselves. These Mormon theologians, unable to think beyond the realm of the physical, distort biblical passages to support their views. They refuse to allow any aspect of God to be incomprehensible to man. Mormon doctrine asserts that there are many worlds which are controlled by different gods. It appears that Mormon theology is actually henotheistic. That is, it exalts one God (the Father-God) above the other gods in the universe.

The Holy Spirit causes problems in the Mormon system. While they say that the Father and the Son each have physical bodies, they are unable to say the same for the Holy Spirit. The Holy Spirit is usually regarded as an impersonal substance of spiritual "fluid" which is dispensed in varying degrees to individuals.

Jesus Christ's deity is minimized in Mormonism. Mormons say He is really not so different from other men. He is eternal, but the spirits of all men are eternal in the same way. Mormon theology teaches that the gods produced spirit children from eternity, but that they had to wait for incarnate men to provide bodies for them by procreation. Christ was one of these spirit children (the spirit brother of Lucifer) who received a body and is now elevated to the level of deity. The real difference between Christ and men is one of time rather than nature. He is referred to as "our elder brother."

Most Mormons believe that Jesus Christ is the natural offspring of Mary and Adam (or Adam-God, the god of our world), not the Holy Spirit. (It was the Adam-God who came into the Garden of Eden and brought Eve, *one* of His celestial wives.) Christ was a polygamist (he married the two Marys and Martha) and produced children. If He had had no offspring He would not have been exalted to the level of deity, according to Mormon reasoning.

Mormons teach that Christ's death and atonement only removes guilt for past sins. This places man in a position in which he can earn his own salvation by means of good works. Justification by faith is clearly denied in Mormonism. Salvation involves faith in Christ, repentance, baptism by immersion, obedience to the teaching of the Mormon church, good works, and baptism by the Holy Spirit through the laying on of hands. Hear the words from an official Mormon text: "Salvation in the kingdom of God is available because of the atoning blood of Christ. But it is received only on condition of faith, repentance, baptism, and enduring to the end in keeping the commandments" (*What Mormons Think of Christ*, B.R. McConkie).

Salvation is progression toward becoming a god. When one attains godhood, he is able to create and populate worlds of his own, and thus the process continues forever.

Mormons deny the doctrine of original sin and actually teach that the fall of man was a good and necessary thing. Man had to disobey one of God's commands (do not eat the fruit) in order to obey another (procreation). Thus there is no imputed sin nature from Adam, and children are born in a state of complete innocence. However, all children eventually sin and reach an age of accountability for their sins.

Polygamy is an important doctrine in Mormonism. Since the Mormons were forced to abandon this practice in 1890, they have substituted the practice of "celestial marriage." Marriages must be sealed in the Mormon secret temples in order for them to endure for eternity. A man can seal up for himself several wives for the future life by engaging in special rites in Mormon temples. This arrangement is also thought to benefit the women, since apart from celestial marriage they cannot attain the highest glory. Procreation now and in the hereafter is considered essential (this violates Christ's teaching—see Matt. 22:30).

Perhaps the most widespread practice in Mormon temples is baptism for the dead and laying on of hands for the dead. Since Mormons believe that baptism by immersion in the Mormon church is necessary for salvation, they compile elaborate genealogies of their "Gentile" ancestors and baptize them by proxy. Millions of the dead have in this way been "baptized" and thus assured of salvation.

According to Mormonism, all people will be resurrected, and those who have solemnized "celestial marriages" through the Mormon church will keep their wives in the next world. There will be no new marriages.

Mormons lean toward universalism in that they minimize hell and say that all men will go to one of three heavens. Unbelievers go to the telestial heaven, religious non-Mormons go to the terrestial heaven, and good Mormons go to the celestial heaven. The celestial heaven is itself subdivided into three sections corresponding to one's services rendered the church on earth as deacon, teacher, priest, elder, bishop, the 70, apostle, or president. The highest eventual reward is for one to become a god and to create and rule a separate planet with his family.

Biblical Evaluation
(1) Mormon theology is far removed from biblical Christianity. It is a system which denies or perverts every cardinal Christian doctrine.

(2) Mormonism places Joseph Smith's writings on a higher plane than the Bible. It says that wherever the Bible is at variance with Mormon doctrine, the Bible is incorrectly translated.

(3) Mormonism denies justification by faith and offers a works system in which salvation is actually progress toward godhood.

Things to Keep in Mind

(1) Mormons present their doctrines in a subtle way, so as to preserve a veneer of orthodoxy.

(2) Mormonism is growing because it provides significant benefits. It offers social security—the church always takes care of the needs of its people. It strives to build the family unit and provides many programs for Mormon youth (scouting, recreation, dances). This results in a very low rate of juvenile delinquency. The church challenges its laymen to be actively involved and provides a host of things for them to do. Mormonism is pervaded with the idea that everything practiced in the church is a result of divine revelation. These are appeals the evangelical Christian church ought to have.

(3) Since the teachings of Mormonism cannot be reconciled with the Bible, Mormons can be delivered from this cult by an honest study of the Bible. They should be challenged to compare the Bible with the teachings of Mormonism.

(4) No Mormon can claim that he *has* eternal life in Christ. Their works system of salvation leads to lack of certainty. This is an important area for Christians to develop with Mormons, because the New Testament emphasizes that certainty of salvation is available for those who base their salvation on Christ's finished work on their behalf (John 20:31).

12

JEHOVAH'S WITNESSES

Background and Teachings

Jehovah's Witnesses, best known for its door-to-door approach to evangelism, is a rapidly growing "Christian" cult whose members are instilled with missionary zeal and urgency.

The founder of the organization that came to be known as Jehovah's Witnesses was Charles Taze Russell (1852–1916). Raised in Allegheny, Pennsylvania where he was indoctrinated in the teachings of the Congregational Church, Russell became the manager of several clothing stores in North Pittsburgh.

Early, Russell had a strong fear of hell, but he later abandoned the idea of eternal punishment when he got involved in the teachings of Seventh-Day Adventism. He began to teach Bible classes (which is how he got the title

"Pastor" Russell, though he was never ordained), and to write books and pamphlets. His teaching and writing was strongly influenced by Adventism, especially in his view of hell and the time of Christ's coming.

When Russell began to disagree with the Adventists on several points (especially the Atonement), he launched his own magazine, *Zion's Watchtower and Herald of Christ's Presence*. Five years later, in 1884, he founded Zion's Watchtower Tract Society and incorporated it as a non-profit religious organization. In 1896 the Society was re-named the Watchtower Bible and Tract Society, and in 1908 the headquarters were moved to Brooklyn, New York.

Russell promoted his modified Adventism extensively through his voluminous writings. His most important work was a seven-volume series called *Studies in the Scriptures*. The first volume appeared in 1886 and the seventh volume was published in 1917 after his death. The last several years of his life were spent in extensive traveling and speaking.

An extremely egotistical man, "Pastor" Russell made absurd claims about himself and his writings. He allowed his followers to class him with such men as St. Paul, Wycliffe, and Luther. He said that if people had to make a choice between reading his books and reading the Scriptures, they would do better to choose his books. His wife successfully sued him for divorce in 1913 on the grounds of adultery, conceit, egotism, and domination. He personally controlled the finances of the Tract Society since he owned 990 of its 1,000 shares of stock. He was charged with fraudulent activities by the *Brooklyn Daily Eagle* and clearly perjured himself in court. Under oath he testified that he knew the Greek alphabet, but when he was unable to identify the letters of the alphabet on re-quest, he was forced to retract.

It is not surprising, then, that Jehovah's Witnesses dis-claim any connection with Charles Russell. They dislike being branded "Russellites," yet the facts of history prove that he was their founder and organizer. It is also obvious that his doctrines are the same as the doctrines of the Jehovah's Witnesses movement today.

"Pastor" Russell was succeeded as president of the Watchtower Bible and Tract Society in 1917 by Joseph Franklin Rutherford. Rutherford was a lawyer and an assistant judge in Booneville, Missouri and later moved to New York. Soon after Rutherford became president of the Society, several Russellites left and started a number of smaller sects. Rutherford warned them that they would suffer destruction if they did not return. During Rutherford's leadership from 1917 to his death in 1942 at age 72, he increased his power and control of the movement until he reached the point of unquestioned authority. Any who opposed him were ousted immediately.

Taking his cue from Isaiah 43:10, Rutherford decided in 1931 to call his organization Jehovah's Witnesses in an attempt to eliminate any connection with "Pastor" Russell.

Rutherford also scathingly denounced all organized religions and generated among his followers a tone of unmitigated hostility toward Christian churches. This hatred of other religions and institutions has become an earmark of this cult and has caused a good deal of trouble for the Witnesses.

Rutherford's work differed from Russell's in that he had almost no public ministry. He was surrounded by an air of mystery, but he was at least as effective as Russell in providing guidance as an organizer and administrator.

Rutherford was an even more prolific writer than Russell. He wrote many books and booklets and these enjoyed a circulation of millions of copies per year. His writings supplanted those of Russell, but the doctrines were embellished, not changed.

Nathan Homer Knorr became the third president of the Watchtower Bible and Tract Society in 1942. Knorr proved to be a strong administrator, and under his leadership the Jehovah's Witnesses stressed the training of their people. He was a less conspicuous figure than his two predecessors and he changed the image of the movement. The constant torrent of Watchtower literature that poured from the presses during Knorr's administration was anonymous. Just as Rutherford minimized the writings of Russell, so Knorr ignored most of the works of Rutherford. Frederick William Franz is the Society's current president.

✗Jehovah's Witnesses are trained to become ordained ministers at the Gilead Missionary Training School in South Lansing, New York. All laymen are trained on Sundays in "Kingdom Halls," and other studies are available during the week.

The doctrines of Jehovah's Witnesses place reason above the teaching of the Bible and reject anything in Scripture that is beyond man's understanding. This has led to a systematic denial of most of the doctrines of historic Christianity, especially the doctrine of the Trinity and the God-Man. Jehovah's Witnesses deny the deity of Jesus Christ and of the Holy Spirit; they also deny Christ's bodily resurrection and second coming.

Though they claim that the Bible is their final authority for truth, the Jehovah's Witnesses' real authority is their official system of interpretation. The literature and doctrine of the Witnesses act as *infallible interpreters* of Scripture, and no deviations are tolerated. The original doctrines of Russell are imposed on the Scriptures with the practical result that no Jehovah's Witness has a right to his own inductive judgment. Jehovah's Witnesses officially claim that there is no infallible human authority, but in practice they slavishly follow an authoritarian system.

Jehovah's Witnesses have produced their own "translation" of the Bible, known as *The New World Translation*. As with other Witness literature, this translation is being widely distributed around the world and its producers are anonymous. Thus, there is no way of knowing the credentials of its translators and whether they worked from the original languages or from interlinear editions and other translations. In spite of the astonishing claims made for this translation, it is clearly not a competent piece of work. It often distorts passages in order to make them conform to the erroneous doctrines of the Jehovah's Witnesses. Here are examples:

(1) John 1:1 is rendered "the Word was a god" in order to deny the deity of Jesus Christ, but this is contrary to Greek grammar. There is no indefinite article in Greek corresponding to our *a* and *an*. So when John writes, "The Word was God," there is no call for including an English indefinite article. The only reason for using an English indefinite article would be if more than one true God were revealed anywhere in the Old or New Testament. Then *a* god (i.e., one among others) might be translated. But the Bible nowhere suggests the existence of more than one true God. Therefore the standard translation is the only one that can make any sense in the Bible.

(2) *The New World Translation* of the New Testament uses the name "Jehovah" for God. While the Witnesses believe that Jehovah is the only true name for God, this word is never used for God in the original Scriptures. In the Old Testament it is actually a combination of the Hebrew consonants for *YHVH* and the vowels from *Adonai* (meaning Lord). Thus the Tetragrammaton *(YHVH)* is better rendered *Yahweh*. But this word does not occur in any of the New Testament manuscripts, contrary to *The New World Translation*.

(3) This translation adds words that are not in the Greek (e.g., Col. 1:16, "By means of him all *other* things were created") in an unscholarly attempt to support Jehovah's Witnesses' dogmas. It also distorts or deletes many other words from the original text for the same purpose.

The doctrine of the Trinity is denied by Jehovah's Witnesses in no uncertain terms. They say that Satan is the originator of this doctrine. Witnesses reject the concept of the Trinity because they cannot reconcile it with their reasoning. They come up with ludicrous questions and childish arguments designed to ridicule the concept of God as the Three-in-One. In order to maintain this teaching they must distort some passages and ignore others.

One result of their rejection of the Trinity is that they must deny the deity of the Holy Spirit. Jehovah's Witnesses clearly do this, teaching that the Holy Spirit is an impersonal force of God, not a Person. Their *New World Translation* consistently distorts the Greek pronouns by referring to the Holy Spirit as "it," "which," and "that." They teach that the Spirit is "not of God, not a member of a trinity, not coequal, and is not even a person." They liken Him to a radar beam or a controlled force.

Another corollary of rejecting the Trinity is the denial of Jesus Christ's deity. Using their inaccurate translation of the Bible to play down His divinity, they distort the meaning of such terms as "only begotten," "greater than I," "firstborn," and "Son of God" to support their unbiblical conclusions about Him. They assert that Christ was the first creation of Jehovah, and that Jehovah used Christ to create everything else. Before His incarnation He was known as Michael, the captain of Jehovah's hosts. ⚹

Jehovah's Witnesses also distort the doctrine of the Virgin Birth, saying that Christ simply changed His nature from a spirit creature to a human, when He was known as Jesus. The Jehovah's Witnesses therefore deny the central truth of Christianity, that God became a Man and offered Himself for our sins. In order to maintain this false position they must ignore or abuse many passages of Scripture, including Isaiah 7:14; 9:6; Micah 5:2; John 1:1; 8:58; Philippians 2:11; Colossians 2:9; Titus 2:13; and Hebrews 1:3, 8. Jehovah's Witnesses desperately cling to their grammatical arguments and proof texts in order to deny Christ's deity because they know if Christ really is Jehovah God they are doomed.

Though Jehovah's Witnesses believe that Christ was sinless, they minimize His redemptive work on the cross.

They teach that Christ offered only a partial atonement for sins. His death removed the effects of Adam's sin and put man in a position to work out his own salvation. Christ did not provide a true ransom for sins but merely gave man an opportunity to merit his salvation either now or in the Millennium.

Jehovah's Witnesses also distort the biblical doctrines of the bodily resurrection and return of the Lord Jesus. They claim that Christ was raised as a spirit; the body of Jesus "dissolved in gases," and the man Jesus is forever dead. It follows from this that the Witnesses also believe that Christ's return to the earth would be a spiritual and invisible return. As in the case of other doctrines, the Jehovah's Witnesses must engage in considerable exegetical gymnastics in order to arrive at this position.

But there is more: Witnesses teach that Christ's second coming to the earth has already taken place! It involved three stages: in 1874 Christ came to the "upper air" and later caught up the apostles and dead members of the 144,000, who will be immortal; in 1914 Christ ended the times of the Gentiles and began to reign; and in 1918 he came to the spiritual temple and began the judgment of the nations.

Jehovah's Witnesses are now eagerly awaiting not the return of Christ but the imminent battle of Armageddon in which Christ will lead Jehovah's forces to victory over evil. Only the faithful Witnesses will escape death in this battle. Then there will be an earthly resurrection of all the dead (the heavenly spiritual resurrection of the 144,000 members of the body of Christ will have been completed). Everyone who was annihilated (the Jehovah's Witnesses' concept of death) will be recreated and given a second chance during the Millennium to believe and obey Jehovah. Those who fail during the probationary period will be permanently destroyed. All who remain on the earth after this will be "Jonadabs" who will enjoy a perfect earth forever. The 144,000 will remain in heaven with Christ.

Satan and his demons will be released to test the faith of those on earth at the end of the Millennium, and they will be destroyed. Thus, for Jehovah's Witnesses the goal of all history is the vindication of the name of Jehovah.

Jehovah's Witnesses emphatically deny the biblical concept of hell and claim that Sheol and Hades mean only "the grave." They fall into one of their common errors at this point, that of forcing a word to have only one meaning regardless of its context. This they do despite the many passages which clearly teach that hell is a place of torment and conscious separation from God (see Matt. 8:11-12; 13:42, 50; 22:13; Luke 13:24-28; 16:19-31; Rev. 14:9-11).

Jehovah's Witnesses deny conscious punishment and argue instead for painless extinction (absence of being). This implies a superficial view of the evil of sin and of the holiness of God. It also involves the corollary teaching that man does not possess an immortal soul. They claim that man *is* a soul. But the Bible teaches that the soul exists as a conscious entity after it departs from the body (cf. Luke 20:37-38; Rev. 6:9-11), and that it will be joined to a glorified resurrection body.

Jehovah's Witnesses are known for their negative views on blood transfusions and human government. They make the incredible application from Leviticus 17:13-14 that since the Israelites were commanded not to eat blood, Jehovah's Witnesses should refuse blood transfusions. And they believe that it is idolatry to salute the flag of any nation, because they should show no allegiance to any government except Jehovah's (but see Rom. 13:1-7; 1 Peter 2:13-14).

Biblical Evaluation

(1) As we have seen, the theology of the Jehovah's Witnesses denies or distorts almost every significant biblical truth, including the Trinity, the deity of Christ, the Virgin Birth, the Resurrection, the Second Coming, the work of the Cross, the deity and personality of the Holy Spirit,

salvation, eschatology, the nature of man, and hell.

(2) The Jehovah's Witnesses arrived at their position by imposing a false system of doctrine on the Scriptures. This system is directly traceable to the writings of Charles Taze Russell. It is therefore not incorrect to call them Russellites in spite of their protests to the contrary.

(3) This cult violates every sound principle of hermeneutics (biblical interpretation) to support its teachings. Its leaders are especially guilty of taking strings of verses out of context and of making Hebrew and Greek words mean only what they want them to mean. Because of their policy of anonymity, none of their writers and "translators" can be made to answer for their many blunders in exegesis and translation.

(4) This is another works system (autosalvation) because it minimizes the efficacy of Christ's redeeming blood.

Things to Keep in Mind

(1) Jehovah's Witnesses are impelled with a great sense of urgency which makes them bold and aggressive. As a result, their movement is growing rapidly. They are zealous missionaries because their only test of "faithfulness" is the degree to which they canvass neighborhoods and promote their system. They believe that the destruction of Armageddon is coming one day, and they work diligently in order to be counted worthy to escape this judgment.

(2) Uninformed Christians are easy prey for the Witnesses, who know proof texts for all of their doctrines. Christians should spend more time in systematic Bible study so that they may know how to biblically support true doctrines. Believers should also know how to examine the *contexts* of passages used by the cult.

(3) We must challenge Jehovah's Witnesses to be willing to abide by the verdict of the Bible regardless of the official teaching of their organization. Jehovah's Witnesses are not allowed to think independently. The Society,

not the Bible, becomes their real authority for truth because it offers its interpretations as infallible.

(4) The deity of Christ should be the central issue in any discussion with Jehovah's Witnesses. We should be able to present a clear biblical case for Christ's deity because their whole system crumbles when Christ is seen to be Jehovah (Yahweh) God.

CHRISTIAN
SCIENCE

Background and Teachings

Biographies of Mary Baker Eddy, the founder of Christian Science, fall into two basic categories: official and unofficial. Early biographies written by her contemporaries have been suppressed because they reveal too much about her real character and life. The church has attempted to destroy these books and to rewrite Mrs. Eddy's history. Nevertheless, the best documented books and the facts of history reveal that her life and practices contradicted the teachings she promoted.

Mary Ann Morse Baker was born in 1821 in Bow, New Hampshire. She was raised by strict Congregationalist parents, and her youth was marred by various illnesses and spinal problems. At an early age she reacted against her faith.

In 1843 she married a businessman named George Washington Glover. Glover died of yellow fever in 1844, and Mary Baker Glover bore their child a few months later in 1845. This traumatic event, coupled with her illnesses, seriously affected her emotionally and mentally. The child, named George, was practically abandoned by his mother who sent him off to school and to live with relatives.

Then in 1853 Mrs. Glover married a dentist named Daniel M. Patterson. This proved to be an unhappy marriage, partly because of her physical and emotional difficulties. Patterson left her 13 years later, and after 7 more years of separation Mrs. Patterson secured a divorce (1873).

During her years as Mrs. Patterson, two important events took place which affected the course of her life. The first occurred in 1862 when she went to Portland, Maine to be healed of her spinal illness by so-called "Dr." Phineas Parkhurst Quimby. P.P. Quimby, influenced by a French mesmerist named Charles Poyen, had developed a system of mental healing he called "The Science of Health" or "Christian Science." Mrs. Patterson was cured through Quimby's technique, and she became an ardent disciple of Quimbyism. She spent many hours compiling notes from the teachings and manuscripts of Quimby, and it is evident that her book *Science and Health*, first published in 1875, contains much of Quimby's material.

Quimby died not long after he healed Mrs. Patterson, and about that time her abundant praise for him began to cease. She later denied that her theories came from him and claimed that her system of healing through the mind was superior to his mesmerism. Nevertheless, Mary Baker Eddy's system is heavily dependent on the teachings of P.P. Quimby. The main difference is that she infused it with religion.

The second important event took place on February 1, 1866, when Mrs. Patterson claimed that she had been pronounced incurable and given only three days to live because of a fall on an icy sidewalk. On the third day she read Matthew 9:2 and suddenly found herself miraculously healed. This, she said, was her discovery of Christian Science.

This story is more than a little suspect, however, since the physician in question denied under oath that he pronounced her to be in dangerous physical condition. He also said she visited him four times later in 1866 to receive medical treatments. Furthermore, a pupil of the late P.P. Quimby received a letter from her two weeks after her fall saying that she had not yet recovered.

In 1877 at the age of 56, Mary Baker Glover Patterson married Asa Gilbert Eddy, a sewing machine salesman. From 1866 to 1882, Mrs. Eddy taught the principles of Christian Science for large fees in Lynn, Massachusetts. She published her book *Science and Health* in 1875 and officially formed The Christian Scientists. The name was changed to the Christian Science Association in 1877, and in 1879 she incorporated it as the Church of Christ, Scientist. Asa Eddy became the first Christian Scientist "practitioner."

Soon a number of her students in Lynn, Massachusetts began to revolt, and Mrs. Eddy decided to move to Boston. There she established the "Massachusetts Metaphysical College" where she taught from 1881 to 1889.

Asa Eddy died of a heart attack in 1882, but Mrs. Eddy contested the autopsy report and claimed that he died of "arsenic poisoning mentally administered." She found a physician who confirmed her claim, but on investigation it was found that this physician, a "Dr." C.J. Eastman, had no medical credentials. Eastman was then sentenced to 10 years in prison for illegally running a medical college. Another damaging fact was that Mrs. Eddy violated her own teaching in *Science and Health* that no Christian Science practitioner should be involved in a postmortem examination.

Mrs. Eddy's years in Boston marked the turning point

in her career. Many churches were founded and the membership began to increase dramatically. By 1900 the Christian Science Church had well over 200,000 members, and Mary Baker Eddy was its uncontested authority. Many of her followers came to regard her as an equal to and successor of Christ, and she began to make such claims herself.

Mrs. Eddy amassed a large fortune from the members of her church through a number of means. For instance, she demanded that all Scientists regularly promote and sell her works (which she regarded as being at least as inspired as the Bible). She also required each Christian Scientist to purchase new editions of her *Science and Health*, even though the changes between editions were almost negligible. There was also the well-known "teajacket swindle"; "Mother" Eddy requested *all* Christian Scientists to contribute to the purchase of three jackets for her for Christmas.

In her last years Mrs. Eddy declined mentally and physically. She died in 1910 at the age of 89. Her personal fortune was then valued at over 3 million dollars, none of which went to charity.

Almost immediately after Mrs. Eddy's death, a number of divisions arose among Christian Scientists over who should take the lead. The already existing Board of Directors assumed control and established a self-perpetuating directorate, thereby preventing any individual from sitting on Mary Baker Eddy's throne. Several groups reacted against this. One dissenting group called itself the Christian Science Parent Church and claimed that Mrs. Annie Bill was Mrs. Eddy's rightful successor. Another group was led by a Mrs. Stetson. In time, however, these groups faded away. Today, the five-man Board of Directors has authority over more than 3,000 branches of the Boston "Mother Church" and more than 8,000 Christian Science practitioners.

Mrs. Eddy claimed that she was inspired by a direct revelation from God when she wrote *Science and Health*, and she placed it on a par with the Bible. (She believed that she was the woman of Revelation 12 because she was being given the "key to the Scriptures.") She also said that the ideas contained in it were original with her and that plagiarism is wrong. A close look at *Science and Health with Key to the Scriptures* reveals, however, that Mrs. Eddy plagiarized the ideas and writings of others. The manuscripts of P.P. Quimby and his ideas were the true basis for her work. She also copied a great deal of material from a manuscript written by Francis Lieber entitled *The Metaphysical Religion of Hegel*. Her writing is an odd combination of elements from the philosophy of Berkeley and Hegel and the mental therapy of Franz Mesmer and Phineas Quimby. Another example of Mrs. Eddy's plagiarism is her 1895 annual message to the Christian Science Church (contained in her *Miscellaneous Writings*). This message is almost a word-for-word copy of a sermon found in *Murray's Reader*.

Mary Baker Eddy was not well educated, and in spite of the claims of her followers, she knew almost nothing about philosophy, logic, theology, Hebrew, Greek, or biblical history. *Science and Health* is full of repetition, mystical jargon, rambling sentences, and ambiguity designed to give the impression of profundity. The material is disjointed and far removed from any logical sequence. The earliest editions are full of grammatical errors which were corrected in subsequent editions. All this is quite strange if this book was indeed inspired by God. Why were so many editions and revisions necessary?

Science and Health with Key to the Scriptures presents itself as the only correct interpretation of the Bible. The Christian Science Church claims to be the only true church, the modern restoration of primitive Christianity. Nothing could be further from the truth. Christian Science actually repudiates every cardinal doctrine of the Bible.

Mrs. Eddy claimed that the Bible was her only authority. Yet she discredited it by emphasizing the thousands of "mistakes" that have crept into the text. She referred to the Genesis 2 Creation account as "a lie." It is clear from her approach to the Bible that she approved it when she thought it supported her teaching but repudiated those passages which refuted her position. Mrs. Eddy interpreted the Bible in a nonliteral, spiritualized sense, and she generally distorted it by taking phrases and verses completely out of context. Since *Science and Health* is regarded as the inspired and infallible interpretation of the Bible, it is more authoritative in the eyes of Christian Scientists than the Bible. In their worship services, the Bible and *Science and Health* are read alternately by two readers.

Christian Science denies the Trinity and the deity of Christ. Mrs. Eddy wrote in *Science and Health* that the doctrine of the Trinity is heathenistic and polytheistic. For her, the Triune God simply consists of Life, Truth, and Love. The Christian Science view of God is impersonal and *pantheistic*. God does not have a mind; He *is* Mind. God is Principle, Life, Intelligence, Spirit, Substance, Mother. God is not personal because Mary Baker Eddy could not conceive of an infinite being who has limitless personality. As for the Holy Spirit, *it* is nothing other than Christian Science itself! And angels are simply "thoughts from God, winged with Truth and Love."

Mrs. Eddy's ignorance of biblical theology and terminology led her to say that Jesus was the Son of God, but *not* God. She drew a false distinction between Jesus (the human) and Christ (the divine idea). Jesus the man was personal but the Christ is impersonal. Mrs. Eddy taught that "a portion of God could not enter man." Her concept of the Virgin Birth was that Mary conceived a spiritual idea of God, and gave to her ideal the name of Jesus. "Jesus was the offspring of Mary's self-conscious communion with God." Mrs. Eddy accepted the position that she was herself the equal and successor of Jesus Christ.

Because the Christian Science system claims that such things as sin, disease, and death are illusions of mortal mind, it reinterprets Christ's miracles of healing. Christ healed by showing people that there is no disease. He removed the illusion from their minds.

Christian Science denies the doctrine of the vicarious atonement of Christ. *Science and Health* states that "the material blood of Jesus was no more efficacious to cleanse from sin when it was shed upon the 'the accursed tree' than when it was flowing in his veins as he went daily about his Father's business." Christ's crucifixion was efficacious only in the sense that it demonstrated true affection and goodness to mankind. Mrs. Eddy further adds that Jesus *did not die* as a result of the Crucifixion, for death is illusory. Also, the Resurrection was not bodily but spiritual. Jesus only appeared to have a body after His resurrection because He had to accommodate Himself to the disciples' immature ideas of spiritual power.

Mrs. Eddy's pantheistic system rules out the possibility of evil. "Man is incapable of sin, sickness, and death." "All sin is insanity in different degrees." This, of course, includes a denial of the existence of evil creatures such as Satan and demons.

The system of Christian Science is based on a number of logical fallacies. It is a form of absolute idealism which claims that matter as such does not exist. The basic syllogism used to arrive at the conclusion is this: God is all, God is Mind, therefore Mind is all. Another syllogism follows from this: mind is all, matter is not mind, therefore matter does not exist. Mrs. Eddy is also guilty of logical fallacy known as the rule of inversion. Here is one example: since God is good, good is God.

In spite of her attempts to think evil away, Mrs. Eddy had to come up with something that at least explained why the "illusion" of evil, sin, disease, and death is so prevalent. She concluded that "Mortal Mind" is the culprit. Mortal Mind is full of error because it is opposition to Divine Mind, the good. But why does Mortal Mind which sees evil and disease as real even exist? It exists because of "Malicious Animal Magnetism" (M.A.M.; she got the idea of animal magnetism from Franz Mesmer). This is the "devil" in Christian Science, the source of error and hostility. For instance, Mrs. Eddy believed that M.A.M. was the reason she had false teeth, wore eyeglasses, and sometimes used morphine to alleviate pain. In her later years, she became so paranoid of M.A.M. that she behaved strangely and frequently changed her place of residence. She thought of it as a fiend that was trying to close in on her.

Christian Science philosophy is quite inconsistent. Since it teaches that God is all, there is no room for such things as Mortal Mind or Malicious Animal Magnetism. This system excludes by definition all evil, including even the illusion of evil. But Christian Scientists speak of M.A.M. and these illusions as *evils* that must be overcome!

The only way to be consistent with Christian Science philosophy is to stop clothing or feeding the body since the body itself is only an illusion of Mortal Mind. Furthermore, Christian Science forces its adherents to deny the data of their five senses with regard to evil, sickness, and death. Why then should they believe their senses when they hear and read about the principles of Christian Science?

Eddyism concentrates on healing but ignores other problems such as hunger and poverty. Followers of Christian Science are not to rely on material methods of treatment of illnesses. They frown on hospitals and medication, yet they permit surgery.

Christian Science claims many cases of healing. Some of the cases are genuine because psychosomatic illnesses were involved. Many others, however, cannot be substantiated. Mary Baker Eddy made impressive claims, for example, but she never gave particulars of names, places, times, or witnesses. When challenged by physicians to heal the kinds of infirmities she previously claimed to have healed, she suddenly became silent. Many of her friends and close relatives (including her own granddaughter) suffered painful deaths, and yet Mrs. Eddy could have healed them if there were any truth to her claims. She herself periodically relied on doctors and medication, and ultimately she was unable to prevent her own death.

Many people have suffered and died because Christian Science practitioners told them not to see doctors or have surgery.

Christian Science teaches that man is not in a fallen state and that he is incapable of sin. Consequently he has no need of a savior. Instead, salvation consists of mental deliverance from error. Furthermore, prayer is an unnecessary thing. Christian Science definitely discourages prayer to a personal God. *Science and Health* says "Don't plead with God. God is not influenced by man." "Shall we ask the divine Principle of all goodness to do His own work? His work is done."

According to this system, marriage is a temporary thing which should continue until people reach a higher state of spiritual awareness. Baptism and the Lord's Supper are occasionally practiced, but no material elements like water, bread, or wine are used.

Incidentally, Christian Science is not the only system which developed from P.P. Quimby's teachings. A number of similar groups appeared in the 19th century. Some of these were Unity, Divine Science, Home of Truth, and Practical Christianity. Except for the Unity School of Christianity, most of these groups were amalgamated under the heading "New Thought." The pantheistic doctrines of New Thought are very close to those of Christian Science because of the mutual influence of Quimbyism. Salvation in New Thought consists of one's discovery and awareness of his inner presence. The cult promotes the belief in success and prosperity.

Biblical Evaluation
(1) Though the Bible is used in Christian Science worship services, the real source of authority is the work of Mary

Baker Eddy, particularly *Science and Health*. This book uses biblical jargon but sets it in a pantheistic framework. It systematically repudiates every important biblical doctrine.

(2) God is impersonal, according to this cult, and the deity of Jesus Christ is denied.

(3) Man is not sinful since sin, evil, sickness, and death are only illusions of Mortal Mind.

Things to Keep in Mind

(1) Christian Science appeals to many because it promises healing. It also capitalizes on people's fear of sin, disease, old age, and death. It has the appeal of idealism, and it has a moral emphasis which makes it attractive to some.

(2) One of the most important factors in the development of Christian Science is the popular ignorance of what it really teaches. It makes effective use of literature, mass media (for example, the *Christian Science Monitor* which was founded in 1908), and reading rooms. It does not spread by means of missionaries as such.

(3) Christians who have opportunities to work with people in this cult should be able to demonstrate from the Bible the deity and saviourhood of Jesus Christ. Clear biblical statements should be contrasted with the teachings of *Science and Health*. Christian Scientists should be made to realize that they are gambling their eternal destiny on the hope that Mary Baker Eddy is right and Jesus is wrong. This gamble is foolish for two reasons: (1) Christian Scientists gain little if they are right and lose everything if Jesus is right. (2) This cult is based on obvious logical fallacies and pseudophilosophical jargon.

(4) The fact that some people are healed does not mean that the system of Christian Science is right. Some illnesses apparently are caused by incorrect and unhealthy mental attitudes and are healed naturally when these attitudes are corrected. Also, many religions and cults (including Satanism) claim similar results. The question of *authority* must be resolved.

SEVENTH-DAY
ADVENTISM

Background and Teachings

Evangelical scholars differ over the question of whether Seventh-Day Adventism should be classed as a cult or as a Christian denomination. Adventism has undergone significant changes over the decades, and today appears to hold an orthodox view of the cardinal Christian doctrines. Thus, it would seem improper to classify Adventism in the same category with such cults as Mormonism, Christian Science, and Jehovah's Witnesses. Nevertheless, definite doctrinal problems and emphases remain which make it hard to view the Seventh-Day Adventists as just another branch of evangelical Christianity.

A number of people were influential in founding the Seventh-Day Adventist Church, which grew out of the widespread excitement in the 1840s that Christ's coming was imminent. Many people in America and abroad had come to the conclusion that Christ was due to return sometime in 1843 or early 1844. One of these people was William Miller (1782–1849), a New York farmer who became a Baptist minister. He was an avid student of the Bible, but he lacked theological training. Taking the "2,300 evenings and mornings" of Daniel 8:14 to mean 2,300 years, he concluded that Christ would return sometime between March 21, 1843 and March 21, 1844.

Miller began to spend all his time lecturing. An Adventist periodical called *The Signs of the Times* promoted his teachings. But March 21, 1844 came and went without Christ's return.

A few weeks later, however, a follower of Miller named Samuel Snow restored the hopes of the Millerites by suggesting that the real date of Christ's return would be October 22, 1844. A new fervency appeared. A number of Adventists gave up their jobs in the "last days" and spent their time attending church meetings. Some writers say that the Millerites wore white ascension robes and climbed mountains at this time, but the historical evidence is to the contrary. When October 22 passed, the Adventists' hopes were again crushed. This came to be known as the Great Disappointment of 1844.

It should be obvious that it is a mistake to place a date on the second advent of Christ (see Matt. 24:36, 42, 44; 25:13). But some of the Millerites refused to learn this lesson. It is to the credit of William Miller that he admitted his error and removed himself from any further chronological speculation. He never accepted the Seventh-Day Adventist doctrines and he remained a devout Christian until his death.

After Miller died, the influences of three people combined to form the Seventh-Day Adventist movement. The first of these was Hiram Edson, who received a "revelation" the morning after the Great Disappointment that Miller was right about the time but wrong about the place. Edson said that Christ indeed began to cleanse the sanctuary as Miller had predicted, but the sanctuary is in heaven, not on earth. Christ had moved from one "apartment" of the heavenly sanctuary to another and had begun a final work known as "investigative judgment." Thus, He is presently "investigating" the works of believers to determine who is worthy of eternal life. When He is through with this work, He will return to the earth. Edson's reinterpretation of Daniel 8 was expanded and promoted by O.R.L. Crosier.

A second formative figure in Seventh-Day Adventism was Joseph Bates, who taught that the Saturday Sabbath was a perpetual ordinance which the church should practice today.

The third figure influential in forming Seventh-Day Adventism was Mrs. Ellen G. White. Her "inspired" interpretations of the Bible are known by Seventh-Day Adventists as "the Spirit of prophecy" (this term comes from Rev. 19:10). Born Ellen Gould Harmon in Maine in 1827, she married James White, one of the leaders of the Adventist movement. Seventh-Day Adventists believe that Mrs. White had a unique gift of prophecy and most of the doctrines especially identified with Seventh-Day Adventism today are a direct result of her highly revered interpretations and "revelations." Ellen White was the foremost leader of the Seventh-Day Adventists until her death in 1915.

The Adventists set up their headquarters in Battle Creek, Michigan in 1855, and there arrived at the name "Seventh-Day Adventists" in 1860. In 1903, they moved the headquarters to Takoma Park, Washington, D.C. Today there are over 3 million Seventh-Day Adventists around the world. Their members give sacrificially to the church to support extensive missionary and literature programs. Adventists also place strong emphasis on education (they have a large school system) and on health and welfare projects. They also make effective use of radio and television.

Certain psychological difficulties have accompanied

this movement as a result of its history, particularly in connection with the Great Disappointment of 1844. Because of the failures in ascertaining the date of Christ's return, the Adventists were humiliated and renounced by most Christian groups. This produced a separatist attitude which was reinforced by the special revelations of Ellen White. Seventh-Day Adventists came to regard themselves as the remnant people and made repeated attacks on the Christian churches. These attacks only further estranged them from other Christians. In addition, the Seventh-Day Adventists' tactic of camouflaging their identity in the media and in their public lecture series encouraged charges of deception and propagandizing.

In their recent material Seventh-Day Adventists make it clear that they have an orthodox biblical position regarding the important doctrines of the inspiration and authority of the Scriptures, the deity of Christ, the Trinity, the bodily resurrection and second coming of Christ, and the way of salvation. However, there are several Seventh-Day Adventist doctrines which are definitely unbiblical, and some of these will now be considered.

One problem is the Seventh-Day Adventist position on the writings of Ellen G. White. Seventh-Day Adventists insist that the "Spirit of prophecy" was given to her, and that her interpretations of the Bible are inspired.

Though some Seventh-Day Adventists go so far as to place Mrs. White's writings on a par with Scripture, this is not the official position of the church, which claims that the Bible is its only source of authority. Theory differs from practice, however, and in a practical sense, Mrs. White's interpretations of the Bible are accepted without reservation by Adventists as completely authoritative. Apart from her "revelations" and writings it is doubtful that the Seventh-Day Adventist church would exist today. Whatever follows the standard Adventist phrase "Ellen G. White comments" is regarded as the last word in interpretation regardless of how many biblical scholars disagree.

The most distinctive doctrine of Seventh-Day Adventism is that the church should worship on Saturdays. Adventists claim that Sunday worship will soon be required by law. When this happens, those who yield and do not worship on Saturday will receive the mark of the beast.

Seventh-Day Adventism received its sabbatarian emphasis from Joseph Bates and Ellen G. White. Their attempts to support this doctrine from the Bible and history are weak. Mrs. White claimed that Sunday worship was instituted by one of the popes, but there is no evidence to support this. It is clear from the writings of the early Christians that the first and second century church worshiped on Sunday, which they regarded as the Lord's Day, evidently because Christ rose from the dead and first appeared to His disciples on the first day of the week. His disciples were assembled on the following Sunday and Christ once again appeared to them. The Holy Spirit came and the church was born on a Sunday (the Day of Pentecost). Christians assembled on the first day of the week (Acts 20:6-7), and Paul told them to make their offerings on Sunday (1 Cor. 16:2).

According to the New Testament, the Adventists' rebuke of the churches for not keeping the Saturday Sabbath is entirely out of place. We read, "Therefore let no one act as your judge in regard to food or drink or in respect to a festival or a new moon or a Sabbath day–things which are a mere shadow of what is to come; but the substance belongs to Christ" (Col. 2:16-17). Romans 13:8-10 and Galatians 4:9-11 also refute the sabbatarian position.

Perhaps the clearest rebuttal of Sabbath legalism comes from Romans 14:4-6: "Who are you to judge the servant of another? To his own master he stands or falls; and stand he will, for the Lord is able to make him stand. One man regards one day above another, another regards every day alike. Let each man be fully convinced in his own mind. He who observes the day, observes it for the Lord, and he who eats, does so for the Lord, for he gives thanks to God; and he who eats not, for the Lord he does not eat, and gives thanks to God" (see also vv. 10-13).

Paul clearly stresses that it is wrong to judge other Christians for not worshiping on a particular day. Unfortunately, Seventh-Day Adventists have been heavy in their condemnation of other Christians in this matter, and some even say that one's redemption may be at stake. They teach that salvation is a free gift but that evidence of salvation is obedience to God's commandments including Sabbath-keeping, the fourth of the Ten Commandments. They blow this issue all out of proportion.

In addition, Adventists are not consistent in their obedience to Old Testament laws. For instance, they don't observe the Passover even though this feast is emphasized as strongly in the Old Testament as the observance of the Sabbath. Part of the problem is that they draw a false dichotomy between what they call the "moral law" (the Ten Commandments) and the "ceremonial law" (the rest of the Mosaic Law). They claim the moral law is still valid while the ceremonial law is not. This false assumption has led to a spirit of legalism among Adventists as well as a divisive attitude that they are the only commandment-keeping church. But the New Testament refers to the entire Law as a unit, and either the entire Law is in force today or it is not in force at all. (This is not to say that believers are lawless; they are under "the law of Christ" [1 Cor. 9:21], which in the New Testament includes nine out of the Ten Commandments, but does not include the Sabbath.)

Adventists promote White's teaching of the "investigative judgment," in which Christ transferred the record of the sins of believers to the heavenly sanctuary in 1844 and began to review the cases of believers to see who is worthy of receiving eternal life. This places all Adventists under the threat of judgment, contrary to the clear teaching of passages such as John 5:24 and Romans 8:1.

Along with this teaching a number of Adventist writers have said that Christ's work of atonement has not yet been completed. It will only be completed when the sanctuary is finally cleansed after the investigative judgment is finished. Then the sins of believers will be blotted out and Christ will return to the earth in glory. At this time Satan will be annihilated because he caused sin to enter the universe (Seventh-Day Adventists view Satan as Azazel, the scapegoat of Lev. 16).

This brings up two more Seventh-Day Adventist doctrines (shared, incidentally, with the Jehovah's Witnesses): soul-sleep and the annihilation of the wicked. A misuse of Old Testament terms and New Testament texts has produced the doctrine that all the dead are unconscious in the grave. A number of passages (Luke 16:22-30; 2 Cor. 5:1-8—"to be absent from the body and to be at home with the Lord"; Phil. 1:23—"to depart and be with Christ, for that is very much better"; and Rev. 6:9-10) strongly refute this position.

Seventh-Day Adventists teach that the wicked will be raised from the grave and burned alive in a great fire which will cover the earth. The righteous dead will also receive resurrected bodies but they will spend the Millennium in heaven. The wicked will eventually die (complete annihilation) rather than bear eternal torment, and then the new Jerusalem will come down on the earth. This annihilation concept is refuted by a number of Scriptures, including Matthew 8:11-12; 10:28; 18:8; 25:41; Mark 9:47-48; John 3:36; 2 Thessalonians 1:9; Revelation 14:9-11; 20:10. Seventh-Day Adventists make the mistake of equating "destruction" with "annihilation," but this is contrary to the meaning of the Greek word.

Seventh-Day Adventists are known for their strong emphasis on health. Like the Mormons, they prohibit the use of alcoholic beverages, coffee, tea, and tobacco. They also follow the food restrictions of the Law of Moses. This means that they abstain from foods such as pork, oysters, clams, crabs, lobsters, and rabbits. Many Seventh-Day Adventists are vegetarians.

Adventists have concluded that "Michael" is another title for Christ rather than the name of an angel. The problem with this view is that Jude 9 says that Michael did not dare rebuke Satan. This could be true only if Michael were an angel and not Christ Himself.

Seventh-Day Adventists have arrived at these doctrines because of the system of Ellen G. White, not because of an inductive study of the Bible. Their theories of the sanctuary and investigative judgment were developed to compensate for their initial chronological errors related to Christ's return. Adventists try to support Mrs. White's "revealed" interpretations by taking verses out of context and ignoring their relationship to other passages of Scripture.

Adventists acknowledge that people in other churches may have salvation in Christ, but their system implies that they may lose their salvation if they do not change their minds about the Sabbath, among other things.

Biblical Evaluation

(1) Seventh-Day Adventism cannot be labeled a non-Christian cult. Its teachings about the person and work of Christ, the Trinity, and the inspiration of the Scriptures are essentially biblical. It also teaches that salvation is by grace through faith in Christ, but the problem here is the emphasis on keeping the Old Testament commandments to give evidence of salvation, or to retain it.

(2) Seventh-Day Adventist doctrines of the nature of man (man *is* a soul), soul-sleep, the annihilation of the wicked, the sanctuary, investigative judgment, the scapegoat, and the Sabbath are unbiblical.

(3) Seventh-Day Adventists have revered Ellen G. White and her writings to a dangerous extent. In practice, her interpretations are accepted as divinely authoritative. Adventists have distorted several scriptural teachings in order to support Mrs. White's "visions."

(4) A legalistic spirit in Seventh-Day Adventism places

its followers under the law. Saturday worship is such an issue that it is practically made a test of one's salvation.

Things to Keep in Mind

(1) Unlike the Mormons, Jehovah's Witnesses, and Christian Scientists, a Seventh-Day Adventist may well be a born-again believer. Many genuine Christians are in the Seventh-Day Adventist Church.

(2) Seventh-Day Adventists are to be commended for their strong emphasis on moral purity, the family, physical well-being, and their missionary, medical, welfare, and educational programs.

(3) Adventists place an inordinate emphasis on the Sabbath. They make such an issue out of this and other distinctive Seventh-Day Adventist doctrines that they sometimes develop an unhealthy attitude toward other churches. Christians should know how to defend the fact that they are no longer under the sabbatical law.

(4) Seventh-Day Adventists should challenge us to study and know the Scriptures, so that we can handle accurately the Word of truth (2 Tim. 2:15).

15

UNITY SCHOOL OF CHRISTIANITY

Background and Teachings

Unity is a huge mail-order religion claiming over 1.5 million adherents around the world. It is noteworthy that most subscribers to the Unity School doctrine are members of non-Unity churches. Their influence is thus uniquely effective in the Christian community. Supposedly built on the foundation of Christianity, Unity developed in the late 19th century from the same roots as Christian Science and New Thought. All three of these religions grew out of the writings of Phineas Parkhurst Quimby, a mental healer from Maine.

P.P. Quimby himself had derived much of his teaching from the ideas of Franz Anton Mesmer (the term *mesmerism* is associated with him) and Charles Poyen. Mesmer worked with the subconscious mind and with the power of one mind over another. Poyen was a French hypnotist who came to New England to teach about the power of mesmerism (hypnotism).

Mary Baker Eddy plagiarized Quimby's manuscripts after his death and this became one of her basic sources as she developed Christian Science. Julius Dresser and Warren Evans were disciples of Quimby who developed the New Thought cult. And Myrtle and Charles Fillmore generated the Unity School of Christianity out of Quimby's metaphysical system. It is therefore no surprise that these three cults share much in common, including their jargon.

Myrtle Fillmore was raised in New England in the Methodist Church. Her husband Charles suffered from several physical problems, and when she herself contracted tuberculosis, they moved to Texas and then Arizona in an attempt to restore their health. During this time Charles Fillmore earned and lost a substantial fortune as a real estate salesman.

The Fillmores moved to Kansas City in 1884, and three years later Myrtle Fillmore heard a lecture which convinced her that "I am a child of God, and therefore I do not inherit sickness." Unity literature claims that with this revelation, Mrs. Fillmore was immediately healed and received the ability to heal others. Her husband soon became a convert of this religious healing system.

In 1889 the Fillmores rented a hall in Kansas City to promote their discovery. Charles Fillmore got out of real estate to devote full time to this new system of "practical Christianity." The Fillmores published a magazine first called *Modern Thought* (1889), then *Christian Science Thought* (1890), and then *Thought* (1891)—Mary Baker Eddy objected to their use of Christian Science terminology.

The movement took the name Unity in 1895, and it began to grow rapidly through its strong publication program. In addition to many tracts, booklets, and books, Unity publishes six magazines: *Unity, Unity Daily Word,*

Weekly Unity, Good Business, Progress, and *Wee Wisdom* (for children).

The Unity Church Universal was established by the Fillmores in 1924. Myrtle Fillmore died in 1931, and Charles married Cora Dedrick, his secretary, a few years later. He led the organization until his death in 1948. Unity has its headquarters in Kansas City, Missouri. The Unity School of Christianity runs a training school, a correspondence school, "Silent Unity" (a 24-hour prayer room), a broadcasting station, the world's most complete vegetarian cafeteria, a massive printing operation, and has a large staff.

The Fillmores dabbled in a number of things and their Unity system is thus an odd combination of Christian Science, the teachings of Swami Vivekananda (Hinduism, Yoga, vegetarianism, reincarnation), spiritualism, New Thought, and theosophy. Like Christian Science, Unity is a pantheistic metaphysical system which emphasizes mental healing. But contrary to Christian Science, Unity teaches that matter is real, not an illusion. Unity also affirms the reality of sin, disease, and death, but it says they can be overcome through right thinking and living.

According to Unity, the Bible is only one of many books which contain spiritual truth. Unity recognizes the scriptures of several other religions in addition to the Bible, but Unity still prefers to be called a "School of Christianity." Its literature spiritualizes the Bible to make it fit the teachings of the Fillmores, constantly twisting words and phrases to distort their meanings. Thus, the Unity School appeals to the Bible but at the same time flatly denies every important biblical doctrine. Unity also claims that its adherents can reach such a level of communication with God that the Bible becomes unnecessary for them.

Unity borrows terms from Christian Science to describe God. According to Unity, God is not a Person but a principle. God does not possess life, intelligence, and will; God *is* life, intelligence, and will. God is being, love, mind, truth, goodness. Each person has access to God because God is in each person. This teaching is pantheistic, and Unity is inconsistent to even use the personal pronoun "He" when speaking of God. Unity says God is a principle or force which is in everything. This is far removed from the biblical teaching of the Triune, infinite-personal God. Unity's pantheism makes God impersonal and repudiates the doctrine of the Trinity.

The next logical step is the denial of the deity of Jesus Christ. Unity claims that the man Jesus was *not* the Christ. Jesus was only a man who possessed a spiritual identity known as the Christ, according to Unity. This is a direct contradiction of 1 John 2:22 which says, "Who is the liar but the one who denies that Jesus is the Christ? This is the antichrist, the one who denies the Father and the Son."

Unity claims that all men have the Christ within them if they will only realize it. The difference between Jesus and other men is that Jesus realized and practiced His potential for perfection while others have not. Any man can attain the same perfection as Jesus if he will gain dominion over his thoughts and recognize that he has the Christ within. Each man is the son of God.

This means that because men are not sinners in need of a Saviour, Christ did not die to pay for our sins. Instead, Jesus simply demonstrated how atonement can be achieved between God and man. Atonement means at-one-ment; it is the reconciliation produced by "a reuniting of our consciousness with the God-consciousness." Salvation occurs when one believes this doctrine and thereby removes himself from the illusion of sin. At this point he receives healing from error and infirmities. The goal of Unity is a perfect union with the mind of God. Heaven and hell are unreal.

Unity also denies the doctrine of the second coming of Jesus Christ. It claims that there will be no judgment. Like Christian Science, it discards as a primitive practice the idea of prayer to a personal God. Prayer is a part of this religion but it is related to control of the thoughts.

The most distinctive doctrine of Unity is that of reincarnation. Unity denies the resurrection of Christ and the future resurrection of men because it replaces resurrection with reincarnation. After death a person's spirit is reborn in another human body on earth. The life he lived in his previous incarnation will partly determine the conditions, opportunities, and health of his new life, and this new life will similarly affect future lives. The idea is that after enough cycles of reincarnation a person will eventually reach perfection. Each successive rebirth should further cleanse the soul.

In order to support their position that reincarnation is a Christian doctrine, the teachers of the Unity School must seriously distort passages from the Bible. For instance, they argue that Christ is a reincarnation of David since He is called the "Son of David." They also cite certain "evidences" for reincarnation. These include feelings of having been in a place before, or a knowledge of events and people that has not been learned or experienced. Unity also appeals to the fact that people are not born with equal abilities or opportunities. It concludes that these inequities are caused by sins in earlier bodies because God would not directly create some people with advantages over others. But the "evidences" of reincarnation cited by Unity are subjective and inconclusive.

Biblical Evaluation

(1) Unity claims to embody Christianity, but it is actually a non-Christian cult which rejects every imporant doctrine of the Bible. It has an impersonal, pantheistic concept of God. The god of Unity is not the God of the Bible. Unity denies the deity, virgin birth, substitutionary work, bodily resurrection, and second coming of Jesus Christ. It also rejects the biblical teaching that men are sinful and in need of a Saviour.

(2) The Unity doctrine of reincarnation has no biblical support. It is refuted by such passages as 1 Corinthians

15 and Hebrews 9:27. It is only a substitute for salvation, judgment, and eternal punishment.

Things to Keep in Mind

(1) Unity appeals to tolerance and "love." It also promotes the gospel of mental healing and financial prosperity. It is an egocentric system which claims to produce "practical" results. With this veneer it subtly but thoroughly undermines crucial doctrines of the Bible.

(2) Unity is so influential because of its extensive literature campaign. It is able to permeate Christian denominations with its doctrines because its adherents are not required to leave their churches.

(3) Unity's authority is not the Bible but the mongrel system of teachings put together by Myrtle and Charles Fillmore. This system is imposed on the Bible by a spiritualizing and allegorical method of interpretation.

THEOSOPHY

Background and Teachings

The Greek word *theosophia* means "the wisdom of God," or "divine wisdom." The word "theosophy" seems to have been used first in the third century by Ammonius Sacchus, a philosopher and teacher of Plotinus. The latter thinker, the founder of Neoplatonism, believed in union with the infinite through meditation. Theosophy is an odd combination of several things, including Buddhism, Hinduism, Spiritualism, and Gnosticism. Though this cult uses Christian terminology to communicate its mystical Eastern concepts to a Western audience, it is vehemently opposed to every major tenet of biblical Christianity.

The modern movement of Theosophy began in the 19th century through the efforts of Helena Petrovna Blavatsky, who was born in 1831 in Ekaterinoslav, Russia. At an early age Helena became interested in magic and the occult. Her mother died when she was 12 years old, and five years later in 1848 she married a 48-year-old Czarist general named Blavatsky. She abandoned Blavatsky after only three months of marriage.

After living with her grandparents for a short time, Helena began a period of extensive travel. During these years (1848–1873) she journeyed to India, Tibet, Paris, London, Cuba, Mexico, the United States, and Canada. She cultivated her interest in mystical things by her studies in these countries, and became a spiritualist medium. For a decade she was controlled by a spirit-guide named John King. In her years of travel she lived with different men and had a child out of wedlock.

In 1873, H.P. Blavatsky settled in the United States, where she continued to function as a medium. In Vermont she impressed a Colonel Olcott, who later left his family to stay with her. She received a number of mediumistic revelations from the "Master Serapis," and these led her and Olcott to found the Theosophical Society in 1875. Blavatsky's New York apartment-headquarters came to be known as the Lamasery. She influenced many through her writings, which included a multivolume set called *The Secret Doctrine* and a shorter two-volume work called *Isis Unveiled*.

Blavatsky moved to India in 1879 and relocated her world headquarters to Madras. Thereafter, Hinduism and Buddhism began to occupy a larger place in her system, and her anti-Christian sentiments became more pronounced. "H.P.B." later went back to Europe and founded the Esoteric School of Theosophy in London.

The American section of Theosophy (called the Exoteric Section) was headed by Colonel Olcott, and the Esoteric Section in England and India was led by Blavatsky till her death in London in 1891 at the age 60. After her death, William Q. Judge took over the work in America and Annie Wood Besant (1847–1933) became the leader of the work in India and England. Annie Besant left her husband to become immersed in Theosophy, and she became its most prominent figure aside from Blavatsky. A prolific writer, she accomplished much in India and rose to a high level in Indian politics.

Mrs. Besant claimed in 1925 that her adopted son Krishnamurti was the reincarnated Messiah. However, Krishnamurti renounced this title in 1931 at the American headquarters of the Society in Krotana, California. George S. Arundale succeeded Annie Besant after her death in 1933, and he was succeeded in 1945 by C. Jinarajadasa. There have been a number of divisions among the Theosophists, with several offspring organizations resulting. Because of this it is difficult to accurately determine the current number of practicing Theosophists in the world (one estimate is 35,000 members in 60 countries), but it appears that Theosophy is on the decline.

Theosophy is a thoroughly eclectic system. It is most heavily influenced by Hinduism and Gnosticism. Some of the prominent Gnostic elements in this religious cult are its low view of matter and its teaching that the universe consists of a number of emanations from God. There are seven different levels in the universe ranging from the physical plane, the astral plane, the mental plane, and on up to the plane of the divine.

Theosophy's view of man and the universe is evolutionary. The idea is that each individual, and mankind as a whole, is slowly evolving through the various planes toward a union with the Absolute. This process requires innumerable cycles and reincarnations and, therefore, great quantities of time.

According to Blavatsky's mediumistic "revelations," mankind on earth is now in his third "rootrace." The first rootrace was called the Lemurian race. The Lemurians were the first true men to appear as a result of evolution. Their history stretches back millions of years.

The Atlanteans were the second rootrace. Theosophists claim that the Atlanteans lived on a huge continent as long as 800,000 years ago, and they have produced maps of Atlantis from this period and prior to its destruction about 15,500 years ago. The later maps show that Atlantis diminished in size from a continent to a large island. Millions of Atlanteans perished when the island catastrophically submerged.

With the destruction of the second rootrace, the third rootrace, the Aryans, began. Each race goes through several "subraces," and we are now in the fifth subrace of the Aryan rootrace.

In the beginning of each subrace, the spirit of the Supreme World Teacher of Christ enters the body of a disciple and assists humanity's spiritual development. In this way each subrace gradually progresses in its spiritual evolution. Each new Christ or incarnation of the World Teacher reveals more of God than the one before. The five Christs of the five subraces in the Aryan rootrace were Buddha (India), Hermes (Egypt), Zoroaster (Persia), Orpheus (Greece), and Jesus (theosophists say that the Christ came on Jesus at His baptism).

Theosophists are expecting the appearance of another Christ in the near future because they believe that our fifth subrace (representing the intellectual man) is about to be superseded by a sixth subrace (representing the spiritual man). The revelation given by this coming Christ will exceed that given by Jesus during His time on earth.

The goal of each Theosophist is to eventually progress through the seven planes of existence. The third plane (mental) is the abode of the angels or "devas," and it is the Theosophic version of heaven, called Devachan. Since each person has a part of God within him, it is the destiny of all men to progressively achieve a union with God as a result of transmigration, an evolutionary process which requires many reincarnations.

A person's moral debt or *karma* must be overcome in this process. Those who practice Yoga will work out their karma more quickly than those who do not. Yoga includes special postures, control of the breathing, and meditation. Thus, Theosophy follows Hinduism's teaching of self-salvation through meditation, mystical experiences, knowledge, and effort. Each person must work out his own karma through his lives on earth and also through his lives between incarnations into new bodies. Sin or karmic debt is purged between incarnations in Kamaloka, the Theosophists' version of purgatory. Kamaloka is a temporary hell which involves various degrees of torture designed to make the next incarnation higher than the one before.

There is no concept of forgiveness of sins in Theosophy. Each person must achieve his own salvation. Theosophists are adamantly opposed to the biblical teachings about the vicarious atonement of Christ and the mercy and grace of God. The idea that Jesus Christ died to pay for the sins of men is repulsive to them. They believe that this doctrine robs people of their self-respect.

Each person has both a "natural body" which consists of four parts (the physical body, the etheric double, the astral body, and the mental body) and a "spiritual body," which consists of three parts which are now in the process of evolution. The evolutionary process of transmigration will move men further from the material level and closer to the spiritual level. Because of this, every individual is a potential "Christ." The only difference between Jesus and other men is that He was further along the evolutionary cycle. Denying the bodily resurrection of Jesus Christ, Theosophy has replaced resurrection with endless reincarnations.

What is Theosophy's authority for all this knowledge of the human races and the process of spiritual evolution? One authority is the Hindu scriptures as contained in *The Sacred Books of the East*. Theosophists believe that all other scriptures come out of the Hindu scriptures; therefore, the Hindu books can be studied with more profit than the Bible. But even *The Sacred Books of the East* can only be properly understood at the mouth of a guru (spiritual teacher) who imparts the true knowledge.

Theosophy's second authority for its teachings is direct "revelation" from higher spiritual beings, known as the Mahatmas (also called the Masters, the Initiates, and the Adepts). These are "divine men" who are on the verge of nirvana but who remain on earth (somewhere in Tibet) to help the spiritual development of humanity. These Mahatmas actually possess the bodies of selected individuals on earth. Madame Blavatsky, for example, was said to be possessed by at least three Masters: Serapis, Morya, and Koot Hoomi. Thus, Blavatsky claimed a kind of "inspiration" for her teachings and writings. She repudiated anyone whose revelations contradicted her own. She alone possessed the key to open up the Vedas and other Hindu scriptures.

Theosophy's god has no intellect, emotions, or will because it has no personal attributes. This Gnostic religion speaks of a cause (impersonality) which is inferior to the effect (personality). It teaches that all religions are fundamentally the same because everything is a part of God. Though prayer to Krishna or to Buddha is the same as prayer to God the Father or Christ, Theosophists are taught that prayer is ultimately quite unnecessary. They rise above prayer as they attain the divine within.

According to Theosophy, the angels, like men, were not specially created by God. Instead, they are the evolutionary products of worlds older than earth.

Biblical Evaluation

(1) Blavatsky and Besant claimed for themselves special authority for their teachings. Theosophists reject the Bible but accept these women's writings. But theirs is an inferior authority since it is not backed up by any substantial evidence. The biblical writings are supported by various miracles, by many fulfilled prophecies, by history and archeology, and by the life and resurrection of Jesus Christ. One must reject Christ's claims and teachings in order to be a follower of Blavatsky.

(2) The impersonal "god" of Theosophy is not a sufficient cause to explain the effect of the personality of man and the complexity of the universe.

(3) Theosophy offers no hope of full redemption. It offers only an endless series of reincarnations sandwiched between periods spent in the tortures of Kamaloka. The autosoteric notion that one can work out his own karma reveals a superficial view of the meaning of sin. The god of Theosophy is neither holy nor loving. This contrasts strongly with the infinite-personal God of the Bible. The Bible reveals that God has Himself provided a way of salvation which offers certain hope of resurrection and glorification rather than a painful path of reincarnations and self-effort. But as long as Theosophists trust in their own works and righteousness, they will not be in a position to receive Christ's free gift.

(4) Theosophy denies that Jesus is the Christ (see 1 John 2:22). It teaches that the Supreme World Teacher possessed the body of Jesus of Nazareth at His baptism. Theosophists fail to realize that the title *Christos* is a reference to the personal Old Testament Messiah, and not to some divine spirit which possesses certain men.

(5) Theosophy has no answer to the problem of evil because it teaches that everything, including matter and evil, emanated from "God." God is directly blamed for evil.

(6) Theosophists enjoy no personal relationship with God since the god of Theosophy is impersonal. Fellowship with Him is replaced with efforts to attain mystical experiences of the unity of all things. This religion produces a good deal of pride because it teaches self-salvation through esoteric knowledge.

Things to Keep in Mind
(1) Before one submits to the teachings of Madame Blavatsky, one should compare her life with the life of Jesus Christ. She was a woman who had little patience and an explosive temper. She abandoned her first husband and

lived with various men. Her morals and language were far from sinless. Blavatsky was also guilty of extensive plagiarism in her writings. She was a self-centered woman.

(2) It is possible that the "Mahatmas" or spirit beings who possessed Blavatsky were in fact demons. Certainly their "revelations" deny the critical truths of the deity of Jesus Christ, the substitutionary Atonement, and the Resurrection.

(3) Though thoroughly anti-Christian in background and teaching, Theosophy proceeds deceitfully and parasitically by its practice of using (misusing) Christian terminology.

PART THREE

Occult Religions
and Systems

The six cultic activities decribed in this section are generally less highly organized than the movements we have considered so far. Christians, by contrast, belong to churches in order to be in good standing. There are, of course, societies that exist for the purpose of propagating occult views, including spiritualist "churches" for example. But many recognized adherents of occult views do not belong to an organized group.

The word *occult* means "secret," and a common thread that runs through the occult movement is the secret nature of the beliefs and practices of occult practitioners. By "secret" we do not mean that the positions taken are not available in most instances. Rather, the beliefs and practices are secret in the sense that performance of the rites is considered to be effective only when performed by those who are deeply initiated in the lore of the cult.

Such an elitist leadership structure implies that success in occult practices requires precise manipulation of objects, substances, words, spirit entities, and the minds of those who subject themselves to practitioners. This subjection to initiated experts need not be person-to-person, but often can be mediated through written or visual materials.

There are good grounds for considering that such occultism is not all fraudulent. Moreover, as will be noted, it is apparent that in many cases the "manipulators" of these systems are themselves manipulated by demonic powers over which the practitioners have no control.

17

WITCHCRAFT AND SATANISM

Background and Teachings

Witchcraft, sorcery, divination, and magic are ancient and universal. Every culture, primitive or civilized, East or West, has had its share of magicians, sorcerers, and witches.

The varieties of witchcraft are so many that they defy systematic analysis. Yet some constant factors can be found: the lust for power, for knowledge (especially of the future), and for control over opposing forces. There is usually an appeal to an external and often mysterious source of power. The proper rituals, spells, and charms must be followed in order to produce the desired results. These things are true whether the conjurer is a sorcerer, a Satanist, a medicine man, a witch, a shama, a magus, or a witch doctor.

In the West, witchcraft is often called "The Old Religion," pointing to the fact that witchcraft existed long before the Christian church began to spread. As Christianity became more dominant in Europe, witchcraft and occultism were suppressed but not eliminated. Many who were called Christians continued their pagan practices and the practitioners of witchcraft borrowed a number of ideas and rituals from the church.

Satanism and witchcraft began to grow with the decline of medieval society. Even some priests got involved. Several new cults like the Luciferians and the Templars appeared, teaching Gnostic doctrines which encouraged homage to Satan. Black magic, Satan worship, and various forms of witchcraft were especially prevalent in Europe from about 1250 to 1700. Many people became fearful, and the church began to retaliate. The papal inquisition against witches reached its greatest intensity in the 16th and 17th centuries. During these years, tens of thousands of accused witches were put to death, usually by fire. Confessions were often extracted under torture, and many were condemned without sufficient evidence.

A number of Renaissance magicians became famous, and their writings are still revered by some occultists today. Men such as Cornelius Agrippa, Paracelsus, and Giordano Bruno used magic in an attempt to attain knowledge about the secrets of the universe.

Satanism and witchcraft declined and went underground for a few centuries, but revived about the beginning of the 20th century. Aleister Crowley (1875–1947) played an important part in this revival of the black arts. Crowley, who made a pact with Satan, referred to himself as the "Great Beast" of Revelation, and even branded one of his mistresses with the mark of the Beast. Crowley and his disciples were heavily involved with drugs, demonism, and sexual perversions.

Since Crowley's time, witchcraft and Satan worship have found increasing numbers of adherents in Europe and America. Hundreds of new witches' covens have appeared. A wide variety of people are involved, including many business and professional people. More books on the subject are available to the general public than ever before. Many high schools and colleges offer courses on witchcraft, magic, and occultism.

Three currently popular witches are Sybil Leek, Louise Huebner, and Alex Sanders. The best-known promoter of Satanism is Anton La Vey, who founded the First Church of Satan in San Francisco, and rose to fame as the author of *The Satanic Bible.* For La Vey (born in 1930) and his followers, Satan symbolizes a force which can be tapped to achieve power and success. Sexual indulgence and hedonism play a central role in La Vey's satanic rituals.

Books on witchcraft do not agree about the genuineness of the powers behind it. Some writers claim that witchcraft is nothing more than legend and ritual. An intermediate view is that witchcraft may involve the combined psychic power of groups of people. There is some truth to these two positions, but they do not explain all the phenomena in witchcraft. Many witches claim to traffic with outside spiritual forces, and it appears that in some cases they do. The Bible calls these spiritual forces demons.

One of the ancient beliefs in witchcraft is that spirit beings sometimes incarnate themselves in humans or animals and appear to worshipers in various forms. The most important of these beings is said to appear in the form of a horned god, usually half-man and half-goat. He is identified with Lucifer or Pan (the Greek god who came to represent the mystical personification of nature).

The word *witch* is derived from the Old English word *wicca* which meant "wisdom" or "knowledge." This word is usually used of females who engage in witchcraft, while the term *wizard* or *warlock* is used of males. However, some warlocks prefer to be called witches.

There are various forms of witchcraft, and some practitioners are more committed to the forces of darkness than others. Some witches believe they are practicing "white magic" (their spells are used for the benefit of others) as opposed to "black magic." In most cases, however, witches desire to attain their own ends through the practice of their craft. They believe certain powers of evil affect the destinies of men, and that the person who gets in contact with these powers can use them for his own purposes.

People who engage in witchcraft have various motivations for doing so, but some of the most common are the desire to gain power over other people and material things, the appeal of mysterious adventure, sexual pleasure, and the promise of occult knowledge.

There is a catch, of course. These things are not free. Most of those who are serious about witchcraft know that some kind of contractual arrangement is involved. Just as they are served by the dark powers (demons), so they must also serve these beings.

Some witches are given great power through demonic agency. By using the proper spells they can have demons inflict pain, disease, despair, and suicidal thoughts on others. Or they can manipulate people and situations to their advantage.

The more a practitioner of witchcraft thinks he is in control of these powers, the more deluded he becomes. He may convince himself that he is master of the situation, but he actually becomes subject to the forces he thinks he has conquered.

Most of what has just been said about witchcraft is also true of Satanism. In general, Satanism and witchcraft do not differ as much in kind as they do in degree. A witch may be uncertain about the source of power he or she is tapping, but a Satanist freely acknowledges that the power comes from demons or from Satan himself. Witches often worship the horned god, Pan, or Lucifer, but the Satanist knows his true identity.

Some Satanist groups are more "orthodox" in their views of Satan than others, regarding Satan as a real spirit being with an intellect, a will, and emotions. Others think that Satan is only a symbol of a dark force of nature that can be mobilized for personal gain.

There is also a great deal of variety in the *practice* of witchcraft and Satanism. Because of these variations, most of what follows should be regarded as general information.

Satanism is a more direct perversion of Christianity than is witchcraft. Satan is substituted for God, and his servants often imitate and mock Christian practices and institutions. For instance, witches and Satanists generally organize themselves into local covens consisting of 13 members (a parody of Christ and His 12 Apostles).

Most covens consist of both men and women, and they are headed by high priests and priestesses. Members of a coven are required to attend a weekly (usually Friday night) or monthly meeting known as the esbat. Special meetings, larger and held less frequently, are called sabbats or grand sabbats. (This word may be derived from the word Sabbath, but there is disagreement over this.) Dates for the sabbats vary from country to country. In England the most important sabbats are held on February 2 (Candlemas), May-eve (Roodmas), August 1 (Lammas), and November-eve (All Hallow E'en).

There are innumerable variations in the order and content of esbat and sabbat meetings, which are presided over by the high priests and priestesses. Depending on the group, they range from silliness and clowning to great seriousness and horror. Esbats and sabbats are often held outdoors in remote locations, preferably by a clump of trees and near a source of water.

These meetings are held at night (a reflection of Satan's delight in darkness), generally beginning at midnight and lasting until dawn. There are many stories of unusual means of arriving at sabbat meetings, including the use of levitation and "astral projection" (out-of-body experiences). In any event, some covens portray this idea of levitation by riding broomsticks.

Special attire at these meetings may be black robes or nothing at all. In some cases, the witches or Satan worshipers array themselves in animal skins. They may wear ritual masks.

A large circle with mystical symbolism is usually drawn on the ground, and the worshipers stand inside it. There they recite certain oaths. The most popular chant is "Yod He Vav He—Blessed be." This chant utilizes the four Hebrew letters which make up the tetragrammaton YHVH—the most important Old Testament name for God.

Some old accounts describe how the devil would appear at this point in the form of a tall man, a goat, a bull, or a cat. The worshipers would then offer him candles and kiss his posterior in a perverse act of homage.

Early in the sabbat meeting there is usually some kind of general confession. Those present may mockingly renounce any good deeds they have done. This is followed by a ritual dance (another act of devotion) which is often primitive or degraded. Discordant and bizarre music is sometimes used, and the dancers may attempt to achieve an ecstatic frenzy. This reveling may be followed by a sexual orgy and then a feast, preceded by a blasphemous "grace." Sometimes the participants will mock moderation by stuffing themselves, though some groups use unsavory food.

Following the feast may be some version of a black mass, which can be simple or elaborate. Many covens use strictly prescribed rituals and rites, and the words must be recited properly. Some rituals use Latin, and in a few cases, renegade Catholic priests are involved.

Black masses generally open with a group renunciation of God and Jesus Christ. Sometimes a blasphemous sermon follows. Accoutrements may include various black vestments, "holy water" (usually including urine), black candles, toads, inverted crucifixes, torches burning with a sulfurous blue flame, incense, crucibles which burn nightshade (belladonna), perfumed material, and sulfur.

A house used for celebrating black masses usually has a special room containing a permanent altar (covered in black), dark heavy curtains, and symbolic images of the devil.

Witches or Satan worshipers generally use some kind of missal (either a manuscript or printed). A few of these missals are bound in human skin, usually that of an unbaptized infant. Christian hymns are sometimes sung backward or in the name of Lucifer, Beelzebub, and other demons.

Stolen items from Catholic churches are frequently used. For instance, a ciborium (the eucharistic chalice) will be filled with a mixture of wine and blood or bitter beverages and passed among the members of the coven. Black mass participants will desecrate hosts (the eucharistic wafers) by cutting and stabbing them with a knife. Sometimes black triangular wafers are used instead.

Almost always a naked girl, representing the sacrifice, lies on the altar during this portion of the sabbat. She is not killed, but a ceremonial animal sacrifice (perhaps a dog or a cat) is offered to the devil. The animal is killed above the girl and the blood allowed to spill on her body. In rare cases (this was more common a few hundred years ago), an unbaptized human infant is sacrificed instead of the animal. In earlier times the infants were obtained for this purpose through midwives or purchase. Sometimes they were the witch's own offspring.

An esbat or sabbat meeting usually includes an opportunity for members to express grievances against enemies and to cast vengeful spells. Charms, herbs, unguents, poisons, and potions are often used in witchcraft. Sometimes wax or cloth images of enemies are made and then destroyed, as in voodooism. These practices and others sometimes lead to violent crimes. The Manson murders are the best-known example; other brutal crimes inspired by witchcraft and Satanism have received little attention.

One of the central themes of witchcraft is the conjuration of demons for specific purposes. Special rituals, invocations, and books of magic are used in this connection. Divination through crystals, planchettes, Ouija boards, and Tarot cards also plays an important role in witchcraft.

Another key part of witchcraft and Satanism is the recruitment and initiation of new members. People are promised knowledge, wealth, power, honor, pleasure, and vengeance on their enemies if they become devotees of the devil.

Initiation of new members requires a formal pact or contract with the devil. This contract may be verbal or a written document signed in the blood of the initiate. Blood is used because it is thought to be a sacred and irrevocable seal. The contract binds the initiate with blasphemous oaths to the service of the dark powers. This may involve striking his name out of the book of Christ and inscribing it in the devil's. Books with names thus signed in blood are kept in secrecy by the chief officer of a coven or by the grand master of a district. Some contracts are made for life and others for a number of years.

An initiate is usually required to undergo a perverse baptism (the mixture may consist of water, salt, and sulfur), at which time he may receive a new name. Sexual intercourse is often involved in the initiation ceremony as well. The initiate may receive a small devil's mark on a normally hidden part of the body.

Many witches and wizards receive animal "familiars" which are said to assist them in divination and casting spells. These animals (birds, frogs, especially cats) in some cases are demonized. Some witches also claim to experience sexual relations with incubi and succubi (demons which assume male and female forms). Others claim the power to transform themselves into animals, usually wolves.

Many witches, wizards, and Satanists are involved in a hierarchy of four stages and perhaps a fifth, known as the Illuminati. However, other practitioners of witchcraft are independent of covens and higher organizations.

Biblical Evaluation

(1) The Old and New Testaments repeatedly allude to witchcraft and sorcery. From the earliest Old Testament books through Revelation, the Bible speaks of magic, sorcery, divination, necromancy in a hostile and condemnatory manner. All forms of witchcraft and demonolatry are explicitly denounced. The Bible mentions divination by witchcraft, sorcery, astrology, human and animal entrails, rods and arrows, water in a cup or basin, teraphim (household idols), and necromancy.

(2) The Bible also acknowledges the reality and power behind some forms of witchcraft and magic. For instance, the ability of Jannes and Jambres to duplicate some of the plagues of Moses demonstrated a genuine force and learning behind their sorcery. In the New Testament, Simon Magus, Elymas the magician, and the medium at Philippi also had certain powers. However, the Scriptures frequently emphasize that the power behind sorcery and witchcraft is limited, unlike the power of God.

(3) Some biblical passages describing the reality and danger of the various forms of witchcraft are Exodus 22:18; Leviticus 19:26, 31; 20:6, 27; Deuteronomy 12:31; 18:10-11, 14; 1 Samuel 15:23; 28:3, 7; 2 Kings 17:17; 21:6; 23:24; 1 Chronicles 10:13; Isaiah 8:19; 19:3; 47:12-13; Jeremiah 27:9-10; Daniel 2:2; Malachi 3:5; Acts 8:9, 11; 13:6, 8; 16:16; Galatians 5:20-21; Revelation 21:8; 22:15.

(4) Satan is now the "ruler of this world" (John 12:31; 16:11). He fell because of his pride and his desire to be equal with God. He acts as a counterfeit of God and demands that demons and humans worship him. Many witches and Satanists have given themselves over to Satan as their master, creator, and god. His followers pray to him, work "miracles" through demonic power, and "prophesy" (practice divination).

Things to Keep in Mind

(1) We must remember that many diverse phenomena are subsumed under the category of Satanism and witchcraft.

Much of it is superstitious and psychological. It attracts large numbers of cranks, charlatans, and dilettantes. But after all allowances have been made for these factors, there remains a significant number of related phenomena which cannot be explained apart from the supernatural.

(2) Many people who are involved in witchcraft claim to practice "white magic" instead of "black magic." They do not believe that they are in league with demonic powers. To the extent that they do utilize genuine power, however, they are dabbling with forces which are more diabolic than they suspect. The difference between white and black magic is more in degree than in kind. There is great danger in all forms of witchcraft because sorcerers are involved with powers much stronger than they. In order to effectively use these powers for their own desires and ends, they must to some extent yield to and serve them. Satan's gifts are never free. Those who willingly receive them often become his slaves, whether they like it or not.

(3) There is also the danger of demonic control. The New Testament makes it clear that demons can possess people. Unlike the servants of Christ, the servants of Satan are not free; they are controlled by malicious forces.

(4) It is important to be aware of the basic reasons for which people go into witchcraft. These may vary with different individuals, but most seek some or all of the following benefits:

(a) Power over people and things; an ability to manipulate one's environment and circumstances for his own ends.

(b) Mystery. For most people religion has lost the mysterious communion with the supernatural. Witchcraft and Satanism claim to have an alternative. They provide experiences with the eerie and the unknown. They offer something out of the ordinary: the spice of adventure with the occult world.

(c) Sexual indulgence and gratification of the drive for pleasure.

(d) Financial success.

(e) Knowledge through divination and communication with higher powers.

(f) Pride and intellectual arrogance.

(g) A means of rebelling against the restraints of society. In a pragmatic sense, Satanism and witchcraft actually *work* in enough cases to attract people. But a relationship with Christ provides a far better solution to human needs and problems, and His followers are on the side that will be victorious.

18

---◆---

ASTROLOGY

---◆---

Background and Teachings

Astrology is one of the most ancient cults, though it has gone through considerable change over the centuries. In its earliest stages, natural astrology was essentially the same as astronomy. Men of learning (usually priests) studied the sky, accumulated information, and tried to understand the workings of the heavens. Because centers of learning were also the centers of religion, natural astrology soon became corrupted by pagan myths, deities, and magic. As a result, two forms of astrology began to coexist: natural astrology (astronomy) and religious astrology.

In the Mesopotamian Valley, where the ancient Chaldean-Babylonian civilization once flourished, great towers or ziggurats were built (the Tower of Babel may have been the first), and Chaldean priests charted the movement of the heavens from the tops of these ziggurats. They believed that the sun, moon, and stars were like deities who controlled their fate. If the priests could understand and predict the movements of these celestial bodies, they could use this knowledge to control their own destiny. This kind of astrology has been variously termed mundane astrology, embryonic astrology, and astrobiology. Its main concept was that the configurations of the heavens correspond to and determine the phenomena of the earth. The worship of deities like Bel (or Ba'al) and Astarte was thus combined with astronomy.

At this stage, astrological divination concerned nations and major events rather than individuals. But when Babylon was conquered by Medo-Persia, a new form of astrology emerged. This new astrology focused on the birth horoscopes of individuals and attempted to make specific predictions of future events for individuals based on the time and place of their birth. This is now called natal, genethliacal, or juridical astrology. This form of divination was only one of many (for example, divination by hepatoscopy, the examination of animal livers), but it gradually increased in popularity.

The knowledge necessary for casting individual horoscopes came from the Babylonians even though the Persians were the first to cast them. Among other things, the Babylonians were responsible for associating the lunar cycle with the seasons and for establishing the ecliptic (the sun's apparent path through the stars in the course of a year). They also determined the movements of the planets.

In the late Persian period, the 12 signs of the zodiac were formulated. The zodiac, an imaginary belt which centers on the ecliptic and includes the paths of the planets, is 16° to 18° wide, and is divided into 12 equal sections or "signs" of 30° in length. At some point these 12 signs were given names and made to correspond to 12 constellations in them. When this was done—more than

2,000 years ago—the signs corresponded to the constellations, but this is no longer true.

The 12 signs of the zodiac are measured eastward from the spring equinox (March 21st), and they are: Aries, Taurus, Gemini, Cancer, Leo, Virgo, Libra, Scorpio, Saggitarius, Capricorn, Aquarius, and Pisces. Not long before the birth of Christ each of the 30° signs was subdivided into three decans. The decan measurement (10°) was a contribution to astrology from Egypt.

Persia was conquered by Greece in the fourth century B.C., and by the third century the Greeks gathered knowledge about astrology from Chaldean priests, especially Berosus. Astrology fit nicely into the pantheistic materialism of the Greek Stoic philosophers. The 12 signs were divided into 4 groups of 3 signs each, to represent the 4 elements. This produced the fiery, earthy, airy, and watery signs. In addition, the zodiacal signs were related to various planets, colors, plants, metals, and stones.

The Alexandrian astronomer Ptolemy (Claudius Ptolemaeus) refined astrology to its present form in the second century A.D. The Ptolemaic system held that the earth is at the center and the sun, moon, and planets revolve around it. Ptolemy's *Tetrabiblios* was an attempt to turn astrology into an exact science, and this work is still revered by astrologers today.

Astrology enjoyed a strong influence in Europe and among the Arabs during the Middle Ages. In the Renaissance, astrologers were important in the courts of Europe. Astrology declined after this period, but revived as a result of the occult explosion of the 19th and 20th centuries. The modern astrology of the West is a direct descendant of Babylonian polytheism and astronomy.

Astrology blends in well with Spiritualism, Edgar Cayce and the Association for Research and Enlightenment, Numerology, I Ching, The Tarot, Theosophy, the Kabbalah, witchcraft and magic, palmistry, and Rosicrucianism.

Astrology is no longer based on the worship of the stars and planets as gods, but this was its origin. In recent years astrology has been popularized by figures such as Carl Jung (Jung used horoscopes in his diagnoses of mental illness), Evangeline Adams, Myrna Kingsley, Carroll Righter, Sidney Omarr, and Llewellyn George, to name only a few. Even Hitler played a role in the resurgence of astrology. He was taken with the concept of cosmic destiny and depended heavily on astrology for the fulfillment of this destiny.

More popular in Europe and America today than ever before, astrology has become the major divination technique of the Western world. There are several astrological associations, including the American Federation of Astrologers and the International Scientific Astrological Research Association. Astrological magazines such as *American Astrology, Astrological Digest,* and *Horoscope* have wide circulations. About two thirds of American daily newspapers carry astrological columns. Millions of Americans purchase books on astrology, even books on horoscopes for dogs and cats.

At least 40 million Americans dabble in astrology. More than 12,000 professional astrologers, plus tens of thousands of part-time astrologers, serve them. Hundreds of millions of dollars per year are spent on horoscopes (many computerized) and other astrologically related items. The situation in Canada, England, France, Germany, and several other countries is similar.

In addition to Western astrology, different astrological systems were developed in other parts of the world. The Chinese arrived at an astrological system centuries before the Babylonians. Astrology in India is also ancient, and even now it is a determinative factor in Indian religion and society.

As we have seen, the central activity in astrology is the determination of horoscopes. These horoscopes, drawn with the help of an ephemeris, a book of tables showing the position of the sun, moon, and planets for different years, chart the position of the sun, moon, planets, and zodiac at the time and place of an individual's birth. The most important element in a horoscope is the sun-sign. Also important is the "ascendent," that is, the zodiacal constellation which was on the eastern horizon at the time of birth. On the horoscope, this ascending constellation is placed in the first "house." The next constellation in the zodiac is placed in the second house, and so on to the 12th house. The 12 houses should be distinguished from the 12 signs and from the 12 constellations of the zodiac.

The position of the planets is another ingredient of a horoscope. This includes what constellations the planets were in at the time of birth and the relationships of the planets to one another. The latter is known as the "aspects." The "good" aspects are the sextile (two planets separated by 60°) and the trine (120° separation). The "bad" aspects are the opposition (180° separation) and the square (90° separation). The conjunction (very small separation) can be good or bad depending on the two (or more) planets involved.

Horoscopes are used in several ways. Natal, or genethliacal, astrology deals with the casting and interpretation of horoscopes for invididuals. Mundane astrology is concerned with whole countries. Horary astrology attempts to answer specific questions, especially related to the best time for journeys, financial decisions, and marriages. Astrology is used to predict how a person's character will develop, what events are likely to take place, and even how one will die.

In the last century, there has been an increasing interest in star-ages. Because of a phenomenon known as the precession of the equinoxes, the sun moves into a new constellation on the first day of spring (the vernal equinox) every 2,160 years. This is because the earth's axis wobbles like a spinning top in slow motion. Each wobble cycle takes about 26,000 years to complete. Thus, at the time when astrology was being formulated, the sun appeared in the constellation Aries on the first day of spring. A little before the time of Christ, the sun passed from the border of Aries to the border of Pisces on the vernal equinox.

It is difficult to be precise about what year a new star-age begins, but the next star-age will be the Age of Aquarius, when the sun moves into Aquarius on March 21. Several dates have been given as the beginning of the Aquarian Age, including 1904, 1910, 1917, 1936, 1962, and 2000. In any case, astrologers have developed a cyclical view of history because of these star-ages. Each of these ages is said to be characterized by its own form of worship and religion, government, ethics, and philosophy.

Because Aquarius the Water Bearer is a man, the new religion of the Aquarian Age will be humanism and brotherhood. Astrologers claim that the age will be one of harmony, peace, and salvation of mankind. The ethical system of this golden age will be characterized by freedom. But this cyclical concept of history is in reality a fatalistic and pessimistic view. It offers no ultimate goal or meaning for history, because with the completion of one 26,000 year cycle, a new cycle just like it will follow.

A number of cultic and mystical writings relating to the Aquarian Age have surfaced in the last century. One example is *The Aquarian Gospel of Jesus, the Christ of the Piscean Age*, published in 1911 by Levi H. Dowling. This book purports to be a series of "revelations" about the "hidden" life of Jesus. There are several other bizarre "Aquarian revelations" about the Cosmic Christ.

Astrology has replaced the personal Creator with an impersonal cosmos. A philosophy which teaches that there is an exact correspondence between the macrocosm and microcosm, it is sometimes summarized by the expression, "As above, so below."

Astrology is also friendly to the idea of reincarnation. Many astrologers state that one's horoscope is determined by the "karmic debt" accumulated in his previous incarnation. This cyclic and fatalistic concept is also extended to nations and ultimately to the whole universe.

The universe is slowly but inexorably moving in an evolutionary cycle in fulfillment of its cosmic destiny. Sometimes religious terminology is used to describe this.

Individuals, nations, and civilizations rise and fall according to the stars. This is a fatalistic, impersonal system of forces and influences which really has no room for free will. Human freedom is only an illusion. Many astrologers, of course, see this problem and try to avoid it by saying that if a person can become aware of his cosmic destiny through astrology, he will be able to use this knowledge to shape his future. This concept is inconsistent with the astrological system, and yet astrologers desperately cling to it because of their egotistic desires to be the masters of their own destinies. On the other hand, astrologers can use this astral determinism to shirk responsibility for their immoral behavior.

There are a number of serious flaws with the whole system of astrology, and several of these will now be listed.

(1) There is a basic problem with *authority* in astrology. The whole history of astrology is imbued with a combination of polytheism, mysticism, divination, and quasicience. What, then, is the astrologer's authority for truth? How do astrologers know that their method of interpretation is valid? What is the basis, for example, of saying that the sextile and trine aspects are good and the opposition and square aspects are bad? Is it because of mythology?

(2) There are several systems of astrology. Chinese and Hindu astrologers would not interpret a given horoscope in the same ways as Occidental astrologers. Not all Western astrologers agree that there are 12 zodiacal signs. Steven Schmidt in his book *Astrology 14* claims that Cetus the Whale and Ophichus the Serpent Slayer should be added to the zodiac for a total of 14 signs. But some argue for only 8, others for 10, and a few for 24. It is clear that many things in astrology (signs, houses, aspects) are arbitrary.

(3) Astrology is based on the Ptolemaic concept of an earth-centered universe. Centuries after Ptolemy, Copernicus proved that the solar system is actually heliocentric (the earth and other planets move around the sun), not earth-centered.

(4) Astrology is out of date for another reason. The early astrologers were not aware of precession and therefore failed to take it into account in their system. The 12 signs of the zodiac originally corresponded with the 12 constellations of the same names, but due to precession, the constellations have shifted about 30° in the last 2,000 years. This means that the constellation of Virgo is now in the sign of Libra, the constellation of Libra is now in the sign of Scorpio, and so on. Thus, if a person is born on September 1, astrologers would call him a Virgo (the *sign* the sun is in at that date), but the sun is actually in the *constellation* Leo at that date. So there are two different zodiacs: one which slowly moves (the sidereal zodiac) and one which is stationary (the tropical zodiac). Which zodiac should be used?

(5) Astrology is based on five planets plus the sun and moon (sometimes erroneously called the seven planets). However, three new planets have been discovered since astrology assumed its present form. Uranus was discovered in 1781, Neptune in 1839, and Pluto in 1932.

(6) There is no question that the universe is orderly and that the sun and moon affect many things on earth. But the concept of celestial influences is carried to an extreme by astrologers. What kinds of forces are astrologers talking about when they speak of planets influencing life and behavior on earth? These so-called "planetary vibrations" and "electromagnetic attractions" have yet to be discovered by astronomers. Planets do exert a gravitational attraction, but this influence is negligible compared to the thousands of environmental forces on the earth.

(7) Astrologers actually ignore most of the pertinent astronomical, biological, and other scientific data now available. Astrology is a simplistic and stylized game far

removed from the astronomical realities of the universe.

(8) Another flaw in astrology is that many people are born in places on the earth's surface which prevent them from having a genuine horoscope. In lands above the Arctic Circle, the planets and zodiacal constellations cannot be seen for long periods. What, therefore, do astrologers say about Eskimos and Laplanders born during these periods?

(9) Astrology also fails to deal adequately with the problem of twins. Twins have the same horoscope (even a birth interval of several minutes would make no real difference), and yet their destinies may be radically different.

(10) Astrologers claim to be able to predict people's destinies and the general manner of their deaths, but this claim breaks down whenever there is mass destruction of humans (the Jews in Nazi Germany, the victims of the atom bomb in Japan, and the people killed by earthquakes). The individual horoscopes involved would by no means have predicted violent deaths for all these people.

(11) Though astrologers use statistics to support their predictive claims, their desired correlations are often not to be found. The horoscopes of large groups of scientists and artists, for example, do not show significant variations from the horoscopes of the general population.

(12) Astrology would make more sense biologically if horoscopes were reckoned from the time of conception rather than the time of birth. All the hereditary factors are determined at conception. In addition, the time of birth is frequently determined by physicians, since labor can be induced or delayed. If astrologers made this logical change, however, they would run into difficulties. It might not be so easy to determine the exact time of one's conception.

(13) Often events do *not* happen as predicted by astrologers. For example, astrologer Jeane Dixon has made many blunders in her predictions (World War III did not

begin in 1958, and Lyndon Johnson was not renominated in 1968, to cite two). When events in a person's life go contrary to the predictions in his horoscope, astrologers try to rationalize the mistake. They have so many escape hatches that it is often difficult to prove when astrology fails.

(14) Astrological columns are often filled with trite and trivial injunctions. The advice may be so absurdly general that it is worthless. Other times it is simply good psychological advice that would be good for anyone regardless of his astrological sign.

(15) Different astrologers give different readings of the same chart. This is because of the conflicting interpretations offered by various source books and because of the strong subjective element involved in interpreting horoscopes. This is why a comparison of the advice given by several astrological columns for any given sign and day will frequently reveal contradictions.

(16) The effectiveness of astrology is in direct proportion to the gullibility of the adherents. Bogus horoscopes are as enthusiastically received by the unsuspecting as genuine horoscopes.

Biblical Evaluation

(1) There are few direct Scripture references to astrology, but it is categorized in the Bible along with other forms of false divination (see Deut. 18:10-14). The Bible repeatedly warns against the attempt to gain knowledge by illicit means of divination.

(2) One central reference to astrology in the Bible is Isaiah 47:8-15. In this passage God condemns Babylon and tells of its impending judgment. Babylon is told that its astrologers will be of no avail in predicting or preventing the coming judgment. "You are wearied with your many counsels, let now the astrologers, those who prophesy by the stars, those who predict by the new moons, stand up and save you from what will come upon you" (v. 13). God is not predictable because He is

not subject to the movements of the heavens or the laws of nature. He is free to act as He wants. Thus, astrology and other forms of divination are inadequate and fraudulent substitutes for true revelation from God.

(3) Jeremiah told God's people, "Do not learn the way of the nations, and do not be terrified by the signs of the heavens although the nations are terrified by them" (Jer. 10:2). This is a reference to the ancient religious form of astrology. Though astrology has changed since then, it is still full of elements directly derived from its pagan origins.

(4) The Bible says that one reason Israel fell was because she participated in the sinful worship of the surrounding nations, and this worship included religious astrology. Like the other nations, Israel began to worship "all the host of heaven" (2 Kings 17:16-18; 21:2, 5-6). When King Josiah of Judah did away with the astrologer priests "who burned incense to Baal, to the sun and to the moon and to the constellations and to all the host of heaven," he received the approval of God (2 Kings 23:4-5, 24-25; see also Zeph. 1:4-6).

(5) The Book of Daniel also exposes astrologers, classifying the Chaldeans (master astrologers) with magicians (soothsayer priests), conjurers, and sorcerers. All of these groups are ridiculed in Daniel 2 for their futile, false, and evil art.

(6) Israel is condemned (Amos 5:25-26) because of its worship of Sikkuth and Kiyyun (Saturn). This is also mentioned in Acts 7:43.

(7) In spite of the clear biblical testimony against divination by astrology, several modern astrologers try to prove that the Bible in fact supports the practice of astrology. The evidence they use is quite flimsy. Astrologers often claim that many of the patriarchs and prophets such as Abraham, Joseph, Moses, David, and Daniel were astrologers. But all the biblical testimony concerning these men proves just the opposite. Astrologers also claim to see references to the constellations of the zodiac

in passages such as Genesis 1 and 49. Several say that the 12 tribes of Israel represent the 12 astrological signs. Again, a simple in-context study of these passages refutes these assertions. Another example of the futile attempt of astrologers to find biblical support for their system is their appeal to the trek of the magi and the star of Bethlehem in Matthew 2. But there are no astrological allusions in this passage.

(8) Astrology is a form of idolatry. It demands a person's faith and takes away from faith in God. It is a reliance on the creation rather than the Creator. It is a religious system which replaces the will of God with obedience to supposed cosmic influences. It is a substitute for God's revelation, and it encourages a worldview contrary to the Scriptures. Astrology also discourages people from trusting God for the future.

(9) Some Christian writers claim the Gospel is outlined by the zodiacal constellations, but this requires a quite fanciful and subjective interpretation. The heavens reveal God's glory, but they are not sufficient to bring one to faith in Christ.

Things to Keep in Mind

(1) There are several reasons for the recent growth and appeal of astrology. One is that it is a substitute for faith in God. Modern man has rejected God in this "post-Christian era," but people still long for contact with something above and beyond themselves. Astrology tries to offer a substitute for the security which God provides. Astrology does well in times of fear and anxiety.

Another appeal of astrology is that it makes no moral demands. It implies that people are not fully responsible for their behavior. It also feeds the self-centeredness of people who want to go their own way. Astrology appeals to the intense curiosity of people, claiming to give insight into other people and into the future.

(2) Astrology is a system which eliminates a personal Creator. In place of God, an impersonal set of forces con-

trols a slowly dying universe. Contrary to the popular myth that the universe is surging upward in order and complexity, the reality is that the universe, if left to itself, will eventually become cold and lifeless.

(3) The fatalism of astrology is intense. Astrologers optimistically speak of the dawning of the Aquarian Age which will supposedly be imbued with peace and brotherhood. But they fail to mention that about 2,000 years later the earth will go into another star-age, the Age of Capricorn, the Goat. This will be followed by the Ages of Sagittarius, Scorpio, Libra, and the others. When this cycle is through it will be followed by another and another. This is a fatalistic and cyclic view of history. Astrology has no genuine basis for its optimistic view that things are getting better and better.

(4) Astrology has "exchanged the truth of God for a lie, and worshiped and served the creature rather than the Creator, who is blessed forever" (Rom. 1:25). Through astrology, many have robbed God of the glory due His name. This is quite foolish, since they are turning to inferior "gods." God is in charge of nature, not vice versa. Christ is seated "far above all rule and authority and power and dominion, and every name that is named, not only in this age, but also in the one to come" (Eph. 1:21). Thus, every person without Christ is a slave to the dominion of Satan, the "prince of the power of the air" (2:2) and the "ruler of this world" (John 12:31). But Christ offers liberation from this bondage to everyone who turns to Him.

19

SPIRITUALISM

Background and Teaching

A number of scholars prefer the term *Spiritism* rather than *Spiritualism* to designate this ancient cult. But spiritism more properly describes the worship of spirit beings which is found in many countries today. Voodoo worship in Haiti is one example of spiritism. Spiritualists, on the other hand, claim to have communication with the spiritual world. Most adherents of this cult therefore designate themselves by this name and distinguish themselves from spiritists. In 1976 the several national and international Spiritualist denominations reported more than 200 churches and clergy in the United States with a total membership of 10,000. This does not include unaffiliated Spiritualists. Membership worldwide is in the millions.

Spiritualism is perhaps the oldest religious cult in existence. Every civilization known has practiced it to one degree or another. Mediums and familiar spirits are mentioned in many ancient sources, including the Bible and the literature of the Egyptians, Babylonians, Chinese, and Greeks.

Spiritualism in its modern form was developed particularly through the efforts of the Fox sisters in Hydeville, New York. In 1848, Kate and Margaret Fox claimed that they were in contact with the spirit of Charles Rosma, a man who had been murdered some years before. This spirit communicated by means of strange rapping noises in response to questions asked by the Fox sisters. They began to hold special sessions for the public. This generated an intense interest in Spiritualism which spread across the nation. It is interesting that Spiritualism developed in the Northeast in the mid-19th century, because this was essentially the same area and period that produced such other cults as Christian Science, Mormonism, Jehovah's Witnesses, and Theosophy.

Another early promoter of modern Spiritualism was Andrew J. Davis, whose book on the subject became quite popular. Spiritualism soon spread to Europe, and it flourished especially in England and France. As it grew in Europe and America, a number of very prominent people began to get seriously interested in spiritualistic seances. Some of these were Sir Arthur Conan Doyle, Horace Greeley, Elizabeth Barrett Browning, James Fenimore Cooper, and William Cullen Bryant. Several scientists also took notice of the movement and some of these conducted scientific investigations of mediums and spiritualistic phenomena. This has resulted in a certain amount of hard evidence which confirms some extraordinary phenomena.

Spiritualism suffered a setback late in the 19th century when one of the Fox sisters, Margaret, announced that the famous rappings were produced by cracking her toe joints (she later retracted this confession). Spiritualism was also hurt by the fact that magicians began to duplicate most of the phenomena which occurred in seances.

Nevertheless, the movement continued to grow, and a number of Spiritualist associations were formed, including the National Spiritualist Association and the International General Assembly of Spiritualists. There are now almost a score of Spiritualist "denominations" in America alone, and most of these are member groups of the Federation of Spiritualist Churches and Associations, formed in 1944. In addition, many mediums and Spiritualists are independent of all Spiritualist organizations.

Spiritualism waxes and wanes in popularity, but it does especially well in times of war (e.g., World Wars I and II). A large percentage of Spiritualists are Catholics or ex-Catholics. Estimates of the number of practicing Spiritualists vary, but there may be about half a million in the United States and several million in the world (Brazil alone has about 3 million).

The main idea in Spiritualism is that the spirits of the dead are able to communicate with people on earth. They do this through mediums, individuals who are especially receptive to the "vibrations" from the spirit world. Each medium usually claims to have one "spirit-guide," known in the Bible as a "familiar spirit" (see Lev. 19:31; Isa. 8:19; 19:3-4; 1 Sam. 28:7-8; 2 Kings 21:1, 6) who controls him or her during the many seances which are conducted.

The primary purpose of a seance is to call up the spirits of the "recently departed." Appealing to a spirit-guide, a medium usually begins a seance by falling into a trance. Everyone in the group holds hands so that the events which take place are attributed to the spirit world. Then the spirit-guide takes control of the medium and sometimes speaks through the medium's voice. In some seances the spirit may play a musical instrument (often a trumpet) which has been set on the table. The spirit of the dead may also communicate by writing (using the medium's hand), speaking, moving objects, or even appearing in a mistlike form called ectoplasm. Some seances involve the levitation of objects. Lights may go on and off, and various noises may be heard.

Some of the most famous seances were those conducted with the late Bishop James Pike, who used three mediums to contact the spirit of his son Jim. Some of his sessions with medium Arthur Ford were even televised.

In addition to seances, many Spiritualists engage in regular services in the Spiritualist Church. These services include several modifications of practices in Christian churches, including the singing of Christian hymns with the words changed to fit Spiritualist theology.

The theology of Spiritualism has been summed up in the "Seven Principles" adopted early in this century by the National Spiritualist Association. These principles are: (1) the Fatherhood of God, (2) the brotherhood of man, (3) continuous existence, (4) communion of spirits and ministry of angels, (5) personal responsibility, (6) compensation and retribution hereafter for good or evil done on earth, (7) a path of endless progression.

The essential dogma of Spiritualism is that there is a continuity in the life of man, an eternal progression toward the perfection of human spirits. There are several planes of spiritual existence, and each spirit must progressively ascend to higher "heavens." As the spirit attains higher circles or spheres on the way to perfection, it gets less interested in the earthly sphere. Thus it becomes more difficult to communicate with a spirit as time goes on. Each new sphere is farther from the earth.

Spiritualists believe that those who do evil compensate for it in this life and in the next. There is no heaven or hell. No matter how wicked a person may be in this life, Spiritualists emphasize "the doorway to reformation is never closed against any soul here or hereafter." Each spirit can make its existence pleasant or poor just as people do on earth, but all eventually achieve "salvation" by their own efforts.

It is evident from the above that Spiritualists reject the

biblical concept of the sinful nature of man and man's need for a substitutionary atonement, which they believe is a primitive and perverted concept. The idea of the fall of man is false. Man needs only to be united with God, and this can be accomplished without the need of redemption.

Spiritualists not only minimize Christ's work, but they also minimize His person. They consistently deny the deity of Jesus Christ as an equal with God the Father. Jesus was only divine in the sense that all people have a spark of the divine within them. Jesus was a great Jewish medium, but apart from this there was nothing unique about Him. They deny the Virgin Birth and the bodily resurrection of Jesus as well as the biblical doctrine of the Trinity. To them God is the "Great Spirit" or the "Supreme Spirit." God is not personal but impersonal.

Needless to say, Spiritualists have a low view of the authority of the Bible. They claim that the Bible is fallible because of its human origin, but they acknowledge that some of it contains inspired revelations. They view the scriptures of other religions in the same way.

Because of their teachings and practices, Spiritualists have traditionally been hostile to the Christian church. Though their earlier literature was especially antagonistic to Christianity, they have more recently taken a less scathing approach. Some Spiritualists belong to various churches, some are in Spiritualist churches, and others go to no churches at all.

Most Spiritualists deny the teachings of the Bible, but their only real authority for doing so are the mediums who contradict the Bible during seances. These have become their standard of truth even though mediums do not claim the kind of inspiration repeatedly claimed by the biblical writers. Spiritualists cannot answer the charge that they may in fact be dealing with lying, evil spirits (demons) rather than the spirits of the dead.

Spiritualism abounds with deception, magicians' tricks, and fraudulent activities. The Society for Physical Research, for example, can endorse the honesty of very few mediums. Many mediums have been exposed as frauds, but it would be wrong to write off all mediums and seances as hoaxes. There is evidence that the phenomena are sometimes genuine.

Even so, this does not prove the Spiritualists' claims that they are communicating with the spirits of deceased humans. They may be wrongly interpreting their experiences. There are other possible explanations for the genuine phenomena. One is telepathy. In some cases the medium may be able to get information from the minds of the sitters in a seance. Clairvoyance, the ability to discern things not present to the senses, may be involved in some instances. Special psychic abilities are possessed in varying degrees by a few individuals.

Psychic powers, however, will not explain all genuine Spiritualistic phenomena. The Bible clearly says that *demonic* powers are often involved. Even a number of Spiritualists have abandoned their mediumistic practices because they realized they were working with evil and blasphemous spirits. Lying demonic spirits often pretend to be departed human spirits. But most Spiritualists claim that there are no evil spirits or demons.

Spiritualists sometimes appeal to the Bible to support their mediumistic practices. For example, they point to the fact that men like Peter, Paul, and John had contact with the "spirit world" because of their visions (see Acts 10:9-16; 2 Cor. 12:2-4; Rev. 4:1-2). They also refer to King Saul's experience with the medium at Endor (1 Sam. 28). But even a cursory look at this passage shows that it *condemns* rather than encourages Spiritualism. Saul asked the medium to call up the spirit of the dead Samuel. But the Spiritualist medium was shocked when Samuel actually appeared. She realized that Samuel's appearance was not the result of her work or the power of her familiar spirit. The explanation of this is either that God Himself made Samuel reappear at Saul's request in order to pronounce Saul's doom or that a demon was impersonating

Samuel. In either case this passage rebukes Saul for re-
sorting to a medium (also see 1 Chron. 10:13-14).

Biblical Evaluation

(1) The Bible condemns witches, wizards, sorcerers,
seers, fortune-tellers, mediums, soothsayers, diviners,
and necromancers. Here are some related passages:
Exodus 8:18; 22:18; Leviticus 19:26, 31; 20:6, 27; Deuteronomy 18:9-14; 1 Samuel 15:23; 28:3-9; 2 Kings 9:22; 21:6;
23:24-25; 1 Chronicles 10:13-14; 2 Chronicles 33:6; Isaiah
8:19; 19:3; 47:9; Micah 5:12; Nahum 3:4; Acts 16:16-18.

In Leviticus 19:31 we read, "Do not turn to mediums or
spiritists; do not seek them out to be defiled by them. I
am the Lord your God." Mediums and spiritists who
were found among the Israelites were to be stoned to
death (Lev. 20:27). Passages such as 2 Kings 21:6 and
2 Chronicles 33:6 place spiritists and mediums in the
same class with witches, diviners, and sorcerers.

The Scriptures clearly speak against attempts to communicate with the spirits of the dead. "When they say to
you, 'Consult the mediums and the wizards who whisper
and mutter,' should not a people consult their God?
Should they consult the dead on behalf of the living?"
(Isa. 8:19) The Bible does not teach, however, that mediums can actually call up departed spirits.

(2) Spiritualists deny the important doctrines of the
Bible, including the personality of God, the Trinity, and
the deity of Christ. Various mediums have become their
source of authority for truth.

(3) According to 1 John 4:1-3, we should "not believe
every spirit, but test the spirits to see whether they are
from God; because many false prophets have gone out
into the world." Spiritualists fail this test because their
"spirit-guides" do not confess Jesus Christ.

Things to Keep in Mind

(1) Spiritualism has a number of appeals which lead people into its folds. It capitalizes on the desire to be with

loved ones who have died. It promises answers to questions about the next life. It repudiates the idea of heaven and hell. Its roots go back to the earliest civilizations of man, and in recent years it has enjoyed the support of many prominent writers and scientists.

(2) Though much spiritualist activity is demonstrably fraudulent, Christians should challenge Spiritualists to consider the possibility of demonic activity in their seances. We should be able to show how the Bible condemns the activities of Spiritualists and mediums.

(3) It is foolish to seek out lesser spirits by means of involved mystical activities when one can have direct access to the living God through prayer and the Bible.

THE KABBALAH

Background and Teachings

The term *Kabbalah* is given to a mystical religious tradition which came out of Judaism. Kabbalah (also spelled Kabala, Cabala, Cabbalah, Quabbalah) means "reception" or "tradition," and refers to doctrines received by oral tradition. The Jewish Talmud also refers to oral tradition but its concern is with the Law and commentaries on the Law. The Talmud is sociological and legalistic, but the Kabbalah is metaphysical and theosophical. The Kabbalah claims to be the perpetuation of ancient and secret religious doctrines.

Because of the nature of the Kabbalah, many Gentiles have become fascinated by its teachings. It has become an integral part of the teachings and practice of the occult community.

The Kabbalah can be divided into two major branches: the "theoretical" Kabbalah and the "practical" Kabbalah. The former is concerned with metaphysics and mysticism while the latter is more thaumaturgical (the practice of magic).

The theoretical Kabbalah concerns itself with philosophical matters such as cosmogony (the origin of the universe), cosmology (the order of the universe), epistemology (the means and validity of knowledge), and the processes of the universe. It is a Hebrew theosophy (knowledge of God through mystical insight) which shares many things with Gnosticism. The Kabbalah occupies itself with esoteric knowledge, the "innermost secrets." It is a unique brand of occultism built on fanciful and spiritualized interpretations of the Old Testament, particularly the Pentateuch. One of the chief elements in Kabbalism is its erotic mysticism, which regards the sexual act as the ultimate sacrament.

The Kabbalah is not a single book. It is a system of mystical doctrines taken from several sources, though two sources are by far the most important. These are the *Sepher Yetzirah* (the Book of Formation) and *Sepher ha Zohar* (the Book of Splendor). The *Sepher Yetzirah* is believed by Kabbalists to have originated with Abraham. Another tradition says it was written by Rabbi Aqiba at the end of the first century A.D.; however, it should be dated between the sixth and ninth centuries. A six-chapter book, it assigns numerical values and esoteric significance to the 22 letters of the Hebrew alphabet.

Probably written toward the end of the 13th century, the *Sepher ha Zohar* is usually attributed to Rabbi Moses de Leon, a Spanish Jew. The *Zohar*, written in Aramaic, is based on ancient material. It is a huge work consisting of several books, the most important of which is a mystical commentary on the Pentateuch. This commentary is divided into five sections corresponding to the five books of the Law. Each of these sections is further divided into subsections. Several of the other fragments which belong to the *Sepher ha Zohar* are: the "Book of Concealment," the "Greater Holy Synod," the "Lesser Holy Synod," and "Discourse of the Aged Man," the "Luminous Book," the "Faithful Shepherd," the "Hidden Things of the Law," and the "Secret Commentary."

Besides the *Book of Formation* and the *Book of Splendor*, a number of commentaries on these books are included in Kabbalistic literature.

Some prominent Jewish Kabbalists of the 13th to 16th centuries were Aaron ben Samuel, Eleazar of Worms, Isaac the Blind, Abraham ben Samuel Abulafia, Joseph ben Abraham Giquatilla, Menahem ben Benjamin Recanti, Isaac de Loria Ashkenazi, Moses of Cordova, and Issachar ben Napthali. Representing the French, German, and Spanish schools of the Kabbalah, these men reacted against the legalistic spirit of the Talmudists of their day and emphasized faith and mystic freedom.

The mystical and magical elements in the Kabbalah attracted quite a few Gentile students of occultism and esoteric Christianity in Renaissance Europe. These included Raymond Lully, Cornelius Agrippa, Paracelsus, John Reuchlin, William Postel, Thomas Vaughan, and Knorr Von Rosenroth. Many of these scholars saw Christian elements in the secret doctrine of the *Zohar*.

Perhaps the most significant Renaissance Christian student of the Kabbalah was Pico della Mirandola (1463–1494). Kabbalism was the basic source for many of Pico's Theses. The limits of 15th century scholarship were largely responsible for Pico's failure to discern the flaws in the Kabbalistic system, particularly in the area of its interpretation of Scripture.

Down through the centuries there have been many conflicting traditions, schools, and teachings within Kabbalism. Its highly speculative methods of interpretation produced a variety of extravagant teachings, often in opposition to one another.

The *Book of Formation* describes three basic methods of interpreting the Scriptures: *gematria*, *notarikon*, and *themurah. Gematria* is a method which works with the numerical values of the Hebrew letters. The letters of every Hebrew word can be added together in a variety of ways, and the numbers that result can be used to arrive at a "deeper" understanding of the things contained in the Old Testament. *Notarikon* is the system which forms new words or phrases out of the first or last letters of the words in a text. *Themurah,* a system of rearrangement and transposition of the letters of a word, was used to make new words from the original words. The Kabbalists took many different approaches to themurah. In one, the alphabet was divided into two or three equal parts and these parts were placed above each other. Letters in the same vertical column were then substituted for each other, and this was used as a code to form new words from the original words of Scripture.

These interpretive systems were used by many of the Kabbalists to argue that the Old Testament must be divinely inspired because of the intricate numerical relationships which can be derived from it. But their main use was to find hidden and allegorical meanings in the Scriptures.

The central teaching of Kabbalism is its emanation doctrine, an elaborate scheme which describes how the limitless God created a universe by producing a series of 10 descending rays or intelligences which proceeded from Him. These emanations, called *sephiroth,* are regarded as beings personifying the attributes of God. The 10 sephiroth also represent different stages or hierarchies, ranging from the supernal to the world of matter. The emanations on the bottom of the hierarchy are further removed from God and consequently less perfect and sublime.

In philosophical terms, this system is called degenerative monism. The 10 sephiroth are named Kether (the Crown), Chokmah (Wisdom), Binah (Understanding or Intelligence), Chesed (Mercy or Love), Geburah (Severity or Justice), Tiphereth (Beauty), Netzach (Victory), Hod

(Glory or Splendor), Yesod (Foundation), and Malkuth (Kingdom).

The sephiroth or emanation doctrine was developed because Judaism had arrived at an extremely transcendent view of Yahweh. He came to be regarded as so infinitely removed from the visible universe that He was practically unknowable. The Kabbalists reacted against this extreme transcendence doctrine and developed a mystical system by which the transcendent God could also be immanent and knowable to men.

The sephiroth doctrine is used to explain the gap between the infinite God and the finite universe, for it provides several intermediaries between God and the world of matter. Behind all the finite emanations is the Ain Soph, the perfect and unknowable Deity. This Ain Soph produced the first of the emanations through His (Its) will to create and become known. Each emanation successively produced another until Malkuth, the 10th and last, appeared. This system is used to explain not only Creation but also the problem of evil and the path of salvation.

In addition to the 10 sephiroth, there are also 4 worlds or levels of existence, which represent different degrees of divine essence. The highest and nearest the Godhead is Atziluth, the world of supernals. The next world is Briah, the world of Creation. Yetzirah is the world of formation, and the fourth and farthest from the Deity is Assiah, the world of material action.

The Kabbalists made charts to visually portray the interrelationships of the sephiroth and the worlds. The best known of these is called the "Sacred Tree" or the "Tree of Life." In this chart the 10 sephiroth are connected by 22 "paths," which are grouped in three columns or pillars. The central pillar is called the Shekinah of God. The right and left pillars correspond to the right and left sides of a human body, with the first sephiroth (Kether) being the head and the last sephiroth (Malkuth) representing the feet.

Salvation in the Kabbalah consists of the soul's ascent to God through the middle path of the "Tree of Life." This is an ascent from the material world (Assiah) to the supernal world (Atziluth) and beyond into the realm of Deity.

The emanations are regarded as "chariots" (a Kabbalistic image taken from Ezek. 1) by which man can ascend to the halls of the divine kingdom. One ascends the Tree of Life by attaining this esoteric knowledge about God and the order of the creation, and by meditation on the 32 paths—the 10 sephiroth plus the 22 connections among the sephiroth. They are also known as the paths of wisdom, and each path has its own name, symbolism, and function. Contemplative prayer and meditation on these paths is used to achieve a mystical experience of union with God.

In addition to the 32 paths, Kabbalists also speak of the 50 gates of understanding. These gates begin with chaos, and go through stages such as the elements, living matter, intelligence, the psychic, the planets, the stars, the angelic world, till the archetypal world of the Ain Soph is reached. Moses is said to have reached the 49th, but not the 50th gate.

We can see from this that the Deity or Ain Soph is not personal, but an impersonal principle so exalted above human reasoning and perception that it is eternally secret and unknowable. The things we perceive are only emanations from this inscrutable unity. The Ain Soph is a supreme will.

Definite connections exist between Kabbalism and Gnosticism (especially the emanation doctrine). Similarities also may be seen between Kabbalism and Islamic Sufism (especially its concept of absorption into the divine). However, the Kabbalists do not have any leanings toward pantheism. Nature may be the garment of God as the Zohar teaches, but it is not the body of God.

The Kabbalah has an elaborate hierarchy of angelic and demonic beings. Corresponding to Briah, the world of creation, is a series of archangels, listed by name. Each of these archangels corresponds, in turn, to 1 of the 10 sephiroth. Corresponding to Yetzirah, the world of formation, are 10 different orders of lesser angels (and each order also corresponds to 1 of the 10 emanations). Corresponding to Assiah, the world of material action, are 10 orders of "retrograde spirits," or demons. These 10 orders are the false counterparts of the 10 sephiroth.

The general Kabbalistic doctrine of souls is that they existed before they inhabited human bodies. Each soul is told by God what body to inhabit. In one scheme, the soul consists of a vital spirit, an intellectual spirit, and the soul proper. Each soul must accomplish a certain mission, and if this mission is achieved in one incarnation, the soul then dwells near to God. If one incarnation is not sufficient, the soul must be reincarnated again and again until the mission is fulfilled. This concept is sometimes called metempsychosis.

The Kabbalah especially emphasizes the female principle in the Deity as represented in the third and tenth sephiroth (Binah and Malkuth). This female principle is called the Shekinah, and she is regarded as the bride of God. Binah is the Shekinah of the superior world, and Malkuth is the Shekinah of the lower or physical world. The Shekinah acts as a demiurge or subordinate creating deity. Called Elohim and Adonai, she is the daughter of God and the mother of man.

The Shekinah is the middle pillar of the Kabbalistic Tree of Life, acting as the pathway of salvation (the upward ascent of man to God). The mystery of Shekinah relates in turn to the Kabbalistic mystery of sex. This involves a heavy anthropomorphism in which the conjugal relationship between a man and his wife is a reflection of the relationship between the Holy One and His Shekinah. Thus, sex is the highest sacrament in Kabbalism. When one is engaged in the sexual act, he should also have the Shekinah in his mind, because the physical union below is an image of the union which is above. The conception of children is therefore an important thing in Kabbalism, and those who do not have offspring are incomplete in this life. Consequently, their souls must be reincarnated.

The Kabbalah allegorizes the biblical account of the earthly paradise, the angelic fall, the serpent, the Fall of man, the Genesis Flood, the Abrahamic Covenant, the life of Moses, the two temples, Sheol, and so on. Everything is coated with symbolism. It also speaks of a coming Messiah who will bring in a new age.

The mystical teachings of the Kabbalah have been seized by many who are involved in occultism, divination, and witchcraft. It has strongly influenced ceremonial magic in the West (for example, witchcraft and magic constantly use the tetragrammaton, YHVH, in its Kabbalistic sense). Alchemists and astrologers frequently drew from the Kabbalah (the 10 sephiroth came to be associated with the seven planets plus the firmament, the *primum mobile,* and empyrean, the highest heaven). The Kabbalah also influenced Freemasonry, the Tarot, Rosicrucianism, and other mystical orders and practices. Such occult writers and "esoteric Christians" as Saint-Martin, Eliphas Levi, Madam Blavatsky, Annie Besant, Macgregor Mathers, and A.E. Waite frequently alluded to the Kabbalah. The Kabbalah itself has often been used in magic spells and rites.

Biblical Evaluation
(1) The Kabbalistic doctrine of God is far removed from the teaching of the Old Testament. The Ain Soph, stripped of any personal elements, is an unknowable, impersonal will.

(2) The emanation doctrine is a philosophical construct which has been imposed on the Scriptures, rather than derived from them. It was devised in an attempt to bridge the gap between a transcendent and infinite Deity and a finite creation. The Scriptures, however, reveal that the transcendent God is also immanent in His creation.

There is no need for a hierarchy of 10 intermediate emanations (see also 1 Tim. 2:5).

(3) Kabbalism involves bizarre and whimsical methods of interpreting the Old Testament in its search for hidden meanings and esoteric truths. Gematria, notarikon, and themurah are exegetical techniques which have no biblical or logical support. They are entirely subjective, and their usage leads to allegorical nonsense. It is unfortunate that these methods of numerical symbolism are not restricted to Kabbalism. Examples of these excesses can be found in 20th century evangelical Christendom.

Things to Keep in Mind

(1) The Kabbalah is an elaborate and fascinating system, but it consists of traditions which are marked by variation and contradiction. Which, if any, should be accepted, and why?

(2) Only the initiated can truly know the Secret Doctrines. This was originally limited to the "Sons of the Covenant," that is, physical descendants of Abraham, Isaac, and Jacob.

(3) While the Kabbalah is essentially a metaphysical system, it is also connected with magical and occult practices. It has become a regular feature in occultism, and those interested in Kabbalism are usually interested in other mystical-divinatory systems (for example, the Tarot and astrology).

21

---◆---

THE I CHING

---◆---

Background and Teachings

The *I Ching* (the "I" is pronounced like a long *e*) is an ancient Chinese method of consulting an "oracle" for answers to questions, especially about decisions. *I Ching* means the *Book of Changes,* and it is used both as a book of divination and as a book of wisdom.

This book fell into disuse in the East for a number of centuries, and it was practically unknown in the West until only a few decades ago. Its popularity in America and Europe is now surging, however, especially among young people. This is due in part to new translations of the *I Ching*, particularly the one by Richard Wilhelm (Wilhelm's German translation was translated into English by Cary F. Baynes).

Popular figures such as Bob Dylan, Tom Wolfe, John

Cage, and Arlo Guthrie have encouraged use of *I Ching*, and these endorsements have dramatically increased sales of the book. It has been estimated that several hundred thousand Americans use the *Book of Changes*.

The *I Ching* is also being carried along by the wave of renewed interest in the occult. Many who use the *I Ching* are also involved with astrology, Tarot cards, and the Ouija. To them it is like an elaborate and mystical game. Its messages are ambiguous and recondite; even the interpretations must be interpreted. The system is so involved that interpretation of the oracles of the book has become a complex art, requiring years of practice.

The *Book of Changes* existed in a simpler form before the time of Confucius (551–479 B.C.) and Lao-tzu (or Lao-tse; his traditional dates are 604–517 B.C.). Because of this, the *I Ching* strongly influenced Confucianism and Taoism, the two main branches of Chinese philosophy.

Four authors of the *I Ching* are cited in Chinese literature. The first is Fu Hsi, a legendary figure of China's prehistoric period. The second is King Wen, who lived about the 12th century B.C. The third contributor is King Wen's son, the Duke of Chou. In fact, the *I Ching* was once known as *Chou I*, the *Changes of Chou*. Confucius himself was the fourth contributor to the *Book of Changes*. He edited and added commentaries to it just as he edited the other books included among the *Classics* (including the *Book of History*, the *Book of Poetry*, and the *Book of Rites*). The *I Ching* that we now know is the version edited and annotated by Confucius in the 5th century B.C. In addition to Confucius' commentaries, other treatises and commentaries grew around the *I Ching* in the centuries before and after Confucius. All this literature came to be known as the "Ten Wings."

About two centuries after Confucius' time, the *I Ching* came to be popularly used as a book of divination and magic. Then in the third century A.D., a scholar named Wang Pi emphasized that the *Book of Changes* should be used as a book of wisdom and not a book of divination.

Since that time the *I Ching* has been used in both ways. Various editions of the *Book of Changes* exist. The best separate the text of the *I Ching* from the Ten Wings or commentaries.

Used as a book of wisdom, the *I Ching* does more than merely predict future events. It also provides counsel by answering the question, "What should I do?" The idea is that each situation demands the proper action. There is always a right and a wrong course of action which can be pursued. Thus, the *I Ching* acts as an oracle which calls for the correct decision at any existential moment.

The *Book of Changes* received its name from its underlying philosophy that all things are constantly changing. Everything is in a process of flux, and behind all of this is the supreme ultimate, the *Tao*. Taoist philosophy is clearly embedded in the *I Ching*.

As noted in the chapter on Taoism (chap. 7), the Tao is the primal beginning of the universe, the unity out of which the world of opposites has sprung. Two alternating states of being whose interaction and change produce the world of phenomena are called Yin and Yang. Yin represents concepts such as female, passive, evil, dark, winter, cloudy, earth, completion, negative, soft, and death. Yang represents the corresponding opposites: male, active, good, light, summer, sunny, heaven, beginning, positive, hard, and life. But these opposites complement and interplay with each other since they are thought to be two sides of the same coin. They even change into one another. All these changes and interactions are subject to the Tao, the universal law or way. The *I Ching* is thus used to show a person how to make his life flow smoothly with the universe without tension or conflict. One of the commentaries on the *Book of Changes* says, "Whoever knows the tao of the changes and transformations, knows the action of the gods."

Another underlying concept in the *I Ching* is that events on earth are *images* of events taking place in the worlds beyond our senses. The events of the invisible spheres take place earlier than the corresponding earthly images of those events. The *I Ching* is used as an oracle to discover the events in the unseen world and thus to predict future events on the earth. It is also used to give *judgments* as to the proper course of action at any given time in light of the consequences. Because of this, the one who consults the *I Ching* believes that he can rise above and control the course of events.

The consultor must approach the oracle with a tranquil and receptive mind so that he will be sensitive to the cosmic influences coming through the divining stalks. The stalks of the yarrow plant (Achillea millefolium), used to consult the *Book of Changes*, are thought to be spirit-possessed. In this way they can transmit influences from the suprasensible world.

Carl G. Jung, who wrote the foreword to Wilhelm's translation of the *I Ching*, believed that the process of consulting the oracle involved an interplay between the conscious mind and the mythic patterns of the subconscious. Jung developed a strong interest in the *I Ching* because he thought that it related to his concept of the collective unconscious and the archetypes.

As a book of oracles, the I Ching grew out of an original symbolism in which an unbroken line (_____) meant a yes and a broken line (___ ___) meant a no. The unbroken line came to symbolize yang and the broken line, yin. These lines were put together in sets of two or three lines. Sets of three were called trigrams. Three of the eight possible combinations were:

Each trigram was given a symbolic name, an attribute, an image, and a family relationship (father, mother, first, second, and third son, and first, second, and third daughter). For example, the trigram K'an was named "the Abysmal." Its attribute is "dangerous," its image is "water," and its family relationship is "second son." The trigrams also came to symbolize different animals, parts of the body, colors, and so on.

After the trigrams were developed, they were paired to form 64 hexagrams (6 lines). Each hexagram has its own name and is made up of 2 primary trigrams. For example, hexagram number 59 looks like this:

```
————————————————
————————————————
————————    ————
————————    ————
————————————————
————————    ————
```

Called Huan (Dispersion), it is made up of 2 trigrams. Sun (the top 3 lines) and K'an (the bottom 3 lines). The meaning of the 64 hexagrams are explained in the 64 chapters of the *I Ching*. These explanations or oracles were so obscure in their meanings that they had to be further interpreted. This is where the commentaries and treatises of the Ten Wings come in. But even these commentaries must be interpreted in order to be understandable to the Western mind.

The hexagrams are obtained by using 50 yarrow stalks or 3 coins. With the yarrow stalk method, 1 of the 50 stalks is put aside and not used. The remaining 49 are then randomly divided into 2 heaps, and by a certain process of subdividing the 2 heaps, either 5 or 9 stalks are obtained. Then the remaining stalks are regathered and the process is repeated, this time yielding 4 or 8 stalks. This procedure is followed a third time, yielding the number 4 or 8. These 3 numbers are then adjusted so that 8 and 9 are given the value 2, and 4 and 5 are given the value 3. When these 3 numbers are then added, the resulting number will range from 6 (2+2+2) to 9 (3+3+3). A 6 is an "old yin," a 7 is a "young yang," an 8 is a "young yin," and a 9 is an "old yang." The yins produce a broken line (⎯⎯ ⎯⎯), and the yangs produce an unbroken line (⎯⎯⎯⎯). The number that is obtained will determine the bottom or first line of the hexagram. This whole procedure must be repeated 5 more times to produce the other 5 lines of the hexagram.

The coin method of obtaining hexagrams is much more simple. Three coins are tossed and each throw determines a line. Each head is a yin (value of two) and each tail is a yang (value of three). Thus, three tails would equal a nine.

Once the hexagram is obtained, the oracle is consulted by finding the corresponding chapter out of the 64 in the *Book of Changes*. Interpretation is an elaborate procedure which includes the meaning of the hexagram, the Judgment, the Commentary, and the Lines. In addition, a six ("old yin") and a nine ("old yang") are called "changing lines." This means that they change the hexagram because the changing yin turns into a yang, and vice versa. Thus, the new hexagram must also be consulted in the interpretation. Furthermore, if a six or a nine appears in certain lines ("the beginning, " the "fourth place," etc.), this may also affect the interpretation. Another refinement is that the hexagram can be analyzed by dividing it into its primary trigrams and its "nuclear trigrams."

Biblical Evaluation
(1) The *I Ching* is based on Chinese religious philosophy, particularly Confucianism and Taoism. The ultimate reality in this system is not God but an impersonal, mysterious Tao. The *I Ching* tells people to get in tune with the creation, not the Creator. As a system, it precludes the possibility of a personal relationship with God.

(2) The *I Ching* holds to the Taoist concept that opposites such as good and evil actually complement one another. This is dramatically opposed to the biblical teaching that evil is a curse and a disease whose power will ultimately be overcome.

(3) The *I Ching's* original use was divinatory. It contin-

ues to be used in this way today, as one of several tools for delving into occult (hidden) knowledge. The Bible clearly speaks against divination and the consulting of oracles rather than God.

Things to Keep in Mind
(1) The *I Ching* has been rising in popularity as a part of the occult explosion. It is often used as an entertaining game with a mystical flavor. The procedure for determining hexagrams is interesting (especially the yarrow stalk method), and this makes it very appealing to dilettantes of the occult.

(2) The method of interpreting the oracular message is quite complicated and the results are ambiguous. With a little interpretive creativity, the message can be applied to any situation.

(3) There is a danger in consulting this oracle, since no one can be certain of who or what the "oracle" may turn out to be. Like the Ouija, this method of divination may sometimes turn into an elicitation of demonic forces. Many who use the *I Ching* have never stopped to consider the spiritual implications of their involvement.

22

THE TAROT

Background and Teachings

Tarot cards were once little known and used in America, but recently their popularity has dramatically increased. Full of mystical symbolism, they are used for purposes of divination or fortune-telling.

The origin of the Tarot is connected with the origin of playing cards themselves. Playing cards were probably used first in China, in the 10th century A.D. or earlier. The Hindus developed cards not long afterward; and these cards had 10 suits representing the 10 incarnations of Vishnu. Playing cards appeared in Europe in the 13th or 14th century. They may have been brought from the Saracens (Arabians) to Italy and Spain by the returning Crusaders. Or they may have been brought into Europe by Gypsies. In Europe, playing cards were used for games, for conjuration, and for divination.

The Tarot cards were probably developed in 14th century Italy, where they were known as the Tarrochini. Ordinary playing cards were number cards, but the 22 Tarots were picture cards. These emblematic cards were numbered from 1 to 21, and one of them was unnumbered (the fool, a card related to the joker). They allegorically depicted forces of nature, religious concepts, and virtues and vices. Together they are known as the Trumps Major or the Greater Arcana. These 22 cards are:

I. The Magician	XII. The Hanged Man
II. The High Priestess	XIII. Death
III. The Empress	XIV. Temperance
IV. The Emperor	XV. The Devil
V. The Hierophant	XVI. The Tower
VI. The Lovers	XVII. The Star
VII. The Chariot	XVIII. The Moon
VIII. Strength	XIX. The Sun
IX. The Hermit	XX. The Last Judgment
X. Wheel of Fortune	O. The Fool
XI. Justice	XXI. The World

The 22 Tarots or trump cards are combined with a deck of numbered cards having four suits. These suits are wands, cups, swords, and pentacles. Each of the four suits in the Tarot pack has 14 cards, beginning with king, queen, knight, page, ten, nine, on down to ace. These 56 cards are known as the Lesser Arcana, and their symbolism lies mainly in their suit and rank.

The combination of the Greater and Lesser Arcana adds up to 78 cards. Sometimes the four suits consist of 32, 40, or 52 cards rather than 56 cards. Over the years the names of the suits changed. Wands changed to diamonds, cups to hearts, swords to spades, and pentacles to clubs. The king and queen were kept, the knight became the knave (jack), the page disappeared, and the 10 number cards remained in the standard deck of 52 playing cards. (This 52-card deck became popular in France, spread to England, and from there to the United States.)

In Europe, the 22 Tarot cards are combined with a deck of playing cards for a game called Tarocchi in Italy, Tarok in Germany, and Tarot in France. This game is similar in some ways to pinochle.

There is a sizeable amount of literature on the Tarot, and the writers disagree on several points. One group holds that the 22 Tarots originally came from Egypt. According to this view, they came out of the Egyptian cult of Isis. Other writers suggest that the Tarot was invented by the Gypsies. India and China have also been nominated.

One of the most important writers on the Tarot called himself Papus. In his *The Tarot of the Bohemians*, Papus argued that the Tarot is connected with the esoteric Jewish Kabbalah. He attributed the order of the 22 trumps to the 22 letters of the Hebrew alphabet. Arthur Edward Waite also held the view that much of the symbolism of the Tarot comes from the Kabbalah. For instance, he wrote that the High Priestess (card II) represents the Kabbalistic emanations of Binah and Malkuth, both of which relate to the feminine Shekinah (see chap. 20).

The Tarot, full of rich symbolism and imagery, seems to capture ideas which are universal or archetypal in nature. Some think that it comes out of the subconscious racial memory. In any case, the allegory and symbolism of the Tarot fascinate Tarot users. *The Waste Land* by T.S. Eliot and *The Greater Trumps* by Charles Williams are two literary works which were prompted by the imagery embedded in the Greater Arcana.

There are several sets and sequences of Tarot cards. Many of these sets are French and Italian, but the most popular today is the "rectified" set formulated by Arthur Edward Waite and illustrated by Pamela Coleman Smith. Waite declared that this set of cards, full of Christian symbolism and mysticism, was at once a work of art and a gateway to truth. Waite believed that the Smith Tarot contains several levels of symbolism, and that meditation on the imagery of these cards could lead one into an understanding of the great Mysteries.

Here are four examples of the Christian symbolism which has been seen in some of the 22 Trumps Major: (1) Wheel of Fortune; this card includes the four living creatures of Ezekiel and Revelation along with the tetragrammaton YHVH (Yahweh). (2) The Hanged Man; a man is hanging from a cross by a rope tied to his ankle. The card typifies the mysteries of death and resurrection. (3) The Last Judgment; a picture of the resurrection at the last trumpet sounded by an angel. (4) The Fool; a type of Christ. A.E. Waite calls him "a prince of the other world on his travels through this one."

There is a clear separation between the Greater and Lesser Arcana. The Lesser Arcana (4 suits, 56 cards) does not rise much above the level of fortune-telling. Each of these cards has its own divinatory significance. But even with these cards religious mysticism has been seen. For example, the four suits have been identified with the four symbols of the legend of the Holy Grail: the cup, lance, dish, and sword.

Mystical groups such as Theosophists, Rosicrucians, Kabbalists, and Freemasons have incorporated Tarot symbolism into their systems, usually teaching that the Tarot carries a secret tradition or doctrine. Only a few people have realized these truths even though they are imbedded in the consciousness of all. There seem to be two prominent concepts in this secret doctrine. One is that humanity has suffered a great loss, and because of this, people have a longing within their hearts to recover the treasure. The second is that this loss can be overcome by meditation on the idea that there is really no separation between man and God (or Nature).

As a whole, the Tarot deck speaks of three levels: the microcosm, the macrocosm, and divinity. These suggest that the human condition is a problem which can be solved by an outside, supernatural intervention. In this respect, the Tarot pack points to some valuable truths. Unfortunately it is used in improper ways, especially as a tool for magic, divination, and fortune-telling.

Tarot is used for both mystic and occult purposes. In its occult or divinatory usage, the possibilities are practically inexhaustible, because there are so many potential combinations. Intuition and clairvoyance play a large part in Tarot readings. Each card has mystical and divinatory meanings which come from several sources. Many of these assigned meanings are quite contradictory, and the alternative meanings for these cards cannot be harmonized.

Tarot divination is an art. Several different methods may be used, depending on whether a definite question is being asked of the cards or a general picture of future events and destiny is being sought. One method places some of the cards in the form of a cross. Each of the card positions represents specific things. For instance, the Significator represents the Querent (the person inquiring of the cards). Another card represents "what will come." Consecutive divinations are often used to pursue a matter and get more specific information. The cards are always interpreted relative to the Querent and the question asked.

Several factors are involved in a Tarot reading. Each card has a set of divinatory meanings for the natural or upright position and a separate set of meanings for the reversed or inverted position (the cards are shuffled in such a way that they could be upright or inverted). The 22 trumps are more powerful and important than the Lesser Arcana. The position of the card, the face value of the card, and its relation to the other cards, to the Querent, and to the question must all be considered. Facility in reading the cards must be developed by practice, and the reader's intuitive abilities must also be cultivated.

Biblical Evaluation
(1) The Tarot is rooted in mysticism, occultism, divination, and magic. It relates more to nature mysticism than

it does to a personal God. It ignores the problem of man's sinfulness.

(2) The Tarot system is somewhat Gnostic in that its symbolism is often esoteric—it contains the "secret doctrine," available to only the initiated few.

(3) These cards are so symbolically potent that they can become dangerous when misused and perverted by occultic and divinatory practices. This is especially true when people try to use them to control their destinies.

Things to Keep in Mind

(1) The Tarot cards have several appeals for potential users. They offer the entertainment value of an elaborate game in which a player can develop his skill by practice. Because there are so many subjective factors involved in interpreting the meaning of the cards, users of the Tarot are encouraged to develop their clairvoyance and intuition. The possibilities for divination are inexhaustible.

(2) The message of the Tarot has an appeal because of its mysticism and partial truths. The cards correctly say that man has a problem and that he needs help from the outside. But the solution they offer is wrong. Many who use the Tarot think that it will help them manipulate their destinies. The Tarot is thus used as an occultic tool, and it fits well with other occult systems such as magic, astrology, and the *I Ching*.

(3) Sourcebooks frequently contradict one another when it comes to assigning symbolic values and meaning to the Tarot cards. The various alternatives cannot be harmonized. There is no real *authority* in the system apart from the conflicting ideas of various writers.

(4) When the Querent poses a question to the Tarot, who or what is supposed to be answering? To whom are the questions addressed, and what is the source of power behind the cards? Some books instruct the Querent to have a blank mind while shuffling the cards, so that he can be more sensitive to the influence of the outside forces. All too often, these forces are demonic.

PART FOUR

New Religions and Cults

As we observed in part one, Eastern peoples seem to have led the way in the doctrine of *monism*: "all is one." This view, along with pantheism, obliterates the distinction between the Creator and His creation. Once this difference is erased, the individual is finally driven to the worship of himself.

Lacking any other acknowledged authority by which they can objectively define themselves or the world around them, many have reverted to ancient Hindu lore. Brahman, the infinite world mind, is identified with the Atman, the deposit of Brahman within each individual self.

Thus perceiving himself to be essentially divine, the worshiper's responsibility to the personal Creator is jettisoned. He is free to become "lost" in contemplation of the so-called "infinite." As we shall see, the Transcendental Meditation and New Age movements are sophistications of these themes.

The Hare Krishna group purports to be monotheistic. However, Krishna is an amoral member of the Hindu pantheon whom Hare Krishna followers have selected for worship. The movement is freighted with the usual Hindu concepts of *karma* and *samsara* (reincarnation). Escape from this cycle of reincarnations is by legalistic ritual.

Sun Myung Moon considers himself to be the incarnation of God. Like Mary Baker Eddy of yesteryear, unwilling to worship the true and living God, he finds himself obliged to exchange true worship for the worship of himself as the successor of Jesus Christ. The Way International is also a personality cult that degrades Jesus Christ and elevates a man.

Whatever their apparent differences, this group of religions shares the principle common to all man-made worship: The Creator-creature distinction is erased, and the creature is worshiped instead of the Creator.

TRANSCENDENTAL MEDITATION

Background and Teachings

Transcendental Meditation (TM) is spreading rapidly across the United States. An efficiently run movement systematically following a "world plan," it appeals to a wide variety of people.

TM's advertising claims it can dramatically reduce stress and tension, improve health, increase productivity and self-confidence, heighten intelligence and creativity, and reduce the need for drugs, to name only a few benefits. In effect, TM claims to be a way of meeting every kind of personal need—for an investment of only 40 minutes a day.

One of TM's most important claims is that it is *not religious* and has no metaphysical basis. According to its proponents, one can practice TM within any religious or value system. There is nothing you must believe in order to use it. As we will see, the truth or falsehood of these statements has important implications.

Mahesh Brasad Warma, the founder of TM, was born around 1918 in India and graduated from Allahabad University with a degree in physics in 1940. After his graduation he became the favorite disciple of one of India's leading religious leaders, His Divinity Swami Brahmananda Saraswati, better known as Guru Dev. Guru Dev taught him a little-known technique of meditation derived from the Vedas, part of the scriptures of Hinduism.

Mahesh served his spiritual master until Guru Dev died in 1953. Before his death the Swami commissioned his disciple to develop and spread the meditation technique to the West.

For the next two years Mahesh withdrew into a cave in the Himalayan Mountains. Then he emerged with a technique of yoga which he called Transcendental Meditation.

In 1956 he named himself Maharishi ("Great Sage"), and in 1959 he journeyed to the United States to found the Spiritual Regeneration Movement. He became famous in the '60s when celebrities, such as the Beatles, began to follow him. When they fell away, it appeared the movement would decline.

Maharishi changed his approach and started to devote most of his time to the unspectacular work of training people to become TM teachers and initiators. This investment eventually paid off in a much greater stability and growth for the movement. There are now so many TM teachers and leaders that Maharishi hopes to soon spend all of his time writing books, especially commentaries on the Hindu scriptures.

One of the most important developments in TM was the radical change from a spiritual to a secular image in the late '60s. Before this change, TM primarily attracted young people and college students. But the new "scientific" image has been a boon to the movement since it now also attracts business and professional people, scientists, housewives, government officials, and others. Today famous television and film personalities, sports figures, and political leaders openly acknowledge their practice of Transcendental Meditation.

The umbrella organization for TM is the World Plan Executive Council (WPEC)—the term "Spiritual Regeneration Movement" was dropped when TM changed its image. The WPEC has a multimillion-dollar income from the initiation fees charged by TM centers in Europe and America.

Some of the organizations directed by the WPEC are the Students International Meditation Society (SIMS), for high school and college students; the American Foundation for the Science of Creative Intelligence, for businesspersons; and the International Meditation Society, for the general public.

In addition to these organizations, the Maharishi International University was opened in 1971 at Fairfield, Iowa to assist in the accomplishment of TM's world plan: 3,600 TM training centers around the world with 1,000 teachers trained by each center. The WPEC was also granted licenses for educational television networks on the two coasts. And TM publishes its own magazine, *Creative Intelligence*.

The public interest in TM is kept alive by a systematic program of introductory lectures which are regularly offered in almost every university in the United States and in many public libraries, churches, and community centers. TM is also being taught in some high schools and in the U.S. Army.

Approximately 7,000 TM teachers are initiating new meditators at a rate of about 30,000 per month. Close to 400 World Plan Centers operate in the United States. Clearly, then, TM cannot be viewed as a local or temporary fad. It is a significant movement and its influence is increasing.

The basic TM program is as follows: prospective meditators are attracted to two free TM lectures by local advertising campaigns. Those who are interested pay an initiation and training fee of $55 to $125. At the end of the initiation ceremony, the instructor assigns a secret *mantra* to the initiate. The mantra is a Sanskrit word which is repeated in the meditation periods. Then the initiate must attend meditation classes for three days in a row. There he is taught to meditate for 20 minutes in the morning and 20 minutes in the evening. The new meditator also attends follow-up sessions during the first year. In addition, advanced courses may be taken, ranging from weekend sessions (about $35) to 12-week teacher-training programs (about $1,000). Advanced meditators are encouraged to learn the techniques of *asana* (yoga postures) and *pranayama* (yogic breath control).

Representatives for TM have attempted to present it as a nonreligious technique for personal development and expansion of consciousness. They emphasize the "scientifically proven" benefits of TM. Because the WPEC is presented as an educational rather than a religious organization, it is able to infiltrate public schools, the military, and various religious organizations and churches. It is often used by these institutions in their drug abuse programs.

However, the use of TM in institutions receiving state and federal funding has been challenged by many who claim that TM is in fact a religious program. In 1977, U.S. District Judge H. Curtis Meanor concluded in an 82-page opinion that "no inference was possible except that the teachings of [TM] are religious in nature. . . ." This ruling was later upheld in Philadelphia by the United States Court of Appeals for the Third Circuit. Hence TM is no longer covered by a secular cloak, resulting in widespread loss of the movement's prestige.

But even so, TM's public relations work has been effective because most people know little about comparative religion. Thus, they are easily deceived by names like the

Science of Creative Intelligence (SCI), the name given to the theory behind the practice of TM. However, it does not take much investigation to discover that TM is religious to the core. It is rooted in the Vedantic school of Hinduism, a fact repeatedly confirmed in Maharishi Mahesh Yogi's own writings, including *Meditations of Maharishi Mahesh Yogi*, *Maharishi Mahesh Yogi on the Bhagavad-Gita*, and *The Science of Being and Art of Living*. Because of the religious nature of these books, they have been played down in recent years by the TM movement, but they are just as authoritative for TM as they ever were.

In his writings, Maharishi makes it clear that TM was delivered to man about 5,000 years ago by the Hindu god Krishna. This meditation technique was lost but briefly restored by Buddha. Then it was lost again until the ninth century A.D., when it was rediscovered by the Hindu philosopher Shankara. It was revived for the third time by Guru Dev and passed on to Maharishi.

The TM technique is closely related to *raja yoga* and involves some of its stages. Through TM the meditator withdraws his senses from the outside world, and by concentrating on a single object (in TM it is the private mantra) loses awareness of all but the object of meditation.

Maharishi writes that after enough practice one may pass from this "transcendental consciousness" to higher states such as "cosmic consciousness" and "God consciousness." In *raja yoga* the latter stage is known as *dyhana*, and it occurs when the meditator experiences a oneness of his individual consciousness with all that is (Being). This is why Maharishi has described TM as "a path to God" and "the fulfillment of every religion."

Maharishi also speaks of yet another stage beyond "God-consciousness." He calls this final stage "Unity consciousness," which corresponds to the final stage of *raja yoga*, known as *samadhi*. It is the goal of all yoga (the word means "union"), because when one reaches *samadhi* the individual consciousness has been completely absorbed into Brahman, the all-that-is.

"God" for Maharishi Mahesh Yogi is Brahman, the impersonal absolute of Hinduism. His euphemistic name for Brahman is "Creative Intelligence." Thus, though few meditators realize it, they are engaged in the *practice* of Hinduism. What they *believe* is irrelevant. TM's real objective, according to the teachings of its founder, is not just relaxation or relief from stress. These are just by-products along the path to consciousness of pure Being, the impersonal Brahman.

So Transcendental Meditation fits its name: it is a meditative technique designed to bring people into an awareness of the transcendent. As such it fits right in with most definitions of "religion" because these definitions usually include the transcendent and man's approach to it.

In his books, Maharishi acknowledges that meditation on the mantra is a "very good form of prayer" which acts as a kind of cosmic antenna to higher spiritual forces. It is designed to lead the meditator to "the field of God." Even the mantras are not meaningless sounds. They are Sanskrit words (e.g., *Kirim, Shiam, Hair-dhign*) which have Hinduistic significance, and some of them are actually the names of Hindu deities (e.g. *Ram*).

Another reason for saying TM has religious characteristics is that it is clearly built on the Hindu scriptures. Books like the *Vedas*, the *Brahma Sutras*, and especially the *Bhagavad-Gita* (as interpreted by Maharishi Mahesh Yogi) are authoritative for the movement.

One of the most obvious religious manifestations of TM is the initiation ceremony. Each initiate is told to bring an offering of fresh-picked flowers, fruit, and a white handkerchief to the ceremony. He must take off his shoes before entering the initiation room, which is filled with incense and lit by candles. The only people in the room are the initiate and the TM initiator. The initiator tells the initiate to kneel before a low table which resembles an altar and holds a picture of Maharishi's departed master, Guru Dev. This picture is known in Hinduism as the *murti*, the image of a god in a personal form. Then the initiator takes the offering of fruit and flowers and puts it on the handkerchief, which has been placed under Guru Dev's picture.

Now that the offering has been made, with the initiate still kneeling before the *murti*, the initiator recites a 10- to 15-minute hymn of worship in Sanskrit, known as the *puja* ("worship"). Since the *puja* is in Sanskrit, the initiate does not know what is happening. However, the English translation of the *puja* was recently made known, and it reveals a three-phase worship ceremony. In the first phase, the gods of Hinduism, and the deified men who passed down the sacred tradition are invoked. Gods like Brahma and Krishna are praised along with men like Shankara and Brahmananda Sarasvati (Guru Dev), who are spoken of as gods.

The second phase of the *puja* concentrates on the offerings to Guru Dev. The formula, "Offering ____ to the lotus feet of Shri Guru Dev, I bow down," is found 17 times in this portion of the *puja*, and the initiate's offerings of fruit, flowers, and cloth are specifically included.

The third phase worships and praises Guru Dev as the incarnation of deity. He is called "the Unbounded, the Absolute, the Self-Sufficient, and the Eternal." At the end of the *puja* the initiator bows, gives the initiate his private mantra, and instructs him to meditate for the first time.

TM representatives naturally play down this religious ceremony by calling it a "ceremony of gratitude" to the masters who preserved the knowledge of the TM technique. But the translated *puja* makes it obvious that more than gratitude is involved.

The *puja* is not only a ritual of worship and adoration, but it is also designed to produce an altered state of consciousness suitable for planting the seed mantra deep in the mind of the new meditator. It appears to be a method of transmitting psycho-spiritual power, and it can serve this function even though the initiate (and sometimes the initiator) is unaware of it.

In any case, this private ceremony is mandatory, not optional. No one can receive his or her mantra (and thus practice TM) without obediently going through every aspect of the ceremony.

It is likely that Maharishi Mahesh Yogi's name will be included in the *puja* after his death. Even now, TM workers accord him a great amount of reverence and esteem.

Representatives of TM claim that it can be practiced within any belief system, but the books of their leader contradict this. Maharishi writes that TM is the way of faith for the faithless, the only way out of the field of sin, and the only way to salvation and success in life.

Thus current TM propaganda is quite deceptive, for there are really two levels in TM: public (exoteric) and private (esoteric). The teaching on the public level can change according to what is expedient. Today, TM hides behind a pseudoscientific image which minimizes any religious implications. As Maharishi wrote in his *Meditations*, "Not in the name of God-realization can we call a man to meditate in the world today, but in the name of enjoying the world better, sleeping well at night, being wide awake during the day."

The private or esoteric teaching does not change because it is the religious philosophy which forms the basis for TM. The average meditator only gradually learns about this, the *true* meaning of TM. Maharishi justifies this deception by arguing that the ignorant must be reached on a level they can understand. After they have been meditating awhile, they will become more amenable to the idea of going on to more advanced states. By getting people involved in the *practice*, they may eventually embrace the philosophical *belief* which underlies it.

In his books, particularly *Transcendental Meditation: Serenity Without Drugs*, Maharishi develops the metaphysical basis for TM. His religious philosophy is unquestionably that of Vedantic Hinduism, and there is no way these teachings can be reconciled with those of Christianity. Maharishi is a monist, not a theist. For him, God is not a person but Being itself (Brahman). This Brahman or "Creative Intelligence" is absolute, but it emanates a relative plane of existence, the universe. So the world is an extension of absolute Being but it is less real; it is an illusion. In some ways, man is a part of this illusion. His body and personality are part of this relative existence. But in another way he is a part of the Absolute: he has a transcendent aspect.

Man's real problem, then, is not one of sinfulness but one of separation from his true Being. This separation is caused by ignorance of his true nature, which is divine. "Salvation" occurs when a person is able to raise himself from the gross levels of consciousness to the most subtle (highest) level of consciousness. According to Maharishi the seven states of consciousness are: (1) dreamless sleep, (2) dreaming, (3) wakefulness, (4) consciousness of one's soul, called transcendental consciousness, (5) cosmic consciousness, (6) God consciousness, (7) Unity consciousness. The fourth state of consciousness is publicly advertised as the benefit of TM. The claim is that one can be both physically rested and psychologically alert in this state. Maharishi regards the last three stages as more important, but they are not publicly promoted because of their religious and metaphysical overtones.

Each person must work out his own destiny according to the law of *karma* (the cosmic law of sowing and reaping). So this is a system of self-salvation. It is easy to attain transcendental consciousness through meditation, but more effort is required to achieve cosmic, God, and Unity consciousness. If one reaches Unity consciousness, he is freed from the endless cycle of successive reincarnations. The illusion of separateness from the Absolute is overcome as he becomes unified with the divine Being. At this point the meditator becomes capable of right action—in effect, he becomes sinless.

As we noted at the beginning of this chapter, TM

makes a number of dramatic claims. It is promoted as the panacea for human ills whether physical, emotional, mental, sociological, or spiritual.

TM's literature and introductory lectures cite scientific research and personal testimonials in support of these claims. These "proofs," however, are inadequate. The studies they appeal to are inconclusive because many involved improper scientific procedures (e.g., inadequate selection and control conditions and selective use of data). Furthermore, these studies were done under the auspices of and published by the TM movement. It is doubtful that the TM organization would publish anything unfavorable to its position.

This is not to say that TM produces no beneficial effects. It is evident that it works to a limited extent. But contrary to TM's claims, there are other ways of duplicating the same beneficial results of relaxation and lowering of stress. Even without the mantra, two daily 20-minute periods of restful contemplation and withdrawal from job, school, or family tensions would have a beneficial physiological and psychological effect.

TM promotion cites positive testimonials but minimizes the increasing number of reports of those who found TM harmful and dangerous. Because of the altered states of consciousness it produces, it can lead to psychological and even demonic problems, as some have attested. Most people, unfortunately, are too uncritical. Too many approach it with the idea that "it may sound like hocus-pocus, but it works." They fail to challenge the official TM *interpretation* of the experiences. They should be asking *why* it may work, and whether it produces better, more loving people.

Biblical Evaluation
(1) From the foregoing, it should be clear that there is no way an informed Christian can reconcile the practice of TM with his faith. The authoritative writings of TM's founder strongly contradict the doctrines of Christianity

at every point. These form the basis for the Science of Creative Intelligence (SCI), which is the *theory* behind the *practice* of TM. In spite of some attempts to separate SCI from TM, the two are closely woven together.

(2) TM's view of God is far removed from the loving, personal God of the Bible, who is exalted above His creation and yet concerned with the welfare of His creatures. Unity with the impersonal Brahman of Hinduism is the true objective behind Transcendental Meditation. The concept of a personal, redemptive relationship with the Creator is foreign to it.

TM's objective—undifferentiated unity with pure Being—is actually nothing more than an experience of identification with the creation at its most subtle level. It is an example of people being blinded by their false speculations and thus confusing the creation with the Creator. "For they exchanged the truth of God for a lie, and worshiped and served the creature rather than the Creator, who is blessed forever" (Rom. 1:25).

(3) TM views man as an extension of Being rather than as a creature made in the image of God. Thus, his problem is one of metaphysical separation, not moral separation as in Christianity. Maharishi teaches that proper meditation takes one out of the "field of sin" and leads to union with Being. The Bible, on the other hand, teaches that man's moral guilt before a personal, righteous God must be paid for. No method of self-salvation (e.g., meditation) is adequate, because a sinner cannot atone for his own sins. Man needs the redemption which is available only through the finished work of God's own Son (Matt. 1:21; John 8:24; Rom. 3:21-26; 1 John 1:7-8).

(4) It is instructive to contrast the founders of TM (Maharishi Mahesh Yogi and his master, Guru Dev) with Jesus Christ. Maharishi is an intelligent and charismatic figure, but there is nothing particularly unique about him. He is just another figure in a long line of Hindu "holy men" whose mission is to transmit ancient knowledge. Christ's life, character, and teachings, however, set

Him apart from all other men. His life was imbued with the supernatural from His birth to His miraculous ministry to His death and *resurrection.* Like Maharishi, Jesus was a Teacher. But He was much more. He was also a Revealer and a Redeemer. He gave His sinless life in order that we who do not deserve it might live.

It is significant that Maharishi said in his *Meditations,* "I don't think Christ ever suffered or Christ could suffer. It's a pity that Christ is talked of in terms of suffering." Maharishi, perpetually surrounded by fawning admirers, would be the last to endure agony for the sake of his enemies. Like Guru Dev, when he dies the world will see him no longer. But Christians serve the Suffering Servant who rose again on the third day.

(5) The required worship ceremony for all TM initiates is idolatrous and clearly in violation of Scripture. "You shall not make for yourselves idols, nor shall you set up for yourselves an image . . . to bow down to it; for I am the Lord your God" (Lev. 26:1; cf. Ex.20:2-5). Meditation on the mantra, which Maharishi calls a "very good form of prayer," contradicts Christ's teaching in His Sermon on the Mount: "And when you are praying, do not use meaningless repetition" (Matt. 6:7).

Things to Keep in Mind
(1) There has been an increasing convergence of 20th century Western thought (for example, parapsychology and the new consciousness) with Eastern religious concepts. The desire for spiritual meaning is great, and many people are susceptible to deception and spiritual counterfeits. They are willing to jump into anything as long as it works, and TM's spectacular claims make it especially attractive. Its mass marketing of peace and its simple technique fit well in our consumer culture. Furthermore, it tells people what they want to hear (you can be a success, find the divinity within yourself, you are not morally guilty), and covers up real problems with private experiences. All these factors add to its success.

(2) It is true that people do not need to change their beliefs to practice TM, but the practice of TM can change people's beliefs, especially those who want to go on to more advanced levels. And the beliefs TM can lead people into are not religiously neutral but Hinduistic. TM is not a religion, but it is a *religious practice* in the *raja yoga* tradition of Vedantic Hinduism. This religious tradition has exclusive truth claims which cannot be reconciled with the exclusive truth claims of biblical Christianity. Both cannot be right.

(3) The idea of stress-relief through periods of relaxation is good, but there is much more baggage to TM than that. Increasing numbers of meditators and ex-meditators report unusual and sometimes disturbing experiences associated with meditation. There are accounts of occultic phenomena and demonic oppression.

Those who become involved in TM are too uncritical in their acceptance of the official TM interpretation of meditation experiences. Many have a pragmatic, "I was skeptical but I tried it and it works" mentality. The fact that something appears to "work" does not guarantee that it is genuinely beneficial. It may "work" because of self-deception, psychological factors, or demonic deception. Maharishi wrote of "communication with the higher beings in a different strata of creation" through the mantra. Perhaps these "higher beings" are less benign than Maharishi thinks.

(4) Though there is no single "technique" of Christian meditation, there are obvious differences between TM and meditating on Scripture or on the character of God. The technique of TM renders the mind *passive* as one seeks to turn off all thoughts and images, but Christian meditative prayer and reflection make the mind and spirit *active* as the believer seeks to deepen his appreciation of, and commitment to, Christ as Lord. The Christian's meditation is part of a *personal* relationship with the Lord, while TM is *impersonal* in nature.

24

THE UNIFICATION CHURCH

Background and Teachings

As many as 2,000 religious, mystic, and esoteric cults are vying for the allegiance of young men and women today. One of the most influential of these is the rapidly growing Unification Church founded by Sun Myung Moon.

Moon was born January 6, 1920 in the small village of Kwangju Sangsa Ri in what is now North Korea. His Presbyterian parents named him Yong Myung Moon ("shining dragon moon"). From his youth Moon had a strong religious bent, coupled with what he calls a clairvoyant ability. He attended a Pentecostal Church as a high school student, and on Easter Sunday, 1936, while praying on a Korean mountainside, he had a vision. Moon claims that in this vision Jesus appeared to him and commissioned him to carry out His unfinished task on earth. According to Moon, Jesus was unable to fulfill His mission of bringing salvation to the earth, and therefore a new Messiah must come.

Moon attended a Japanese university during the Second World War. He married in 1944 but in the same year he left his pregnant wife behind in Seoul, Korea in order to preach and build a following in North Korea. Moon returned to South Korea in 1946 and spent several months with a self-proclaimed Korean savior named Paik Moon Kim. Kim's teachings influenced Moon and helped shape his unusual theology. It was this theology, along with Moon's activities, that led to his excommunication from the Presbyterian Church in 1948. By this time his growing pretensions led him to change his name to Sun Myung Moon, meaning "Shining Sun and Moon."

Moon was imprisoned in North Korea in 1948 but was able to escape in 1950, evidently because of the United Nations forces. He claims that his imprisonment was due to his anticommunist activities, but many who knew him then say it was because of his ritual sex practices with members of his communes. According to their statements, Moon engaged in "blood cleansings" in which he had sexual intercourse with women followers in order to purify them.

In 1954 the self-ordained "Reverend" Moon established the Holy Spirit Association for the Unification of World Christianity, better known as the Unification Church. In Korea this is called the Tong-il Church. It was also in 1954 that Moon's wife of 10 years divorced him. In 1955 Moon was again arrested on morals charges involving his sexual church-related rites, but escaped conviction.

With the help of a disciple, Moon published *Divine Principle* in 1957. This book, later translated into English, has become the authoritative scripture of Moon's movement.

During the late '50s, Moon became quite successful financially. By 1976 his business holdings in Korea were estimated at $15 to $20 million. His factories produced air rifles, ginseng tea, machinery, titanium, and paint. Many of Moon's employees were followers who worked on a voluntary basis. In recent years, Moon has been developing his business interests in the United States. Through his disciples (often called "Moonies"), he is establishing small businesses and importing ginseng tea from Korea.

In 1960, six years after Moon was divorced by his first wife, he married an 18-year-old named Hak Ja Han. A number of Koreans, however, claim that Moon had two other wives during this six-year interval and that his present wife is his fourth.

After gaining an extensive following in South Korea and Japan, Moon decided that God was telling him to move to the United States. He imported hundreds of Korean disciples to work for him as he began his annual preaching crusades in America in 1972. In these well-publicized crusades, Moon delivered lengthy and dramatic speeches in Korean, using an English interpreter. Through these crusades and the efforts of Moon's disciples, the North American membership of the Unification Church has grown to several thousand committed followers and tens of thousands of sympathizers.

Moon's cult is not only growing rapidly, but also exerts an influence out of proportion to its membership, enjoying both considerable notoriety and expanding real estate assets. The church owns houses and properties in most of the states, with a concentration in New York and California. On 680 acres of prime land not far from San Francisco, it runs its Eden Awareness Training Center. At a former Catholic seminary in Tarrytown, New York it operates its primary training institute for new members. In Westchester County, New York, the Unification Church has large holdings. The Hotel New Yorker, now Moon property, has become the church's unofficial international headquarters. Moon and his followers have even expressed an ambition to purchase the Empire State Building!

Because the Unification Church has an official religious

status, it is exempt from property taxes. Renovations, repairs, and maintenance on its buildings are also virtually free since these tasks are voluntarily performed by Moonies.

Moon himself, with a net personal worth of $15 million, lives in the lap of luxury on a 25-acre estate in Irvington, New York. Moon also owns a 50-foot cabin cruiser, "New Hope," which he uses for fishing. Moon protects his lifestyle by surrounding himself with highly competent bodyguards.

Moon uses some of his money to hire lawyers and public relations experts in an effort to achieve an image of respectability for his church. The Unification Church has also developed a large number of "front" organizations to accomplish this purpose: Project Unity, the One World Crusade, the New Education Development, the International Cultural Foundation, the Collegiate Association for the Research of Principles, the International Federation for Victory over Communism, and others.

Moon is also trying to win friends and increase his political influence in Washington. Despite these efforts, his church has become the object of increasing investigations in such areas as its tax-exempt status, its "brainwashing" techniques, and the alleged connection of some of its leaders with the South Korean government. It is also under investigation in matters of financial concealment and improper procedures. Sun Myung Moon was convicted of tax fraud in 1983 and was sentenced to 18 months in prison. Whenever the church encounters such obstacles, however, Moon's disciples are taught to compare them with the persecution that Christ endured.

The theology of the Unification Church is a strange combination of pseudo-Christian, mystical, psychological, philosophical, and charismatic ingredients. The final authority in this religious movement is not the Bible but the writings and teachings of Sun Myung Moon. "Man is the visible form of God, and God is the invisible form of man. . . . God and man are one. Man is incarnate God"

(Sun Myung Moon, *New Hope,* Washington, D.C., 1974, p. 5).

Posing as a Christian minister ("Rev." Moon) when he deems it a helpful promotional tactic, Moon's real position is one of open hostility to Christianity. In *Master Speaks* he says, "Our group is of higher dimension than the established churches and naturally there must come vast difference between what we are and what the Christian people are. . . . The Christianity which God has been fostering for 6,000 years is doomed. Up to the present God has been with Christianity. But in Christianity things are stalemated." Moon also declared, "God is now throwing Christianity away and is now establishing a new religion, and this new religion is Unification Church."

Moon regards himself as the most important man alive and the prophet for a new age. He says, "I am the foremost one in the whole world.

"Out of all the saints sent by God, I think I am the most successful one.

"I have talked with many, many Masters, including Jesus, on questions of life and the universe. . . . They have subjected themselves to me in terms of wisdom. After winning the victory, they surrendered."

Moon tells his followers to be open to the new truths he is revealing, especially since these truths will render the New Testament unnecessary. Moon's book, *Divine Principle,* is the bible for the cult, though Moonies are often quite secretive about this volume. Moon gives lipservice to the Bible, but not surprisingly he discourages followers from taking it too seriously. The Bible has its place as long as it is interpreted in accordance with his theology and revelations.

Moon's theology centers around three Adams and three Eves. The first pair was created by God to become the parents of a perfect humanity. But they were not to come together until a period of spiritual maturation was completed. God's plans were thwarted when Eve was seduced by the archangel Lucifer, who became Satan. This act marked the *spiritual* fall of both man and Lucifer. Eve then tempted Adam sexually and this led to the *physical* aspect of the Fall of man. Thus, the Fall was not due to the disobedient act of eating the fruit of the tree of knowledge of good and evil as indicated in the Genesis account.

Eve's offspring by Lucifer was Cain, who according to Moon symbolizes communism. Abel was Eve's offspring by Adam, and Moon makes him a symbol of democracy.

The second Adam was Jesus Christ. Moon denies the Virgin Birth and the biblical doctrine of the Trinity, saying that Jesus was a man, not the God-Man. "We must understand that this (John 8:58) . . . does not signify that Jesus was God Himself. Jesus, on earth, was a man no different from us except for the fact that he was without original sin" (*Divine Principle*, p. 212). Though Jesus was the first man to be obedient to God, a number of failures marred His mission: the three wise men were supposed to rear Jesus until the day He took a wife, but they failed to do so; John the Baptist failed because he did not recognize Jesus as the Saviour; Jesus was not successful in His revolutionary mission of unifying all religions and cultures; Israel rejected and murdered Him on the cross before He was able to find the second Eve and begin the physical restoration of the human race.

According to Moon, Jesus failed in His mission to accomplish spiritual and physical salvation. He did not come to die on a cross, and His crucifixion was against the will of God. Moon rationalizes this by saying that the Old Testament presents two different destinies for the Messiah, and that the passages which speak about the sufferings of Messiah (Ps. 22; Isa. 53) did not have to be fulfilled.

Jesus, Moon says, was an imperfect image of God, who with the Holy Spirit brought about spiritual but not physical salvation. When Jesus saw that He would not accomplish His mission, He began to preach about His second advent. Jesus' resurrection was spiritual, not bodily. He did not ascend to the heavenly kingdom but instead waits in Paradise until another completes His unfinished task of bringing the kingdom to earth.

A third Adam and a third Eve must now come to bring physical salvation. This third Adam is the Lord of the Second Advent. Moon does not explicitly say that he is this third Adam, but he is quite generous with his hints. The third Adam and Eve will be parents of a new humanity—precisely what Moon claims for himself and his current wife. Disciples are told to address them as "True Parents." (Significantly, Moon has stated that instead of praying in the name of the Father, Son, and Holy Spirit, his followers should pray in the name of the True Parents.)

By a strange combination of scriptural eisegesis (reading concepts into the Bible) and numerology, Moon has deduced that the Lord of the Second Advent was born in Korea in 1920. By an odd "coincidence" Moon himself was born in Korea in 1920. Moon further paves the way for concluding that he is the messiah by radically reinterpreting the Scriptures to deny that the Lord of the Second Advent will come in power and glory.

Moon has made a number of dramatic assertions about himself. In addition to implying that he is the incarnation of God, Moon has claimed that he is greater than Jesus Himself.

"Master" (Moon) has said such things as: "The time will come, without my seeking it, when my words will almost serve as law. If I ask a certain thing, it will be done. If I don't want something done, it will not be done.

"The whole world is in my hand, and I will conquer and subjugate the world.

"I am a thinker, I am your brain.

"There is no complaint, objection against anything being done here until we have established the Kingdom of God on earth up until the very end! There can *never* be any complaint!

"Up until now, Jesus has appeared in the spirit world to His followers. From now on, I will appear."

Moon regards the people of the United States as chosen of God. The True Parents desire to begin the new race here by intermarrying their sinless children with selected followers. God has thrown off the Jews as His chosen people because they failed in the opportunity He gave them. The Roman Empire and Britain also failed, and it is now up to America to bring in the kingdom of heaven on earth. In this kingdom, Moon sees a unification of Korea and America, of East and West, as the guiding force of the new civilization.

Moon repeatedly warns, however, that America is in grave danger of spiritual decline and failure. He must turn the United States to the fulfillment of God's program before it is too late. (He seems willing to use politics, deception, and anything else necessary to accomplish this goal.)

The coming messiah is the only hope for America, and Moon sees himself as the one who must usher in the Messianic Age. This new messiah will judge the world, and the standard of judgment will be what people have done with Moon's message. "Master" is therefore very critical of Christians who refuse to accept him and warns that in so doing they doom their churches. He freely compares any opposition he receives to the persecution Christ suffered at the hands of the Jewish leaders.

Moon seems to exercise an almost hypnotic control over the many young people who follow him. This is accomplished through a carefully planned regimen. To make initial contact with prospective converts, the Unification Church uses posters, leaflets, radio, and television to speak about the betterment of mankind, world peace, ecology, and the moral upgrading of the United States. This appeals to idealistic young people seeking clear answers to the ills of mankind.

In the streets, on campuses, and in shopping centers, the perpetually smiling, clean-cut, conservative-looking

Moonies engage college-age people in discussions about a more meaningful life and the peaceful unification of all people. Moon is rarely mentioned at this point. They end the discussions by inviting contacts to dinner and an introductory lecture at a local Unification center. Those who are curious, lonely, or seeking some form of commitment, often accept.

At the center, prospective converts are showered with attention and warmth. Moon's "family" wants to convince them that they love them. This "love bombing" takes the form of pats, hand-holding, and ceaseless smiles. After dinner come prayers, singing, and a lecture. Those who know little about the Bible and history are more susceptible to the lectures because they are not able to detect the errors and distortions.

The evening at the center usually concludes with an invitation to a three-day weekend workshop at a retreat or training center. Those who go find themselves in the middle of an exhausting schedule of relentless lectures, prayers, and singing, broken only for eating and exercise. A potential recruit is never left alone or given time to reflect on what is happening. Peer pressure to conform with the others in the activities is great.

By the end of the three days, the participant is exhausted from lack of sleep, continuous activities, and mental bombardment. In this state his judgment is poor and his decisions are likely to be governed by his emotions. He is begged to stay on and commit himself to the movement. For those who do, longer workshops follow, varying in length from a week to four months.

The program of indoctrination for new converts is rigid, highly organized, and in some ways frightening. Converts are told to give all their possessions, including bank accounts, to the Unification Church. They are also told to isolate themselves from families, friends, schools, and the world in general. The Moonies who are constantly around them become their new family. They are no longer to be exposed to television, radio, films, books, and newspapers, and there is no talk of the outside world. The new environment completely insulates them. Those who want to return to families and friends are told they are yielding to Satan since the latter are his agents. They are told that they must love Moon more than parents or anyone else.

The new believers are subjected to a rigid schedule which includes a heavy dosage of Moon's lectures and *Divine Principle*, hard work, five or six hours of sleep per night, starchy food, harangues for nonconformity to the group, constant drilling, praying, and singing. They are often charged up by the leaders into emotional frenzies. The elements of fear and guilt are also exploited as psychological levers to maintain control over the behavior of the new followers.

All physical needs—housing, food, and clothing—are provided for Moon's followers. They no longer need money, and they make no decisions. Many who have observed these techniques see in them a classic pattern of brainwashing. It is not surprising that there have been nervous breakdowns and some suicides among Moon's followers.

After the indoctrination is complete, Moonies are sent to various centers around the country. The highly disciplined schedule continues, and the emphasis is on communal living, fund-raising, and proselytizing. Moon communes allow no sexual contact, drugs, alcohol, or smoking. Uniformity is stressed, as reflected by the modest and sometimes identical clothing worn.

Everyone is up by 6:30 to go through the morning regimen of group prayer, breakfast, singing, and more prayer, followed by a long day of raising money in the streets and in shopping centers. The workers are driven in vans to the target areas. Under pressure to raise as much money as possible, many of them use "heavenly deceit" to sell more flowers, candles, peanuts, candy, or ginseng tea. Some say that they are raising the money to help orphans or drug addicts. Many Moonies take in several hundred dollars a day, and those who do not make a minimum quota (often $100) stay on the streets until they do. All this tax-free money flows into the coffers of the Unification Church, and apparently none of it goes to helping those on the outside.

When they return to the communes at night, there is more singing, praying, and indoctrination. Prayer is sometimes addressed to the pictures of Moon on the walls. Medical attention is discouraged for those who get sick, and there are sharp disciplinary procedures like long fasting, all-night prayer and repentance, and cold showers for those who get out of line.

The Moon communes offer the security of a perpetual childhood for those who do not wish to cope with the outside world: no drugs, no money, no sex, no choices, and no independent thought. Even one's marriage partner is selected after he or she "matures" in the cult for a certain period of time. Moon and the church leaders choose "willing" couples and arrange mass weddings periodically.

Parents have made numerous attempts to rescue or "kidnap" their children from the tight folds of this cult. Sometimes they have used professional "deprogrammers," with varying degrees of success. A growing number of ex-Moonies have also left the cult because of disillusionment. Many of them are afraid to speak about what went on for fear of retribution.

Biblical Evaluation
(1) The Unification Church is an anti-Christian cult that would better be termed Moonism. It is Moonistic, not biblical, in that Moon claims to be the only one who can decode the message of the Bible. Furthermore, Moon's *Divine Principle* is really the bible for his cult.

(2) Moonism proclaims a system of self-salvation based on human merit. It rejects the grace of God in Christ for another gospel (see Gal. 1:6-9), one based on works. Because Moon claims his followers can reach a level of sin-

less perfection through him, they have no need of turning to Jesus Christ. Forgiveness of sins is not necessary for salvation. According to Moon's teaching on "indemnity," one atones for his own sins through constant effort and can build up enough indemnity to atone for the sins of his ancestors as well. There is a great deal of pressure here because disciples are led to believe that their parents or ancestors may have to spend, say, another 1,000 years in hell if they are disobedient or entertain negative thoughts.

(3) Moon's teachings abound with perversions of clear biblical statements. For instance, he claims that "Jesus did not come to be persecuted and die on the cross" (but see Mark 10:45; Luke 24:26, 46; Acts 2:22-23; 3:18; Heb. 2:9; 9:26-28). Moon claims that John the Baptist denied Jesus (but see John 1:29-37). He claims that Jesus was the bastard offspring of Zechariah and Mary, who had been seduced by him. He claims that Christ was to find the most perfect girl in the world and have a huge family. And he claims that Mary Magdalene was Judas Iscariot's lover but fell in love with Jesus, and that Judas betrayed Jesus because of her. Judas hung himself not out of remorse but because Mary turned on him for betraying Jesus. Moon claims that the Holy Spirit is a female. He denies the resurrection and second coming of Christ. He says that the kingdom of God and the unification of all people and religions will be brought about through human effort, not the work of Christ. These and dozens of similar teachings of Moon not only lack biblical support but are complete fabrications and delusions.

(4) Moon teaches that God is sad and is to be pitied because He is surrounded by the forces of Satan and isolated from His children. He is imprisoned, but He looks to Moon to provide hope and restoration. Moon claims to be the only man who truly loves God.

(5) Moon fits Christ's description of the false messiahs who will come in the end times, trying to mislead even the elect (see Matt. 24:23-27).

Things to Keep in Mind
(1) Cults like Moon's, which purport to be based in part on the Bible, should remind us of our need to know the teachings of Scripture. The truths of the Bible clearly expose corresponding errors in Moonism. Devoted followers of Moon are hard to work with and may close their ears to the words of Scripture, or appeal to the "room for interpretation" or "just come to our workshop" avoidance techniques. Even if we cannot reach them, however, we can certainly warn young Christians about their teachings and tactics so that they will influence Moonies for Christ more than being influenced by them.

(2) Followers of Moon are taught to "fall in love" with him and give him complete devotion. In addition, the church's leaders generate a tremendous fear of satanic possession and loss of salvation. Together, these act as a powerful force to control thinking and behavior of the young believers. The "brainwashing" techniques, and in some cases demonic influence, add to the difficulty of breaking away from the hold of this cult. The freedom that Christ offers to those who serve Him ("You shall know the truth, and the truth shall make you free" [John 8:32]) is in sharp contrast to the mental, emotional, and physical bondage in the Moon cult.

(3) This cult draws away young people from the Christian community because it promises to meet needs the church has failed to meet. People are attracted to the love and acceptance in a "family" environment.

(4) There is a kind of "progressive esotericism" in this cult similar to that found in other pseudoreligious and occult groups. There are various stages of initiation, and followers learn more about Moon's *real* doctrines as they move up in the ranks.

THE HARE
KRISHNA
MOVEMENT

Background and Teachings

The youth of today's Western technological society are showing an increasing interest in Eastern religious concepts. Many are searching hard for spiritual meaning and reality, and purveyors of Eastern ideologies are providing a number of choices that were all but unknown a few years ago. The International Society for Krishna Consciousness (ISKCON) is a good example of one of these new choices.

Members of ISKCON are developing a network of temples and communes (*ashrams*) in urban America and in various cities around the world. These devotees of the Hindu god Krishna (they prefer the spelling Kṛṣṇa) want to overcome the polluted atmosphere of modern society by spreading Krishna Consciousness.

Throughout its entire history Hinduism has been a constantly changing and splintering religion. Two of the most important sects are the Shivaites and the Vishnuites. The former worship Shiva as the highest god while the latter reserve this place for the god Vishnu and his incarnations. Most Vishnuites think of Krishna as one of the incarnations (an *avatar*) of Vishnu. But several centuries ago a further splintering was caused when some Vishnuites decided that Krishna is the supreme god and that Vishnu was actually an incarnation of Krishna.

The man primarily responsible for this new view was Caitanya Mahaprabu (A.D. 1486–1534), who was the key figure in the revival of devotional religion which took place in Bengal. Taking his inspiration from the *Bhagavadgita*, the most influential of the Hindu scriptures, Caitanya emphasized liberation (*mukti*) through devotional love and service to Krishna as the ultimate and personal god. This is known as *bhakti yoga*. Caitanya introduced a devotional method called *sankirtana* which involves chanting aloud and ecstatic dancing, and this practice is continued today among devotees of Krishna.

The Caitanya sect of Krishna worship was criticized by a number of Hindu philosophers, but it is quite alive and has now spread to the Western world. The introduction of the *bhakti* cult of Krishna to the West was accomplished recently by A.C. Bhaktivedanta Swami. Born in Calcutta, India on September 1, 1896, Bhaktivedanta's original name was Abhay Charan De. He majored in philosophy, economics, and English at the University of Calcutta until 1920, and in 1922 he became a disciple of Sri Srimad Bhaktisiddhanta Saraswati Gosvami Maharaja. Saraswati initiated Abhay De into the Caitanya tradition of bhakti yoga in 1933. A few days before he died in 1936, Saraswati commissioned his disciple to spread Krishna Consciousness to the English-speaking people of the world. In 1947 Abhay Charan De came to be known as Bhaktivedanta, and in 1954 he renounced his wife and family and became a monk. At this point he assumed the new title of Swami. He started the League of Devotees in 1962 in Delhi and studied and published portions of the vedic scriptures.

A.C. Bhaktivedanta Swami made his most important move in 1965 when he came to New York. He must have been quite a sight on the Lower East side of Manhattan— a 70-year-old man from India, wearing a saffron robe, begging on the streets, and looking for disciples. Slowly the disciples began to come, and in 1966 he founded the International Society for Krishna Consciousness. In 1968 Bhaktivedanta began a prolific writing program, concentrating on translations of and commentaries on some of the Hindu scriptures. There are now over 30 books by "His Divine Grace A.C. Bhaktivedanta Swami Prabhupada" (his full title) which have been published and distributed by ISKCON.

The ISKCON movement continues to establish new temples around the world, concentrating especially in the United States. They publish a monthly magazine called *Back to Godhead*, which Krishna devotees peddle on the streets. They also distribute records produced by ex-Beatle George Harrison containing the Hare Krishna *mantra* and hymns to Krishna. Their desire is to spread the name of Krishna to every city and town.

One of the biggest claims of ISKCON is that it is the result of an *unbroken disciplic succession* from Bhaktivedanta to Saraswati, back to Caitanya, and from him back to Krishna himself (they believe that Krishna came 5,000 years ago). According to the Hare Krishna movement, one cannot attain true understanding of the Hindu scriptures apart from this disciplic succession. Though he died in 1978, Bhaktivedanta remains as the spiritual master, and only through his teachings can the "authorized, transcendental science of God-realization" be known. He was Krishna's representative on earth and is accepted as Krishna himself. Krishna devotees must surrender themselves completely to his desires and teachings.

Bhaktivedanta was inaccessible to most of his devotees,

but they constantly hoped to see him, desiring especially that he might smile on them. Prabhupada (Bhaktivedanta) lived in comfort and luxury, constantly surrounded by a coterie of servants. He desired to see 108 temples in existence before his death (there are over 70 at present), one for each of the 108 *japa* beads carried by every devotee. He also wanted to bring about the spiritual revival of India.

Now 11 gurus lead the movement. Each guru is assigned to a different geographical district. Since the passing of Bhaktivedanta, the fund-raising methods of ISKCON have become notorious. False pretense and even theft have been the subjects of legal proceedings against the movement. But the new leadership insists that such tactics are correct because Krishna owns everything anyway.

There are several reasons why young people are attracted to the ISKCON movement. For some it may be an expression of disgust with modern technological society. It appears to be a way of breaking away from the anxiety and disappointment of material life. They hope that by joining they will be able to achieve self-realization and discover the spiritual meaning of life. Proselytizing efforts are aimed especially at college students and people who are disenchanted with the drug culture.

Others join because of identity confusion, loneliness, and isolation. ISKCON offers a rigidly structured institution. In the communal life of ISKCON temples, all phases of daily activity are tightly scheduled and the rules must be obeyed. Most activities are done in a group and there is one authority. Everything is well-defined, security is high, and few decisions ever need to be made.

Outsiders (called *karmis*) are encouraged to visit the temple, especially for the Sunday feast. Those who join are lavished with flowers and attention. There is a period of leniency for new devotees, but pressure to conform to the temple rules gradually increases. All the symbols of the prior self are stripped away and a new identity as a

Krishna devotee is created. Conversations about and associations with the outside world are eliminated, all personal possessions are given away, and everyone must wear the same distinctive hairstyles and clothing. Male devotees shave their heads except for one lock of hair (called the *sikha*). Instead of pants they wear a yellow or saffron *dhoti* which resembles a robe. Women wear Indian *saris*, their hair is parted in the middle and braided, and they are allowed no makeup. All devotees wear a string of japa beads carried in a small bag worn around the neck, 12 clay markings on their bodies (called *tilaka*), and a small necklace of beads.

Usually, in order to make advances in Krishna Consciousness, one must enter the temple and follow all regulations. Temple life is marked by communal living and austerity. No gambling, games, sports, or discussions unconnected with Krishna Consciousness are permitted. Anything having to do with science, education, violence, or carnality is spurned. There are no drugs, alcohol, tobacco, coffee, tea, or illicit sex. Dietary regulations prohibit meat, fish, and eggs. Everyone must sleep on the floor, usually in sleeping bags.

There is a strict daily routine with few variations. Devotees rise at about 3:30 A.M. and before breakfast they chant, engage in worship ceremonies, dress the temple deities, and offer food to them. They also attend studies on the Hindu scriptures and Bhaktivedanta's books. This is followed by more chanting with the japa beads, and temple-related work. Some make incense, others sew, paint, clean, cook, and take care of the deities. A number of devotees go in groups to chant and dance on the streets. They ask for money and sell books, incense, and *Back To Godhead* magazines—the sales bring in a good deal of money. Everyone sleeps by 10:30 P.M.

After about six months, a new devotee can be initiated in a special fire ceremony in which he or she receives a Sanskrit name from Prabhupada. A second initiation may follow about six months later in which a male devotee becomes a *brahmin* and receives a secret mantra.

Since the death of Bhaktivedanta the movement has been passing through a phase of liberalization. Proselytes will no longer be required to leave all and dwell in the temple. But they must become vegetarians and build an altar at home. Farms and health food stores apparently have been replacing the practice of public chanting.

Devotees are to incorporate a number of Sanskrit words in their speech, since Sanskrit is the primary language of the Hindu scriptures. Prayers and scripture texts are recited in Sanskrit. In sum, Krishna's children must devote all thoughts and actions to his service and lose themselves in the process.

The system of Krishna worship can be very simple or quite complex depending on one's degree of involvement. It may be as simple as keeping a picture of Krishna and Caitanya in your home and chanting the basic Hare Krishna mantra: "Hare Krishna, Hare Krishna/Krishna, Krishna, Hare, Hare/Hare Rama, Hare Rama/Rama, Rama, Hare, Hare." These 16 words are supposed to produce a transcendental sound vibration. *Rama* is another name for Krishna, and *Hare* means, among other things, the pleasure potency of Krishna. According to Bhaktivedanta, this mantra is the only solution for spiritual realization in this age. Many devotees chant this mantra on each of the 108 japa beads more than 16 times a day.

An additional step in Krishna worship is known as *sankirtana* and is performed in temples, parks, schools, and on the streets. This practice involves hearing about Krishna's pastimes when he was on earth and group chanting, singing, and dancing to the Krishna mantra. Many of the devotees who dance and sing in this way seem to experience ecstatic, trancelike states.

The following are further aspects of this kind of bhakti yoga, or devotional service to Krishna:

(1) Taking *prasada*, that is, food prepared for and offered to the temple deities.

(2) Thinking always of Krishna.

(3) Performing the *aratrika* (greeting the Lord) ceremony two to six times a day.

(4) Worship of the sacred Tulasi Devi plant found in every temple. This ceremony is thought to rid worshipers of sins and diseases. Great care is taken to insure "her" (the plant's) growth.

(5) Service to the temple deities. Each temple has an opulently decorated room which houses two 24-inch statues, one of Krishna playing the flute and one of his favorite lover Radha. These statues are placed on an altar close to three smaller wooden deities and pictures of Caitanya, the disciplic succession, and Bhaktivedanta. The deities are dressed in satin, lace, and jewels. They are bathed, "fed," praised, touched, given changes of clothes, and put to bed. Devotees claim that the deities are special incarnations of Krishna, not idols. They drink the water used to wash the deities.

(6) Certain fast days and festivals are observed during the year. Three of these festivals commemorate the "Appearance Days" of Krishna, Radha, and Bhaktivedanta.

These devotional acts are meant to produce a feeling of humility and personal surrender. They are practiced according to temple regulations, but the goal is spontaneity of worship. The possibility of failure is high, and due to frustrations and disappointments with the ISKCON movement, there is an increasing number of "bloopers" (dropouts from ISKCON).

The power structure of ISKCON is simple. Since Bhaktivedanta's death, the regional gurus now have unquestioned authority over all devotees in their temples. Women are regarded as inferior and placed in a servanthood role to the males or to their husbands if married. They are not allowed to make decisions on their own. Husbands are free to beat their wives when they are disobedient.

Spouses are selected by the leadership. Bhaktivedanta taught that marriage is only for those who cannot remain celibate, since ideally a person should avoid the sex act altogether—it increases the materialistic and bodily concept of life. Within marriage it is allowed only for the purpose of procreation. Children are given spiritual (Sanskrit) names at birth and allowed to do as they please until age five. Then they are taken away from their parents and sent to the ISKCON school to be educated in Krishna Consciousness. The hope is that these children will not have to be reincarnated again.

It was mentioned above that one of the most important doctrines of ISKCON is the disciplic succession from Krishna to Bhaktivedanta. This movement looks down on "bogus yogis" who collect fees from students, teach them that they are one with God in their meditation, and allow them to engage in material gratification. Such yogis are false teachers, not true gurus, since they are not in the disciplic succession. One must come to God through the guru, the spiritual master. Since the spiritual master is God's representative, a disciple learns knowledge and pleases Krishna by pleasing the spiritual master, formerly Bhaktivedanta, who was the external manifestation of Krishna. The devotee who submits himself will in this way attain spiritual life. One who displeases the spiritual master cannot receive the grace needed for advancement.

This teaching was Bhaktivedanta's means of claiming absolute authority. This authority extends to his translations and interpretations of vedic scriptures. His translation and commentary on the *Bhagavad-gita*, called the *Bhagavad-gita As It Is*, often claims to have the *exact* meanings of the verses. ISKCON refuses to recognize any other translations of the *Bhagavad-gita* because they are inferior and do not promote Krishna Consciousness.

The *Bhagavad-gita* is the favorite scripture of ISKCON, and devotees proudly say that it was written 5,000 years ago, many centuries before the Bible. There is no evidence for such a claim, however, and most scholars place it somewhere between the fourth century B.C., and the first century A.D. It is now a part of the *Mahabharata*, the great Indian epic.

Another heavily used scripture in ISKCON is the *Srimad-Bhagavatam,* more widely known as the *Bhagavata Purana.* It was probably written sometime during the 9th or 10th century A.D. Of course, devotees claim it was written by the author of the *Bhagavad-gita* 5,000 years ago. Many of Bhaktivedanta's books are translations and commentaries of the *Srimad-Bhagavatam,* since it deals with Krishna's pastimes during his life on earth. These books and the artwork in them are regarded by ISKCON as the literary incarnation of God (Krishna).

The *Srimad-Bhagavatam* has a number of legends about Krishna and pictures him especially as a cowherd boy with blue skin (the name *Krishna* actually means "black"). As a boy he was given to tricks and pranks such as stealing butter. Later he played on his flute and called cowherd girls (*Gopis*) to leave their husbands and dance with him in the moonlight. He danced in such a way that each *Gopi* had the illusion that he was making love to her alone. His favorite mistress among them was Radha. Devotees regard this illicit love as a human representation of the divine love which overcomes human ties.

Krishna is often pictured with four arms holding a conchshell, a lotus flower, a club, and a disc. The club and disc are used to kill demons. According to legend he died at the age of 125 when he was inadvertently struck in the foot by an arrow.

There is an *avatar* (human incarnation) of Krishna for every age, and the most recent was Caitanya, the golden avatar. The present age, called the *Kali-yuga* ("the dark age"), will last for 432,000 years. In previous ages it was more appropriate to engage in mystic yogic meditation, ritualistic sacrifices, or temple worship. But in this age, according to Bhaktivedanta, the way of salvation is *kirtana:* chanting the Hare Krishna mantra and performing devotional service to Krishna.

Krishna is called "the Supreme Personality of Godhead" by ISKCON devotees. They regard him as the ultimate, personal god and creator of millions of material universes. Beyond these he also created the "spiritual sky" which contains millions of spiritual planets. All the material and spiritual planets are inhabited by living entities including demigods and demons.

ISKCON emphasizes two of Hinduism's most basic doctrines, *karma* and *samsara* (reincarnation). According to Bhaktivedanta's teachings, Krishna the Supersoul created innumerable individual souls (*jivas*). The *jiva* is the real self, not the material body. It does not die but is reincarnated in new bodies after the death of the old ones. The basic problem is that people identify themselves with their material bodies and thus become entangled in illusion (*maya*) and sinfulness. This process of entanglement and self-deception is called *karma*. As long as one is engaged in karma his soul will continue to be reincarnated. The nature of the new body and station in life (if human) is determined by the karma of the previous life. The soul goes through the fourfold misery of birth, disease, old age, and death with every incarnation.

Thus, there is a need for liberation from *samsara*, the cycle of repeated incarnations. One who attains Krishna Consciousness achieves this liberation and receives an eternal, spiritual body. He then dwells in eternity, bliss, and knowledge with Krishna in his residence, Krishnaloka. This is the soul's journey "back to Godhead." If a person engaged in bhakti yoga fails to complete the process of self-realization, he is given another chance. Devotees who fail are guaranteed birth in a family of wealth or high caste.

So sin (karmic debt) is caused by ignorance and self-deception. Devotional service to Krishna is the only way of salvation, and the spiritual birth comes when one is initiated by the spiritual master and attains consciousness of the Supreme Personality of Godhead. ISKCON devotees believe that all other religions are inadequate. They often quote Krishna's statement in the *Bhagavad-gita* (18.66), "Abandon all varieties of religion and just surrender unto Me."

Biblical Evaluation

(1) ISKCON is one of the few non-Christian religious movements that worships a god who is both personal and infinite. It definitely speaks about a personal relationship with Krishna and emphasizes the path of love and service. However, this bhakti yoga is essentially a works system of salvation. The Hare Krishna mantra must be chanted thousands of times; one must serve the spiritual master in various ways; there are numerous dietary and social regulations; the ceremonies must be observed properly; and so forth. This is far removed from salvation by grace through faith.

(2) Those who do not succeed are given innumerable chances (reincarnations) until they do. One must eventually atone for his own sins and reduce his karmic debt, though the process may take millions of years. This is contrary to the biblical teaching that no one can pay for his own sins. Even if reincarnation did occur (Heb. 9:27 says it does not), each new life would increase the number of sins on a person's account since there is no one who does not sin (1 Kings 8:46; Prov. 20:9; Rom. 3:23; 1 John 1:8).

(3) ISKCON teaches that sin is caused by ignorance and illusion, but the Scriptures teach that it is rebellion against God's character, leading to moral guilt before the holy God.

(4) Krishna's life on earth was far from holy, considering that he stole things as a boy in his "playfulness" and made love to numerous women, many of whom were married. There is no comparison between the lives of Krishna and Christ. Nor is there any comparison between their deaths. Krishna died of an arrow in his foot, while Christ was crucified and rose from the dead three days later.

(5) The services to temple deities are idolatrous, in terms of Exodus 20:4-5. Bhaktivedanta denies this because, he said, idolatry is the "worship of a material *form* of God," but in ISKCON one is not worshiping a *form* of

233

God. Rather, he said, "the form *is* God." This is an obvious delusion.

Things to Keep in Mind

(1) There is a good deal of circular reasoning in Bhaktivedanta's statements. His two claims to authority are the disciplic succession and the vedic scriptures. He claims to use all the scriptures of Hinduism, but he is in fact *very* selective in the scriptures he appeals to: the *Bhagavad-gita* and one of the *Puranas*. This is because most of the vedic literature teaches that Krishna is *not* the Supreme Personality of Godhead. He is simply one of the incarnations of the god Vishnu. Bhaktivedanta appeals to the teachings of his particular disciplic succession (there are many such successions) to support his unorthodox use of Hindu scripture. We are left with Bhaktivedanta's interpretation of his own selection of scriptures.

(2) The scriptures used in ISKCON are not historical but legendary. They were certainly not written 5,000 years ago and there is no archeological or historical evidence to support the events mentioned in the *Bhagavad-gita* or in the *Srimad-Bhagavatam (Bhagavata Purana)*.

(3) In this system of reincarnation, Krishna is supposedly not to blame for evil or illusion. But there must have been a first incarnation of every created individual soul (*jiva*), and this places the ultimate responsibility for evil on Krishna, since they were evidently not perfect. Krishna is also to blame for the materialistic world of *maya*.

(4) The basic issue is whether a person should accept Krishna and reject Christ or accept Christ and reject Krishna. One cannot have it both ways. Emotional experiences cannot settle the case. Instead, a comparison should be made between what we know about them, what they taught, and how they lived. Krishna is a legendary figure who taught a works system of salvation. His life was one of questionable morality, he did not suffer for others, and his death was that of an ordinary man. Jesus was a historical Person who offered salvation

as a free gift to anyone who would trust in Him. He led a sinless life, suffered a cruel death on a cross that others might live, and rose from the dead.

26

THE WAY
INTERNATIONAL

Background and Teachings

The Way International is a swiftly expanding cult which claims to be the restoration of first-century Christianity. Many of its teachings about the authority of the Bible, the way of salvation, and Jesus Christ are scriptural, and on the surface The Way may appear to be reasonably sound. But a closer examination reveals a number of important doctrines in this movement which are radically opposed to Christianity. The Way's founder and leader, Victor Paul Wierwille, openly acknowledged that the terms he used are often the same as those of most Christians but that his meanings were quite different.

Wierwille (1917–1985) developed a strong interest in Christianity by the time he graduated from high school. This can be seen in the education he pursued. He studied at Mission House College, Moody Bible Institute, and the University of Chicago Divinity School. He also received a Master of Theology degree from Princeton Theological Seminary and a doctorate from Pike's Peak Seminary.

Wierwille was ordained as a minister in the United Church of Christ and served in a number of churches. However, he was confused because of the conflicting views he encountered in his exposure to various theologians. This built to a crisis in his thinking and ministry until he decided to clean himself out by destroying his entire theological library. He resolved to study only the Bible and seek the power of God in his life. As Wierwille developed his personal interpretation of the Bible, he became convinced that he had recovered the true apostolic understanding of Christianity which had been totally lost to the church since the first century. He also entered in the "abundant life" and began speaking in tongues.

In 1953, Wierwille started to teach the course that would become the standard training for The Way. He called it "Power for Abundant Living" (PFAL), and it was held in Van Wert, Ohio. The course met with success and expanded to other parts of Ohio and eventually to other states. In 1957, Wierwille decided to resign from his United Church of Christ pastorate in Van Wert to devote all his time to his PFAL ministry. He moved to his family's 150-acre farm in New Knoxville, Ohio two years later. By 1961 the farm became the official headquarters of The Way International with its Institute for Biblical Research and Teaching.

The Way grew slowly until 1968 when it tapped into the Jesus Movement. Suddenly thousands of youth started pouring into The Way, and its rapid growth has continued to the present. Though there is no official membership, it is safe to say that tens of thousands of people are active in a large number of groups (perhaps 2,000) in every state and in over 35 foreign countries. Wierwille organized The Way International as though it were a tree. The *trunk* is the New Knoxville, Ohio international headquarters. The *limbs* are the state organizations, and the *branches* are the cities. The *twigs* are the home or campus Bible studies, and the *leaves* are the individual members.

The Way promotes Wierwille's "Power for Abundant Living" course which features him in 12 video-taped sessions of about three hours each. This $85 course is "guaranteed to answer 95 percent of your questions about the Bible and about everything else." There are also intermediate and advanced courses. Enrollment in these courses continues to grow. Repeats are free and some followers take them over and over.

The Way's headquarters provides books, brochures, cassette tapes, films, and records to spread Wierwille's teachings. Using these materials, many small groups of Way disciples work diligently to establish new Bible studies (twigs) and win converts to the movement. These people are "WOW" (Word Over the World) ambassadors. Some have left work, school, and family to become full-time WOW ambassadors, while others do it on a part-time basis. Small "families" of full-time ambassadors typically move to new areas for at least a year until a work is established. The leaders are trained through a program called The Way Corps.

The Way now has special WOW programs, including Medical WOW, Educators WOW, and College WOW. The latter is designed to establish twig fellowships on every college campus in the United States within a short time. Their desire is to make Wierwille's PFAL course available to all college students.

The Way also has a college of its own which was established in 1975 in Emporia, Kansas. Before their senior year, students at The Way College leave to spend an interim year as missionaries for The Way. In addition to these things, The Way sponsors summer training and camping programs, retreats (called "advances"), and prison outreaches. A summer outreach called the Minuteman Program sends groups of PFAL graduates to various cities for a summer to set up twigs and enroll people in the PFAL course.

The Way's printing press, The American Christian Press, publishes *The Way Magazine*, Wierwille's writings, and other literature.

Another growing interest of The Way is the coordination and development of businesses owned by Way members. This will provide employment for other members and create a greater financial base for the organization. Even without this, however, The Way is evidently well endowed financially. The 10 percent tithe from its members, along with the fees from its P.FAL courses, helps maintain financial health.

The biggest promotional events for this movement are the periodic "Rock of Ages Festivals" which feature music by The Way's traveling singing groups. Two of these groups are The Joyful Noise and The Good Seed. The festivals draw several thousand people and the number increases each year.

The Way International disclaims being a church, denomination, or sect. Some of its practices are the same as those of churches, but there are also important differences. There is no special day for twig meetings. They are held often and on an informal basis, usually in houses or borrowed facilities. Water baptism is not administered unless specially requested, but communion is observed in these meetings. Teaching, listening to Wierwille tapes, singing, praying, and speaking in tongues are the main ingredients. The Way ordains men and women ministers, but most of its local leaders are not ordained. Pentecost is the most important day in The Way's calendar, not Christmas or Easter.

Followers of The Way exhibit a great deal of enthusiasm, commitment, and evangelical zeal. It is common to see these people set aside all hobbies and outside interests to devote their available time to the movement. The majority of its members today are in their late teens and early twenties, but there are also older members. The

Way discourages drugs, alcohol, premarital sex, and slothfulness. It offers an abundant life in the here and now, characterized by power, confidence, health, and happiness. This makes it appealing to many people.

As with other "Christian" cults, The Way relies on a second authority for its understanding of the first authority, the Bible. For all practical purposes, this second authority is just as fundamental as the Bible because it professes to be the inspired interpretation of biblical teaching. This interpretation is final, and it is not to be questioned by members of the cult.

In the case of The Way, the second authority is the oral and written teachings of Victor Paul Wierwille. After he jettisoned his theological library to study only the Bible, Wierwille claimed that God's voice came to him and said that He would teach him the true New Testament doctrines as they were originally understood by the first-century apostles. Thus, "Doctor" (as he was often called by his followers) arrived at "the first pure and correct interpretation of the Word since the first century A.D." Wierwille's single-handed recovery of the lost truth can be found in his PFAL courses and in his writings which include *Jesus Christ Is Not God*, *The Bible Tells Me So*, *The Word's Way*, and *Receiving the Holy Spirit Today*.

In his writings and lectures, Wierwille tried to create the appearance of scholarship by referring to the biblical languages (Hebrew, Aramaic, and Greek) and to church history. He said that the Bible is the inspired Word of God, and that it should be interpreted literally. But he also said that the church had lost the original meaning of the Bible, which was available exclusively in his teaching. Only the New Testament epistles apply to Christians today, according to Wierwille, because the Gospels belong in the Old Testament.

The fundamental error in this cult is reflected in the title of Wierwille's book *Jesus Christ Is Not God*. Like the Jehovah's Witnesses, Wierwille explicitly denied the deity of Christ and hence the Trinity. Jesus is the *Son* of God but not God. He did not exist prior to His incarnation; He was miraculously created when God artificially inseminated His mother Mary. Because of this divine insemination, Jesus was a sinless human being. Though He is our Saviour and Redeemer, He is not to be worshiped, for worship is reserved for God alone.

Wierwille convinced himself that he had restored the teachings of the early apostles, but in reality he was teaching a modernized version of a third-century heresy known as Dynamic Monarchianism. The central tenet of this teaching was that Jesus was a unique man who was specially filled with the power of God. So Wierwille's doctrines are not new; they are simply variations on old heretical themes.

Of course, Wierwille tries to turn the tables by arguing that the doctrines of the Trinity and the deity of Christ were introduced to Christianity by pagan converts in the third and fourth centuries. To him, the real heretics were the early church leaders, not the Monarchians and Arians.

To support his teachings, Wierwille turns to the New Testament. He systematically distorts and explains away passages which clearly proclaim the deity of Jesus Christ. One such passage is John 1. "In the beginning was the Word, and the Word was with God, and the Word was God. He was in the beginning with God. All things came into being through Him; and apart from Him nothing came into being that has come into being. . . . And the Word became flesh, and dwelt among us, and we beheld His glory, glory as of the only begotten from the Father, full of grace and truth" (John 1:1-3, 14). These verses plainly teach that the Word is God and He (the Word) is a Person. Verse 14 says that this Person is Jesus Christ. So Jesus is God.

Wierwille goes to great lengths to avoid this conclusion in his chapter on John 1 in *Jesus Christ Is Not God*. Here is his "literal translation" of John 1:1-2: "In the beginning (before the Creation) God was the Word, and the re-

241

vealed Word was in God's foreknowledge (which was later communicated to man in spoken words, written Words, and the incarnate Word). This Word absolutely was in the beginning before the foundation of the world together with the one true God in His foreknowledge yet distinctly independent of Him."

This is a blatant distortion of the passage. Wierwille tried to avoid the fact of Christ's preexistence by watering it down to foreknowledge. But this passage and a number of similar ones do not say this. Wierwille also used the phrase "distinctly independent of Him" in an effort to lay aside the biblical statement that "the Word *was* God." He *imposed* his erroneous theology on passages of Scripture (eisegesis); he did not *derive* his theology from Scripture (exegesis).

Members of The Way are drilled in Wierwille's interpretations of many passages of Scripture so that they have come to rely on his teachings as the key which unlocks the Bible. This process stifles consideration of alternative interpretations of Scripture.

The Way is unitarian in its view of God. He is one in substance and only one in Person (the Father). The Holy Spirit is just another name for the Father, not a Person. However, Wierwille also speaks of "holy spirit" (no capitals). This human holy spirit is an impersonal force which is given to those who believe in Christ. According to Wierwille's theology, the first Adam lost his spirit at the Fall and with it went the image of God in man. Jesus Christ, the second Adam, had a sinless soul because of His unique birth. At His baptism He received a human holy spirit which empowered Him to launch His perfect ministry. Through this power He was able to perform miracles and become our Redeemer. On the Day of Pentecost the ascended Christ imparted the gift of the human holy spirit to His disciples, and this gift was manifested by speaking in tongues.

So people are born only as flesh (Wierwille's term for body-soul), without any spirit. Only when a person is born again by believing in Christ does he receive a (human holy) spirit. The reception of this spirit is *always* accompanied by speaking in tongues. This is the one visible proof of salvation. If one does not have this manifestation, he cannot have received the spirit, and therefore remains flesh.

This human holy spirit is the "power for abundant living." It enables the believer to attain sinless perfection, perfect health, happiness, and success. He is able to do all the things that Jesus did. Tongues and healing are practiced regularly by followers of The Way. The more one speaks in tongues, the more spiritually mature he becomes. Wierwille even developed a special technique designed to produce the tongues experience for those who have not had it.

Wierwille also taught the doctrine of soul sleep which claims that there is no consciousness after physical death since the soul "sleeps" until the resurrection at the second coming of Christ.

Since the death of Victor Paul Wierwille in 1985, The Way has suffered a decline in membership, reductions in donations, crises in leadership, and some splitting into alternative groups. Some doubt The Way will weather these problems, but others think that it may reverse these trends and grow once again.

Biblical Evaluation
(1) The Way rejects two of the most fundamental Christian doctrines—the Trinity and the deity of Christ. This is important, because what a person thinks about Jesus Christ has to do with his salvation. The Way acknowledges that "If Jesus is God, we are *not* saved." A biblical Christian, on the other hand, realizes that if Jesus is *not* God, he is not saved from his sins. Only God in human form could pay the infinite purchase price necessary to redeem us from sin and judgment. Some verses which support the deity of Jesus are: Isaiah 9:6; John 1:1-3, 14; 20:28; Philippians 2:5-7; Titus 2:13; Hebrews 1:8.

(2) The Way often uses the right terminology but in the wrong way. But they do say that Jesus Christ lived a sinless life, rose from the dead, ascended to heaven and will come again, and that one should accept Him as Saviour. It is quite possible that some of those who are in The Way are saved in spite of Wierwille's rejection of Christ's divinity.

(3) Wierwille's doctrine of the Holy Spirit and the human holy spirit are completely unscriptural. Verses such as Matthew 3:16-17; 28:19; and 2 Corinthians 13:14 make it clear that the Holy Spirit is not the Father but a separate Person. He has His own intellect, will, emotions, and ministries. But He is also God (see Acts 5:3-4). Concerning the "human holy spirit," there is no such thing in the pages of Scripture. Contrary to Wierwille's teaching, all people have spirits just as they have souls. Even a cursory Bible concordance study of the word "spirit" will make this clear.

(4) The Way falls into the old error of placing a second authority alongside the Bible and interpreting the Bible exclusively by this authority. Thus, Wierwille's theology is the real bible of the movement.

Things to Keep in Mind

(1) It is unnecessary to systematically refute all of Wierwille's distortions of biblical passages. Instead, we should always be ready to use Scripture *in context* to challenge particular misuses by ambassadors of The Way.

(2) Remember to focus on the issue of Christ's deity. The Way has several problem doctrines, but this is by far the most important. Be prepared to show from the Scriptures that Jesus Christ is God (Isa. 9:6; Matt. 1:23; John 1:1; 8:58; Rom. 9:5; 1 John 5:20).

(3) Followers of The Way are convinced that because they speak in tongues and practice healing, their system alone must be the truth. However, they should be told that truth must not be based on experience but on the teachings of Christ. Many groups, including non-Chris-

tians, speak in tongues and perform healings. Furthermore, it is quite suspicious when one person declares that he has cornered the market on biblical interpretation and truth for the first time since the first century. This mentality produces Wierwillism, not Christianity.

27

THE NEW AGE
MOVEMENT

(By William H. McDowell)

Background and Teachings

Man's ancient fascination with the mysterious has formed the foundation of those religions and cults in this book that can be referred to as "mystical"—such ancient Eastern religions as Hinduism and Buddhism, and such modern Western cults as Unity and Transcendental Meditation. Indeed it would be misleading to perceive the ages-old mystical movement as many absolute, self-contained compartments. Their vocabularies differ in some respects and their leading personalities differ, but there is a common, almost monotonous theme that dominates them all. This is the theme that there are no real distinctions in reality and no objective definitions of truth. Over the doorways of all mystical thought and action can be written in large capital letters: ALL IS ONE.

And this remains as the rediscovered theme maintained by what the late-20th-century generation calls the New Age movement. Here is an assortment of groups and individuals who present anew all of the concepts of earlier mysticism, in various wrappings with novel applications styled to be attractive to Western society. Thus, the term "New Age" has captured the imaginations of tens of thousands of people with the false suggestion that revolutionary verities hitherto unknown or forgotten have been dramatically dawning in our time. Along with this conviction is the euphoric belief that society stands at the brink of unscaled heights of spiritual achievement.

Still, there are those who feel they have good grounds for skepticism about the promises of such New Age apostles as John Denver, Shirley MacLaine, Theodore Roszak, David Spangler, Ken Wilber, and William Irwin Thompson. The world has been around for a long time, and its records are amply available. From these it can be learned that the experiences of past and modern societies that have embraced the essential message of the New Age movement are less than encouraging.

The history of India, for example, insofar as its massive population has been controlled by its home-grown Hinduism, has not recommended that society as one that is evolving to higher things, but rather as an appalling array of hideous disease, death, and decay. Why? Because, in the view of this religious ancestor of the New Age movement, there is no objective truth. In final analysis the East Indian Hindu knows *nothing* and has *nothing* to contemplate but the empty hope that at some remotely distant date, in some future life, he will escape his present, illusory world of misery and be absorbed into the infinite, impersonal world mind of Brahman.

So why are enlightened Western people so excited about the dreary spinoffs from Hinduism that emigrate to our shores? The sobering answer lies in the fact that Hinduism is not truly the ultimate source of the solipsism and nihilism embodied in the New Age movement. The foundations are much older.

In Genesis 3 we hear the insolent suggestion by Satan that God has no right to make statements about truth or morality: "Has God indeed said?" The sequel to this question shows that its goal was to undermine the confidence of the first human pair that anything certain could be known about God or His world. For that matter the entire universe could be a projection of one's own state of mind—a universe as he or she wanted it to be! And this was precisely the option Adam and Eve chose: "You will be like God." Man would henceforth "create" his own reality according to his own desire and conception. So Adam and Eve were the first self-declared humanists. The self-existent God would no longer be permitted to interfere in the affairs of secular man. Consequently, god-less man has been miserable in the real world that was designed by its Creator for a society that loved God and kept His commandments.

But why should this have been a problem for us in the West? Eastern peoples have gone their misguided way. But in the West we have the Bible which persuasively proclaims a self-existent Creator. It would seem that this precious possession should have insulated Western society against God-denying monism and mysticism.

For a long time it indeed seemed that knowledge of the Scriptures performed that very function in our civilization. Our culture was consciously based on recognition of an objective world created by the self-existent God of the Bible and on man's moral responsibility to that God. Western man was far from being sinless or faultless. But he was imbued with the biblical worldview. Inspired by that view, he was building a society that promised the avoidance of those tragedies that afflicted areas of the world where the preexistent Creator was not honored.

However, humanist elements of the Renaissance of five centuries ago had begun to grow weary of that worldview. In the minds of many Renaissance thinkers God had failed, as evidenced by the fact that the kingdom of God certainly had not yet come as expected. Severe injustices prevailed in the world (and the church). So the humanists promised us a better "new age." To achieve this goal they would not confess their sins and failures to the Author of life. Rather, they would altogether do away with the idea of a God-centered world, root and branch.

Once again, as at the dawn of history, God's creatorhood and sovereignty were given the short end. "Man Is the Measure" became the anthem of the new humanist society. Notwithstanding these radical aims, the Scriptures were providentially salvaged and powerfully proclaimed by luminaries like John Wycliffe, William Tyndale, and Martin Luther.

Not content with the secularizing gains wrought by the humanist wing of the Renaissance, later so-called Enlightenment thinkers finished the job. Renée Descartes proposed that we can't really know the truth about the objective world because our senses consistently deceive us. George Berkeley boldly proposed a full-blown solipsism: objective reality was mere appearance created by our own senses. David Hume assured his contemporaries that there could be no certainty of causes and effects. Immanuel Kant proclaimed that God could be known only as a sentimental persuasion. Side-by-side with the Gospel of an eternally self-existent Creator, Sustainer, and Saviour have thus stood the builders of the humanist edifice until now.

In our own time John Denver, Shirley MacLaine, and their associates would like to continue the forlorn humanist traditions of East and West. All that basically changes is the name—the New Age—but humanism all the same, transmuted into a mystical religion whose god is man just as before. Thus the so-called New Age movement is conceived and born.

So the prophets of the New Age are simply restating a contemporary, pop form of the ancient humanism, whether it be sought at the dawn of Creation, in Hinduism, in the humanist wing of the Renaissance, or in Enlightenment philosophy. In its outward manifestation the New Age movement can be characterized as a highly positive romanticism in which many secularists are daring to dream the impossible dream of actually being the divine/human masters of the universe. The advocates of the movement try to dignify their views by appealing to ancient religious movements that share New Age lifeviews.

The new paganism embraced by leading New Age thinkers closes ranks with pre-Christian nature religion or fertility cultism. Judeo-Christian theology is said to be patriarchal (therefore evil) and must be replaced by the nature-cult acceptance of female deity (therefore good). Thus Father-Sky must be replaced by Mother-Earth as the correct theology.

Yet, feminist Rosemary Ruether has shown that the reconstruction of ancient nature-cult religions by New Age enthusiasts, in which female deities are said to be dominant, has had little reference to history ("Goddesses and Witches: Liberation and Counterculture Feminism," *The Christian Century*, September 10, 1980). The record of female goddesses in past nature cults does not suggest they were in a role of supremacy, but simply members of a pantheon. Modern goddess advocates are dealing in blatant romantic fantasy.

The stated theological viewpoint of the New Age movement is Eastern mystical and particularly Hindu. The imported guru-based cults in the West are tantric Hindu. Immigrant Swamis Vivkenada and Ramakrishna were tantrists. Hindu tantrism teaches the experience of divinity through expertly guided sexual exercises. The Eastern movement in the West is thus a restatement of the sexual obsessions of the fertility cults of the Hindu and pre-Hindu Eastern world. Records of the orgiastic excesses of the fertility religions are open for all to read.

Therefore, it must be obvious that the romantically envisioned Hindu foundations of New Age are by no means preoccupied with other-worldly concerns. Many unwary Western people have long been deluded by su-per-spiritual notions about the East. For some the naked truth about this aspect of Hinduism comes as a rude awakening; for others it is precisely the antinomian liberation from healthy moral constraints they have been seeking. Now they feel free to clothe their lust in an imported sex-ridden "religion."

Deena Metzger, for example, advocates "holy" prostitution as an avenue of New Age spiritual celebration. Are we morally shocked? In her book, *Dancing in the Light*, Shirley MacLaine quotes her supernatural spirit guide as follows: "Until mankind realizes that there is, in truth, no good and there is, in truth, no evil, there will be no peace." Also, "Every vile and wretched thing you do broadens your understanding" (Martin Gardner, "Issues Is Her Business," *New York Review*, 1987). So much for morality in the New Age movement.

How is this amoral phenomenon possible in any so-called religion? Let us first remember what we said earlier about the dawn of history. Once we have canceled God, there can be no objective truth and no morality. "When a man ceases to believe in God, he does not believe in nothing, he believes in anything" (G.K. Chesterton).

But don't Hindus and New Age people talk about "god"? Yes, they do. But we need to be reminded constantly that followers of these movements are not only liberated from objective thinking, they are also freed from objective speaking. As Humpty Dumpty declares in *Alice Through the Looking Glass*, "When I use a word . . . it means just what I choose it to mean—neither more nor less." It is almost impossible to hold useful dialogue with a pure romantic. When such people talk about "god," "man," "morality," and similarly basic terms of accepted dictionary meaning, the speakers must be understood by their hearers to be speaking of something wholly different. Indeed, New Age spokespersons are proud to admit, like Humpty Dumpty, that they have broken their ties to any standard meanings of such vocabulary.

So who or what is the "god" of the New Age? Basic to all New Age thinking is the premise that the universe and all contained in it are one unified whole ("all is one"). This oneness is not merely metaphoric but real, and the "Universal Consciousness" which this unity consists of may be called "god" in a purely impersonal sense. There is no conception of an absolute personal god like the God of the Bible. Of course, this rejection of the Creator is pure Hinduism with its basic idea of the infinite, impersonal Brahman as the ground of all being. To be finally absorbed into this impersonal unity, after a long process of reincarnation, is the goal of all Hindus. Individual, personal life is the enemy.

Paradoxically, god-ness in the world is realized by a deposit of the infinite Brahman in every person. This deposit is called "Atman." Thus the Hindu god is actually realized in every human personality. There is no preexistent god who creates, makes laws, and reigns over the universe. The Hindu scriptures are not texts of divine, propositional revelation. These scriptures comprise the collective mystical experience of the Hindu ancients, all testifying to the basic doctrine that all is one without distinction (monism) and that all is god (pantheism). The many varieties of the New Age movement accept this theology as the foundation of their total worldview. In the words of Shirley MacLaine, "You are unlimited. You just don't realize it" (*Dancing in the Light*).

Some exponents of the New Age movement deftly refer to Psalm 82:6, "You are gods," as support for their views. Also they cite Colossians 1:27, "Christ in you, the hope of glory." The reasonable reader will recognize that whatever is meant by texts like these, they certainly don't intend to obliterate or obscure the doctrine of the separate, sovereign Creator of human personalities. Words must be understood always in their contexts, and the biblical context of such language in no way supports the pantheism or monism of the Hindu religion.

The New Age movement has branched out into numerous disciplines beyond narrowly religious and philosophical concerns. Fritjof Capra is a physicist whose books, *Tao of Physics* and *The Turning Point*, seek to establish a relationship between recent scientific discovery and religion. He points out truly that Albert Einstein had shown that space and time are relative. Though admitting that his philosophy has affected his scientific reasoning, Capra has concluded that since Einstein's theory was established, it may therefore be assumed that *everything* is relative, including ethics. He and others also conclude that human consciousness truly creates reality, thus radically destroying the Creator-creature distinction. Man is the creator.

It has been well observed that science depends for its very survival on the external objectivity of reality. Where absolute subjectivity reigns (solipsism), there can be no discovery because there can be no valid observation. Without a worldview that allows for valid observation and description there can be no objective body of learning, and civilization must fail. Only a biblical worldview allows for wholesome scientific enterprise, even by those who may not willingly subscribe to a created universe. Without at least tacit acknowledgment of creation, man is alone with his subjectivity. Definitions have no authority, and verbal communication may as well be meaningless gibberish.

Marilyn Ferguson is author of *The Aquarian Conspiracy*, a book which documents the promising growth of the New Age movement through networking, that is, by use of all available means of intercommunication between unrelated branches and elements of the movement. Following Capra, Ferguson believes she has found the secret of evolution in the view that all of life has autonomous creative energy within itself: Smaller energy particles, she says, "thrust toward ever-higher orders of complexity and integration." But she forgets the long-standing embarrassment of evolutionary thought—that the universe is *not* progressing in vitality, but rather regressing and dying under the inexorable effects of the second law of thermodynamics. So much for Ferguson's scientific romanticism. If only wishing could make it so! But, alas, that groundless wishfulness is exactly the position maintained by the New Age movement.

New Age has also entered the medical and health professions. Ivan Illich, a social critic, has written a book, *The Medical Nemesis*, in which he documents his position that "the medical profession has become a major threat to health." The social consciousness of certain evils of orthodox medicine has opened up the health industry to invasion by New Age philosophy, including promotion of the New Age concept of holistic health. Holistic medicine in general has had a respectable track record in its concern, not merely with the medical tradition of curing disease, but also with promoting positive wellness in the whole person.

The contribution of New Age to holistic medicine, however, is more sinister. For example, some varieties of chiropractic medicine refer to "universal intelligence" as the source of healing techniques. Chinese employment of acupressure and acupuncture has its roots in the Tao, the fundamental doctrine of which is "the One" (monism). Occult religion pervades the healing practices of psychics and mediums. Spiritual and psychological damage as the result of occult healing methods is well established by John Weldon and Zola Levitt in their book, *Psychic Healing: An Exposé of an Occult Phenomenon*.

The widespread contemporary obsession with health provides fertile ground for the New Age narcissistic concern with self. When man rejects sin as the ultimate root of his problems, he tries feverishly to save himself from death (and judgment). "Those who worship health cannot remain healthy" (G.K. Chesterton). To be healthy is good, but health is not an absolute good.

It is not surprising that the New Age movement's worldview inevitably drives its followers to obsession with themselves. After all, what greater self is there to be concerned about in pantheism than one's own self? One of the messages of the false gospel of self is that we have been overburdened with an awareness of guilt. The burden of guilt is destroying us (true). Therefore we must, it is said, use every psychological device to jettison our guilt and enhance our opinion of ourselves (false).

The Bible has given a straightforward and accurate diagnosis of our spiritual malady: We not only *feel* guilty, we *are* guilty. The sooner we confess this fact wholeheartedly to God and receive His remedy in Christ, the sooner we will have peace about our sins—not by ignoring them, but by forgiveness and cleansing in the blood of Christ.

What a tangled web of self-deceit we weave by our tortuous techniques of shoring up self-esteem! One of the greatest lies being marketed by Satan in our time is that guilt is an abnormal illusion rather than a real disorder. Sadly, some (so-called) Christian preachers shy away from addressing the issue of sin in exchange for an exclusive gospel of "love." No sin, no salvation; no salvation, no peace! But the New Age loves the more silken-styled gospel. It provides just the satanic fuel the movement needs to promote its own gospel of the omnipotent self. If New Age-ism flourishes, it is at least partly due to lack of virility in the present proclamation of the Gospel of grace.

Public education is the most effective means of shaping culture in a society of state-controlled, state-required education. This reality is not lost on New Agers like Marilyn Ferguson. Ferguson admits in her book, *The Aquarian Conspiracy*, that the New Age agenda is being aggressively carried forward by administrators, teachers, and counselors in the American education system.

As control of public schools becomes more centralized, traditional values of home, religion, morality, and patriotism are being replaced by New Age doctrines: ethical relativism is idealized; everybody must decide for himself what is ethically good; there is no absolute right or wrong; absolute tolerance is the rule. What is not viewed tolerantly, however, is the Judeo-Christian morality that gave us the benign cultural environment in which New Age ideas could receive a fair hearing.

History textbooks are being washed of those specific events that became the cornerstones of our civilization: Hebrew history and the emergence of the Bible, the person and work of Christ, the first thousand years of Christianity, Byzantine Christianity, the Protestant Reformation, the religion of the Pilgrim fathers. On the other hand, in a federally funded study, Paul Vitz has discovered that occultism, magic, and American Indian religions receive five times more textbook mention than Judeo-Christian subjects.

"Global education" is a term that sounds innocent enough until we investigate the real goals of the proposal. Here is not a curriculum of international studies, but a system for setting forth New Age philosophy. The movement toward global education has captured the consent of leading public education agencies of our time. What are its ambitions?

First, children should early be indoctrinated with a one-world view versus a national political view. Patriotism should be discouraged. Along with this perspective comes militant pacifism. "Good" and "evil" among nations are set forth as relative concepts. Christian ethics is seen as the offender in this effort, since all world societies are viewed as morally equal—a romantic vision that would not have stood up very well during our confrontation with Nazi Germany from 1933 to 1945!

New Age religious leaders are not above the practice of deceit in promoting these educational programs. Dick Sutphen openly advocates changing the occult terminology of New Age in order to make the movement's doctrines palatable to an unsuspecting citizenry. For example, some New Age educators have proposed use of the word "centering" in place of Eastern "meditation" in the classroom, in order to defuse the emotional issue.

Barbara Clark's book, *Growing Up Gifted,* openly asserts that all the New Age doctrines we have discussed previously must be advanced in public education. "Reality is . . . an outward projection of internal thoughts, feelings, and expectations." So much for the hope of real learning under a New Age educational philosophy.

Practices in keeping with the above viewpoints have resulted in violations of the Hatch Amendment in the schools of at least seven major cities. This amendment is designed to protect school children from subversive psychological control. In those cities, New Age practices such as compulsory indoctrination with yoga were cited.

From what has been said about education, it would follow that New Age is vitally interested in the political application of its doctrine. New Age politics is often referred to as "transformationalist politics," a change in political approach that is to be achieved by means of a new consciousness leading to a new worldview. Among the subordinate aims of the new politics are the raising of the consciousness about nature and its preservation and the advancement of feminine equality or superiority. Beyond these concerns are the leading ambitions for a world government to be spearheaded by the United Nations.

Donald Keys is the founder of Planetary Citizens, a society begun in 1972 for the purpose of advancing the New Age political agenda, using liberal-minded elements of society as the unwitting vehicles for his cause. The Planetary Initiative, as it was called, climaxed with a Planetary Congress held in Toronto, Canada in 1983. The manifesto emerging from this assembly declared its goals of one-world government and a radically new economic system.

World Goodwill is another such group, popularized in the books of Alice Bailey, who claims her writings were supernaturally inspired by a Tibetan religious leader. She advocates acceptance of the divinity of man and the rejection of Judeo-Christian views of God, man, and the world. Planetary Citizens and World Goodwill maintain offices at the United Nations Plaza.

Representative Charlie Rose (D-NC) is founder of the Congressional Clearinghouse on the Future, a group that encourages the hearing of psychics and observes psychic phenomena (psi) in Washington. Rose claims that about a quarter of the members of Congress engage in such psi activities as prophecy, healing, and psychokinesis. Former Speaker of the House Jim Wright has taken instruction in prophetic techniques. Psychic guru Anne Gehman has stated that Wright has strong psychic gifts (*U.S. News and World Report*, December 5, 1988).

Senator Claiborne Pell (D-RI), chairman of the Senate Foreign Relations Committee, is a leading spokesman in Washington on behalf of psychic research and an enthusiastic reader of Shirley MacLaine's works. For over three years Pell has employed an aide (at public expense) whose chief activity has been to observe and encourage so-called "consciousness" studies and psi.

Not only the West, but also the professedly atheist Communist world is intensely interested in New Age philosophy and religion. As many as 35,000 people have crowded into a Mongolian football stadium to hear a psychic lecturer. Soviet Russia spent between $70 million and $350 million in 1985 on psychic research, compared to the $500,000 spent by the United States. The KGB has studied the possibility of mentally stopping a frog's heart, as well as telepathically inducing feelings of human pain and suffocation at a distance of 500 miles.

Who would rule a one-world political order? New Age proponents such as David Spangler and William Irwin Thompson say plainly that it must be a hierarchical structure headed by those most spiritually "attuned," that is, who espouse the doctrines of the New Age. Thus is fulfilled the observation of G.K. Chesterton: "Exactly in proportion as you turn monotheism into monism you turn it into despotism."

The aggressiveness of the New Age movement in such areas as medicine, education, and politics can also be observed in the business world. If the Eastern ancestors of New Age are largely absorbed in other-worldly concerns, it is just as true that Western New Age applications of Hindu principles are often materialistic in their goals.

Werner Erhard, as Jack Rosenberg now calls himself since his New Age spiritual awakening, has conducted "est" meetings for about a half-million people. Est stands for Erhard Seminars Training. Audiences of the seminars comprise business and professional leaders of the commercial world, as well as teachers from institutions like Harvard Business School, MIT, and Stanford Business School. Workaday individuals commonly pay hundreds of dollars to attend "the Forum," as Erhard calls it, whose goal is to bring its pupils into touch with "being" during a 60-hour program. This experience of "being" is intended to enable business personnel to be more effective in their fields and thus dramatically increase their incomes.

Neil Chesanow has written "Est Revisited" in *New Women* magazine, in which he describes the marathon experience of indoctrination with Erhard's "being," an irrational procedure in which the individual is emotionally driven to break all ties to the external God or objective morality. Here again we are confronted with the New Age doctrines that all is one, reality is our own personal creation, we are responsible to self alone, and effectiveness comes by "being," not thinking. Since 1984, Erhard's Forum is branching out through an organization called Transformational Technologies, Inc. Thus Erhard has sold many franchises for which buyers pay $20,000 and 8 percent of the gross income for the first five years.

A questionnaire response by over 800 personnel directors has revealed that a significant number (14 percent) regard one or more New Age techniques as effective in human resource management. The same study determined that this group is also inclined to be sympathetic to the underlying New Age worldview. When coerced to participate in company-sponsored New Age motivational programs, some employees have reacted by effectively filing religious discrimination lawsuits against their employers.

Biblical Evaluation

(1) For the Christian there can be no retreat from the basic premise of God's existence given in Genesis 1:1— "In the beginning God created the heavens and the earth." By attempting to remove this premise, the New Ager (perhaps unwittingly) destroys the very basis of knowledge and sanity. Without the Creator-creature distinction we are all of us alone in a meaningless universe in which there can be no legitimate order. The only order that can remain on acceptance of the New Age doctrine of existence is the order imposed by despotic force.

(2) The previous statement is reinforced by a second principle, namely, that the absence of a divinely revealed morality leaves mankind in a state of hopeless moral chaos. Without moral responsibility to the Creator there can be no responsibility except to oneself, as New Age mentors agree. In such a view, law becomes a joke and savagery can be legitimized. New Agers do not fear this condition because, contrary to universal experience, they romantically believe that man is inherently "good," whatever that can mean. Indeed, in order to teach such a doctrine, one would have to be living under an approximate code of Judeo-Christian morality, because only under that system do terms like "good" and "evil" have any comprehensible meaning.

(3) Since, according to New Age, we all project our own reality, redemption becomes superfluous. The doctrine of sin is viewed as an evil concept that induces negative self-esteem. Therefore we need only to recover our self-confidence. Christ could not die for anybody's sins, New Age says, since Christ was only an archetypal

man like Buddha. We need to become like Christ and Buddha. However, Christ and Buddha are radically opposed in their worldviews. Buddha: "Dependence on all gods is unhealthy."

(4) The New Age way to Christhood (or Buddhahood) is by building good karma throughout many reincarnations. Reincarnation, however, is a purely intellectual invention without evidence. On the other hand, the historical evidence that Christ arose from the dead for our justification (Rom. 4:25) is overwhelming.

(5) It is presupposed in New Age that human society is participating in a grand program of evolution to greater things. However, objective science has demonstrated that, far from getting better, the cosmos is in a process of winding down to destruction. Socially also, humanity has become more and more violent and destructive (2 Tim. 3:13), notwithstanding an aggregation of technological insights.

Things to Keep in Mind

(1) New Age adherents are not all alike. Some are militant, possibly demon-possessed, and apparently driven to a counter-cultural position that seeks the destruction of good from motives of sheer satanic spite. These probably comprise a minority. The majority are victims of desperate propaganda. They have been disappointed in life. Their church backgrounds are weak or nonexistent. Their understanding of the Christian Gospel is unclear or confused. Such are easy prey for cults, especially New Ageism at this time. For the Christian, love never ceases to be the rule of operation. Remembering that he too was once without God and going astray, the Christian seeks the redemption and good of his neighbors. These neighbors include New Age disciples.

(2) Christians need to affirm Christian truth that speaks to the issues that New Agers are obsessed with:

(a) Is there any real meaning in the world?

Answer: Yes, there is meaning, because the world

was created by a rational, just, and holy God. The implications of this basic fact need to be clarified for the New Age disciple.

(b) How can I be significant among so many billions of people throughout time?

Answer: The infinite, all-knowing Creator knows all about you, and wants you to know His personal, eternal friendship.

(c) Everybody is dying all around me, and so am I. What hope do I have in such a world?

Answer: Death is not normal; it is the wages of sin. But God wants to give you eternal life. Jesus Christ died and rose again, on account of sin, to provide everlasting and abundant life with Him by trusting in Him.

(3) Remember, societies that have embraced the fundamental doctrines of the New Age, like India, are as a necessary result wallowing in disease and mass starvation. This telling historical fact needs to be pointed out to New Age disciples.

(4) Parents whose children are in public schools need to know and be involved in what their children are being taught. They should be aware of laws that are provided for protection of their children from so-called "Values Clarification" and other teaching vehicles by which occult religions can be forced on children in public schools. Such laws include the Federal Protection of Pupil Rights Act (Hatch Amendment). The NEA opposed this law that prohibits psychological, political, sexual, and religious interference by schools in the lives of children.

COMPARISON OF CULTS, WORLD RELIGIONS, AND THE OCCULT
by Bob Wallace

MAJOR NON-CHRISTIAN RELIGIONS OF THE EAST

DOCTRINE	HINDUISM	JAINISM	BUDDHISM	SKIHISM
JESUS CHRIST John 1:1-3, 14; 8:58 Col. 1:16-20	No recognition of any kind given to Christ.	No recognition of any kind given to Christ. This is regarded as a sect within Hinduism.	No recognition of any kind given to Christ.	No recognition of any kind given to Christ.
TRI-UNITY Luke 3:21-22 1 Peter 1:2 Matt. 28:19 John 15:26	God is an *It* in Philosophical Hinduism, and in Popular Hinduism there are great multitudes of Gods. In the ultimate sense, man is God.	Jainism is an atheistic religion in that it denies the existence of a Supreme Being or Creator. The universe is uncreated and eternal.	No recognition of the Tri-Unity. Most Buddhist sects are either polytheistic, pantheistic, or atheistic. (There are many different forms of Buddhism.)	The Sikh concept of God is monotheistic, but is so mystical and abstract that it borders on pantheism. Sikhs claim that all religions worship the same God under different names.
EVERYONE HAS AN ETERNAL SPIRIT Matt. 25:46 Dan. 12:2 Ecc. 12:7 Rev. 20:11-15	Yes, and it continues through many incarnations.	Same as Hinduism.	Gautama, founder of Buddhism, claimed that men have no souls.	Similar to Hinduism; includes Hindu ideas of karma and transmigration.
BORN A LOST SOUL Ps. 51:5 James 1:15 Rom. 5:12-21 1 Cor. 15:21-22	No recognition of sin and moral guilt. Sin is an illusion.	The living soul is bound to non-living matter by karma that keeps the soul in bondage to matter.	Gautama, the founder of Buddhism, claimed that men do not have souls.	Original sin not recognized. Sins committed, expiated by repeating and meditating on the name of "God"—Sat Nam.

SALVATION John 3:14-17 Acts 16:31 Rom. 3:21-30; 10:4, 9-10 Gal. 2:16	Hinduism is a works system. Forgiveness of sin does not fit into the picture of karma (cause and effect). Each person has many lives in which to reach salvation.	No mercy or grace, only works. One of the most severe systems of legalism the world has known. The ahimsa (non-injury) concept is unworkable as a practical living concept.	Theravada Buddhism: salvation by self-effort. Mahayana Buddhism: salvation of one dependent on the grace of others.	Righteous living required in addition to the grace of Sat Nam to achieve salvation.
SACRED BOOKS (AUTHORITY)	Sruti-revealed script. Smriti-tradition. These groups of books contain many contradictions.	No clear and consistent authority—the three sects do not agree on which books are canonical. None of the books put in written form till 1,000 years after founder's death.	Buddhist scriptures and sayings attributed to Gautama were written about four centuries after his death, and there is no way to be certain they are really his words.	The Granth—a most difficult book to read; worshiped by Sikhs.
SUGGESTED APPROACHES FOR PRESENTING THE CHRISTIAN FAITH	1. Address the Hindu argument that all religions are the same. 2. Emphasize the unique claims of Jesus. 3. Point out that no other religion offers a real solution to the problem of sin. 4. Note that all books of the Bible are harmonious; Hindu scriptures contradict one another. 5. Inform that man is born as a lost human headed for eternity in hell because he inherits the sin of Adam as federal head of the race, he inherits a sin nature, and he will sin during life.	1. The ahimsa concept is unworkable since there is no way a human being can avoid killing living organisms by the millions. 2. Note that though the problem of sin is defined differently, it is important in this religion. The issue is whether a sinner can atone for his own sins. 3. There is no clear and consistent authority as compared to the Bible. 4. Adapt arguments from Hinduism. Point out that we live in a cursed environment, as evidenced by disease, war, injustice, etc.	1. Give a positive and clear exposition of the claims of Christ, and His victory over sin and death. 2. Christ offers salvation; Buddhism does not. Each person must work out his own salvation. 3. Adjust and accommodate for the manner in which Buddhism has become embedded in the culture. 4. Make a strong case for the Bible—archeology, history, and prophecy.	1. Emphasize the personality and work of Jesus, and His substitutionary death on behalf of sinful men. 2. Note that the God of the Bible is NOT worshiped by all religions—the Tri-Unity is unique! 3. Stress should be placed on the vitality of a personal relationship with Christ. 4. Point out that a scripture should be easily readable to all who may be motivated to read it. 5. Adapt Hinduism arguments. Make a strong case for the Bible.

MAJOR NON-CHRISTIAN RELIGIONS OF THE EAST

DOCTRINE	ZOROASTRIANISM	CONFUCIANISM	TAOISM	SHINTOISM
JESUS CHRIST John 1:1-3, 14; 8:58 Col. 1:16-20	(A "Saviour/Deliverer" will come.) No recognition of Jesus Christ. (This religion closest to Christianity of Eastern religions.)	Jesus Christ is not recognized. There is just a hint of God and heaven.	Jesus Christ is not recognized. There is no personal Creator-God. Popular Taoism degenerated into a system of magical practices and incantations.	There is no recognition of Jesus Christ.
TRI-UNITY Luke 3:21-22 1 Peter 1:2 Matt. 28:19 John 15:26	Tri-Unity is not recognized. In its place is a dualism of a Good God and an Evil God.	The Tri-Unity is not recognized. There is just a hint of God and heaven. This is a combination of ancestor worship, animism, and social traditions.	The Tri-Unity is not recognized. There is no Father, Son, and Holy Spirit. Taoism is involved with nature, mysticism, and impersonal principles.	There is no personal Creator-God. Shintoism involves polytheism and nature worship.
EVERYONE HAS AN ETERNAL SPIRIT Matt. 25:46 Dan. 12:2 Ecc. 12:7 Rev. 20:11-15	Yes	Not recognized	Not recognized	Not recognized
BORN A LOST SOUL Ps. 51:5 James 1:15 Rom. 5:12-21 1 Cor. 15:21-22	No	No. Human nature is good.	Not acknowledged	No. The gods made man, and therefore man is good.

266

SALVATION John 3:14-17 Acts 16:31 Rom. 3:21-30; 10:4, 9-10 Gal. 2:16	Salvation by works, not faith. If good works outweigh bad works, one is allowed into heaven. (There will be sinners in heaven.)	Salvation is not needed—human nature is good.	Salvation is achieved by following the Tao—living a life of simplicity and quiet.	Salvation is deliverance from the trouble and evil of the world. No concept of sin and depravity. No Saviour needed.
SACRED BOOKS (AUTHORITY)	The Zend-Avesta (This religion is characterized by empty ritual, ceremonial forms, and by legalism.)	Analects, the sayings of Confucius.	Known as the Tao Tsang, and consists of about 1,120 volumes.	Eighth century Kojiki and Nihongi are entirely unverifiable, based on stories devoid of any historical facts.
SUGGESTED APPROACHES FOR PRESENTING THE CHRISTIAN FAITH	1. Emphasize the problem of sin and the futility of works. Few, if any, can be certain of their salvation with such a credit/balance kind of belief. 2. Zoroastrianism offers ritual and teaching, but Christ offers a relationship. 3. Zoroastrianism teaches that a Savior will come; Christians know that a Saviour *has* come, which should offer a good point of entry. 4. Make a strong case for the Bible.	1. Point out difference between the ethics of Confucianism and the NEED of salvation through Christ. 2. Human nature is NOT good; we are all born as lost souls headed for eternity in hell. 3. Point out/emphasize the totally different characters of Confucianism with its ancestor worship, animism, and social traditions, and the faith of Jesus Christ. 4. Make a strong case for the Bible—archeology, history, and prophecy.	1. Point out that Taoism is not a revelation from a personal Creator; its only authority is human speculation. 2. Emphasize that people think and practice evil things, and this is proven by the evidence of our senses and thoughts. 3. The ministry of the Holy Spirit in convicting men of their sin, and revealing the path to salvation should be made clear. 4. Note that people involved with popular forms of this religion are plagued with demonic possession and fear.	1. One of the most important issues is the problem of sin. The cruelty and moral guilt of man must be acknowledged, and Christ shown to be the solution. 2. Reliability of the Bible as affirmed by archeology, history, and fulfilled prophecy must be contrasted with the pure myths of the Kojiki and Nihongi. 3. Emphasis must be placed on the resurrection of Jesus as a victorious alternative to the centuries of ancestor worship found in Shinto.

DOCTRINE	MAJOR NON-CHRISTIAN RELIGIONS OF THE EAST		PSEUDO-CHRISTIAN RELIGIONS OF THE WEST	
	ISLAM	JUDAISM	MORMONISM	JEHOVAH'S WITNESSES
JESUS CHRIST John 1:1-3, 14; 8:58 Col. 1:16-20	Jesus Christ is nothing more than a prophet of God.	Rabbinic teaching holds that there must be two Messiahs: Son of Joseph, who would die; and Son of David, who would establish the kingdom on earth.	Jesus Christ, spirit brother of Lucifer, received a body of flesh and bone and is now elevated to deity. He is referred to as our "elder brother," one of many gods.	Jesus is a god, not God the Son. He is represented as the first creation of Jehovah. Before his incarnation he was Michael, captain of Jehovah's hosts.
TRI-UNITY Luke 3:21-22 1 Peter 1:2 Matt. 28:19 John 15:26	There is only one God—Allah.	There is only one God—Yahweh.	Mormon theology is henotheistic—it exalts one God (the Father-God) above the other gods in the universe. The Holy Spirit is an impersonal spiritual "fluid."	The doctrine of the Tri-Unity is denied emphatically. The deity of the Holy Spirit is denied—he is likened to a radar beam.
EVERYONE HAS AN ETERNAL SPIRIT Matt. 25:46 Dan. 12:2 Ecc. 12:7 Rev. 20:11-15	Yes	Yes	Yes	They argue for painless extinction, indicating man does not possess an immortal soul, just a combination of breath and flesh.
BORN A LOST SOUL Ps. 51:5 James 1:15 Rom. 5:12-21 1 Cor. 15:21-22	No	Judaism rejects the doctrine of original sin, saying that sin is an act not a state.	Mormons deny the doctrine of original sin and teach that the Fall of man was a good and necessary thing. There is no imputed sin nature.	Adam's sin imputed to mankind, as federal head of the race. However, a sin nature apparently not inherited by the race.

SALVATION John 3:14-17 Acts 16:31 Rom. 3:21-30; 10:4, 9-10 Gal. 2:16	After the resurrection, each man's deeds will be weighed to determine his destiny—heaven or hell.	Man does not need redemption. Repentance (turning back to God) is all that is needed when one fails to live according to the Law. (Torah)	Christ's death and atonement only removes guilt for past sins. Man must earn own salvation by Christ + good works, repentance, baptism by immersion, laying on of hands, and obedience to Mormon teaching.	Christ's death removed effects of Adam's sin, and puts man in a position to work out his own salvation.
SACRED BOOKS (AUTHORITY)	Koran—most important Tauret Pentateuch (of Moses) Zabur (Psalms of David) Injil (Evangel of Jesus)	The Torah The Old Testament The Talmud	The Bible, the Book of Mormon, Doctrines and Covenants, and the Pearl of Great Price. The Book of Mormon is a plagiaristic fraud.	"The New World Translation" of the Bible. An anonymous, gross distortion of Scripture.
SUGGESTED APPROACHES FOR PRESENTING THE CHRISTIAN FAITH	1. Christians must focus on the problem of sin, contrasting what God of the Bible has done about it with what Allah has NOT done. 2. Because of sectarian differences questions should be asked to determine particular views. 3. Point out that the Muslim has no personal relationship with God. 4. Focus on the true deity of Jesus Christ, the lost nature of man, and the salvation offered by Jesus. 5. Point out the error of works righteousness.	1. Get acknowledgment that the original Christians were all Jews. 2. Note that a Jew does not have to give up his Jewishness to become a Christian—Christianity is not a Gentile religion. 3. Point out that the New Testament was written by Jews (except Luke), and that Jesus was a Jew. 4. Focus on the meaning of Christ's sacrificial death and the fact of His resurrection. Emphasize Isaiah 53 as prophetic of Jesus' coming, and the New Testament resolving the Old Testament paradox of two Messiahs (One, twice).	1. Learn and attack the "pillars" of Mormonism; Melchizedek priesthood; nature of God; repentance; works salvation; hell; becoming a god; etc. 2. Point out that the teachings of Mormonism cannot be reconciled with the Bible—challenge them to compare. 3. Show a copy of the Smithsonian Institute publication that proves the Book of Mormon is a fantasy. The archeology of the New World refutes the Book of Mormon. 4. Show evidence of plagiarism from the *King James* Bible in the Book of Mormon.	1. Challenge them to be willing to abide by the verdict of the Bible regardless of J.W. teachings. 2. Present a clear biblical case for Christ's and Holy Spirit's deity, and persist until accepted. J.W. will then crumble. 3. Be prepared to do battle with their "proof texts." Insist on looking at the complete context of each "proof text." 4. Present a clear biblical case for the Tri-Unity & persist until accepted. 5. Demonstrate that their teachings follow exactly those of their founder Russell who was an uneducated opportunist.

DOCTRINE	PSEUDO-CHRISTIAN RELIGIONS OF THE WEST			
	CHRISTIAN SCIENCE	SEVENTH-DAY ADVENTISM	UNITY SCHOOL/CHRISTIANITY	THEOSOPHY
JESUS CHRIST John 1:1-3, 14; 8:58 Col. 1:16-20	Jesus' deity denied. Jesus did not die on the cross—it was illusory. The C. S. Jesus is a principle, an idea, a gnostic Jesus.	Orthodox position in regard to Jesus Christ.	Jesus Christ was not the Christ. Jesus was only a man who possessed a spiritual identity known as the Christ. Christ did not die to pay for our sins.	Denies that Jesus is the Christ. Only difference between Jesus and other men is that He is further along in the evolutionary cycle. Denies His bodily resurrection.
TRI-UNITY Luke 3:21-22 1 Peter 1:2 Matt. 28:19 John 15:26	The doctrine of the Tri-Unity is denied. The soul or mind of man is God. The Holy Spirit is Christian Science itself.	Orthodox position in regard to Tri-Unity.	God is not a Person, but a principle. God does not possess life, intelligence, and will. God is life, intelligence, and will. God is in each person. (pantheistic)	God has no intellect, emotions, or will. No personal attributes. This is also a Gnostic-type religion.
EVERYONE HAS AN ETERNAL SPIRIT Matt. 25:46 Dan. 12:2 Ecc. 12:7 Rev. 20:11-15	Man exists as part of the great Mind, since Mind is ALL.	Man enters into "soul sleep" at physical death, and is regenerated at resurrection. (non-orthodox).	Yes, through endless reincarnations.	Yes, through many reincarnations and interludes in purgatory (Kamaloka).
BORN A LOST SOUL Ps. 51:5 James 1:15 Rom. 5:12-21 1 Cor. 15:21-22	Man is not in a fallen state and he is incapable of sin.	Orthodox position on the condition of the natural man.	Men are not sinners in need of a Saviour.	Personal sin removed by suffering in Kamaloka, and personal salvation obtained through various reincarnations ending in absorption of the individual ego.

SALVATION John 3:14-17 Acts 16:31 Rom. 3:21-30; 10:4, 9-10 Gal. 2:16	Salvation consists of mental deliverance from error. A Saviour is not necessary.	Orthodox position on salvation. (The wicked will be annihilated.)	Atonement reunites our consciousness with the God-consciousness. Salvation occurs when one believes this doctrine and removes himself from the illusion of sin.	Follows Hinduism's teaching of self-salvation through meditation, mystical experiences, knowledge, and effort. Jesus' vicarious death is repulsive.
SACRED BOOKS (AUTHORITY)	The Bible—with numerous corrections to make it fit Mary Baker Eddy's ideas. (Miscellaneous Writings, and Science and Health.)	The Bible—supplemented by the writings of Ellen G. White.	The Bible is only one of many books that contain spiritual truth.	The Secret Doctrine. Isis Unveiled. The Sacred Books of the East (plus direct revelation from the "Mahatmas").
SUGGESTED APPROACHES FOR PRESENTING THE CHRISTIAN FAITH	1. Demonstrate from the Bible the deity of Jesus Christ, and the constitution of the Tri-Unity. 2. Prove from the Bible that man is born as a lost soul headed for eternity in hell. 3. Show that Jesus was the incarnation of Christ, and that He died on the cross to provide a way out for mankind. 4. Demonstrate through Scripture that man cannot achieve salvation through good works; he must change his allegiance from the world to Jesus. 5. Show that this cult is based on obvious logical fallacies and pseudophilosophical jargon.	1. Recognize that the Adventist may well be a born-again believer. 2. Be firm in your knowledge of and argument for not being under the Law. 3. Be prepared to defend your position against soul-sleep. 4. Point out that the Bible does not support the doctrine of the destruction of the wicked. 5. Be armed to defend the doctrine of the eternal spirit. 6. Since the Adventist acknowledges the infallibility of the Bible, a sound grasp of the Scriptures that apply to the above doctrines is indispensable and effective.	1. Skewer the perverted doctrine of the Trinity held by the Unity School by direct reference to the appropriate Scriptures. 2. Point out that Christ Jesus was not a perfect man indwelt by the Christ-consciousness present in every person. We all then are not miniature "christs." 3. Emphasize that "salvation" in the form of endless reincarnations is a doctrine completely foreign to the Bible. 4. Demonstrate that the resurrection of Jesus was not spirit alone but body and spirit, and that this was the foreshadowing of the resurrection of all men.	1. One initial approach is to get an agreement on the Bible. Is it acceptable? 2. Point out that Theosophy's view of man and the universe evolving through the various planes toward a union with the Absolute is absolutely not scriptural. 3. Show that there is no concept of forgiveness of sins in Theosophy, only endless reincarnations. 4. Prove from the Bible that all persons are not innate divinity, and in time become christs. 5. Press to gain an acknowledgment of the vicarious sacrifice of Jesus and its application to salvation for all who believe in Him.

OCCULT RELIGIONS AND SYSTEMS

DOCTRINE	WITCHCRAFT & SATANISM	ASTROLOGY	SPIRITUALISM	THE KABBALAH
JESUS CHRIST John 1:1-3, 14; 8:58 Col. 1:16-20	(Not well-defined.) Jesus recognized at least to the extent of Him being the prime adversary of Satan/witchcraft.	Astrology has replaced the personal Creator with an impersonal cosmos.	Jesus was a great Jewish medium. His deity denied, along with the Virgin Birth and the Resurrection.	Not recognized (Saviour to come)
TRI-UNITY Luke 3:21-22 1 Peter 1:2 Matt. 28:19 John 15:26	Satan is the ape of God. Worshipers renounce God at black masses.	There is nothing in astrology which is comparable to the Tri-Unity, other than the cosmos and secular humanism.	God is not personal but impersonal. God is the "Great Spirit" or the "Supreme Spirit."	Utterly transcendent; the Ain Soph, with ten emanations leading to successive levels to the material world (Gnostic).
EVERYONE HAS AN ETERNAL SPIRIT Matt. 25:46 Dan. 12:2 Ecc. 12:7 Rev. 20:11-15	Not defined	Astrology is friendly to reincarnation, which then infers that man must have an eternal spirit.	A dogma of Spiritualism is that there is a continuity in the life of man, an eternal progression toward perfection of the human spirit.	The doctrine is that souls existed before they were given bodies, and they are reincarnated repeatedly.
BORN A LOST SOUL Ps. 51:5 James 1:15 Rom. 5:12-21 1 Cor. 15:21-22	Not defined	Astrology does not recognize man as a lost person in need of salvation.	There is no heaven or hell. Man is not lost; the doorway to reformation is never closed.	Each soul must accomplish a certain mission, and failing must be reincarnated until successful (metempsychosis).

SALVATION John 3:14-17 Acts 16:31 Rom. 3:21-30; 10:4, 9-10 Gal. 2:16	Not defined	Since astrology does not recognize man's lost condition, there is also no need for salvation or a means to achieve it.	Spiritualists reject the biblical concept of the sinful nature of man and his need for substitutionary atonement.	Salvation consists of the soul's ascent to God from the material world to the supernal world, by gaining esoteric knowledge about God.
SACRED BOOKS (AUTHORITY)	Some form of missal, sometimes bound in human skin.	The signs of the zodiac and their positions before Christ, based on a Ptolemaic system.	None. The Bible condemns witches, wizards, sorcerers, seers, fortune-tellers, mediums, diviners, and necromancers.	Book of Formation, Book of Splendor
SUGGESTED APPROACHES FOR PRESENTING THE CHRISTIAN FAITH	1. Make discreet inquiries to determine why the person is into witchcraft/satanism; power over others, mystery; indulgence/gratification; financial success; pride and intellectual arrogance; rebellion against society. 2. Find a Scripture that will speak specifically to the reason the person is into witchcraft/satanism. 3. Point out that Satan is temporarily the ruler of this world, and get the person to read some of the many passages in Scripture describing the reality and danger in witchcraft/satanism. 4. Describe the plan of salvation.	1. Point out that the Bible repeatedly warns against divination. The Book of Daniel ridicules astrologers. 2. Disprove that the Bible supports the practice of astrology. 3. Show that astrology is actually an error of idolatry; that it relies on the creation rather than the Creator. It is a substitute for faith in God. 4. Explain that a person without Christ is a slave to the dominion of Satan, and that astrology is a tool of Satan. 5. Demonstrate the foolishness of astrology in that it is based on an earth-centered system, and is millennia out of date.	1. Note that the Scriptures clearly speak against attempts to communicate with the spirits of the dead. Make a case for the Bible being the inerrant Word of God. 2. Challenge the spiritualist to consider the very probable possibility of demonic activity in seances. 3. Point out that the Bible condemns witches, wizards, sorcerers, seers, fortune-tellers, mediums, soothsayers, diviners, and necromancers. 4. Challenge the spiritualist to test the spirit-guides/spirits with whether they confess Jesus Christ, or fail this declaration.	1. Point out that the sephiroth doctrine of the Kabbalah is a construct of man to satisfy a perceived conflict between the imminence and transcendence of God, and is not justified by either Jewish or Christian Scriptures. 2. Note that the Bible does not mention the sephiroth, and seems actually to contradict such a notion. 3. Explain that the exegetical techniques of the Kabbalah have no truth value because there is no scriptural justification for Hebrew being the sacred language, and one gets from the technique only what he puts into it through his presuppositions.

DOCTRINE	OCCULT RELIGIONS AND SYSTEMS		NEW RELIGIONS AND CULTS	
	THE I CHING	THE TAROT	TRANSCENDENTAL MEDITATION	THE UNIFICATION CHURCH
JESUS CHRIST John 1:1-3, 14; 8:58 Col. 1:16-20	Not recognized	Not recognized	No recognition given to Jesus Christ. TM is rooted in the Vedantic school of Hinduism.	Jesus Christ was a man, not the God-Man. Virgin Birth denied; the Resurrection was spiritual, not bodily.
TRI-UNITY Luke 3:21-22 1 Peter 1:2 Matt. 28:19 John 15:26	The ultimate reality is not God, but an impersonal, mysterious Tao.	Relates more to nature mysticism than to a personal God.	God is Brahman, the impersonal absolute of Hinduism.	Biblical doctrine of the Tri-Unity denied.
EVERYONE HAS AN ETERNAL SPIRIT Matt. 25:46 Dan. 12:2 Ecc. 12:7 Rev. 20:11-15	Not recognized	Not recognized	Yes, through many incarnations	Yes
BORN A LOST SOUL Ps. 51:5 James 1:15 Rom. 5:12-21 1 Cor. 15:21-22	Not recognized	Man's sinfulness is ignored.	Imputed sin and a sin nature are not recognized. Man's real problem is not sinfulness, but separation from his true Being.	Uncertain

SALVATION John 3:14-17 Acts 16:31 Rom. 3:21-30; 10:4, 9-10 Gal. 2:16	Not recognized. Evil and good complement one another.	No need for a Saviour or salvation.	TM is the only way out of the field of sin, and the only way to salvation and success in life. Man must raise himself to highest consciousness.	Forgiveness of sins not necessary for salvation. One atones for his sins through constant effort. No need to turn to Jesus, turn to Moon.
SACRED BOOKS (AUTHORITY)	The Book of Changes. Used as an oracle to discover the events in the unseen world, which parallel ours, and thus predict the future.	No authority of any kind.	The Vedas The Brahma Sutras The Bhagavad-Gita, as interpreted by Maharishi Mahesh Yogi	Divine Principle
SUGGESTED APPROACHES FOR PRESENTING THE CHRISTIAN FAITH	1. Show that the I Ching concept of good and evil complementing one another is dramatically opposed to biblical teaching. 2. Make a case for the archeological, historical, and prophetical testimony to the Bible. 3. Note that the roots of I Ching lie in Confucianism and Taoism; worthless mumbo-jumbo (ref. those approaches). 4. Point out that the use of I Ching is primarily divinatory, and the Bible speaks against such practices. 5. Get acknowledgment that the results of I Ching are quite ambiguous; they can easily be made to fit any situation.	1. The Tarot is much like astrology in that it is a system of divining the future. 2. The Tarot is rooted in mysticism, occultism, divination, and magic. The Bible speaks against such practices. 3. The arguments used in discussing astrology and spiritualism may be used against the user of Tarot cards.	1. Get an acknowledgment that TM is not a religion, but is a religious practice in the raja yoga tradition of Vedantic Hinduism. 2. Point out that this tradition has exclusive truth claims which cannot be reconciled with those of the Bible. 3. As for I Ching, make a case for the archeological, historical, and prophetical testimony to the Bible. 4. Explain that the technique of TM renders the mind passive; however, Christian meditation and prayer make the mind and spirit active in deepening the commitment to Jesus Christ.	1. Gain acknowledgment of the inerrant nature of the Bible, and of its revealed truth. 2. Point out that the "Rev." Moon fits Christ's description of the false messiahs who will come in the end times, trying to mislead even the elect. 3. Show that the Bible gives a clear picture of Jesus that is totally different than the one that Moon promotes. 4. Get agreement that the Bible teaches that man is born as a lost soul headed for eternity in hell, and that everyone inherits a sin nature and sins. 5. Show that the only way out for man is a salvation not of works but faith in Jesus.

DOCTRINE	NEW RELIGIONS AND CULTS	
	HARE KRISHNA MOVEMENT	THE WAY INTERNATIONAL
JESUS CHRIST

John 1:1-3, 14;
8:58
Col. 1:16-20 | Not recognized | Jesus is the Son of God, but not God. He did not exist before His incarnation (Dynamic Monarchianism). |
| TRI-UNITY

Luke 3:21-22
1 Peter 1:2
Matt. 28:19
John 15:26 | Krishna worshiped as god. This is one of the few non-Christian movements that worships a god that is personal and infinite. | Unitarian in its view of God. One in substance and only one in Person (the Father). The Holy Spirit is another name for the Father. |
| EVERYONE HAS AN ETERNAL SPIRIT

Matt. 25:46
Dan. 12:2
Ecc. 12:7
Rev. 20:11-15 | Yes, through many incarnations | People are born only as flesh without any spirit. One only gets a spirit when one believes in Jesus. Soul sleeps after death until second coming of Jesus. |
| BORN A LOST SOUL

Ps. 51:5
James 1:15
Rom. 5:12-21
1 Cor. 15:21-22 | No imputed sin and sin nature. Sin is caused by ignorance and illusion. | Apparently not |

SALVATION John 3:14-17 Acts 16:31 Rom. 3:21-30; 10:4, 9-10 Gal. 2:16	The way of salvation is chanting the Hare Krishna mantra and performing devotional services to Krishna.	Must accept Jesus as Saviour.
SACRED BOOKS (AUTHORITY)	Bhagavad-gita Bhagavata Purana	Jesus Christ is not God The Bible Tells Me So The Word's Way Receiving the Holy Spirit Today
SUGGESTED APPROACHES FOR PRESENTING THE CHRISTIAN FAITH	1. Emphasize that Krishna is a legendary figure who taught a works system of salvation, and his life was of questionable morality. Jesus was a historical figure who offered salvation as a free gift to those who believe in Him, and He led a spotless life. 2. Point out that the Bible does not support in any way the concept of reincarnation, and that this can be a snare and delusion. 3. Show that the Bible teaches that sin is not caused by ignorance and illusion, but rebellion against God. Describe imputed sin, the sin nature, and sins committed, and prove from the Bible the consequent need for salvation.	1. Focus on the issue of Christ's deity. Be prepared to show from the Scriptures that Jesus Christ is God. 2. Point out that the truth must not be based on experience, but on the teachings of Jesus Christ found in the Bible. 3. Use Scripture in context to refute the concept of a person not having a spirit. 4. Emphasize that the Bible clearly defines the Tri-Unity of God, and the person and deity of the Holy Spirit. 5. Refute the concept of "soul sleep" through scriptural passages in context.

BIBLIOGRAPHY

The following is a brief list of some of the *general* books on religions and cults. More specific works can be found in their bibliographies. If you need an in-depth understanding of a particular religion or cult, don't limit yourself to analyses by nonmembers. Use these, but also try to obtain some of the literature published by the cult. The combination will give you a more accurate perspective.

Anderson, J.N.D. *The World's Religions*. Fourth revised edition. Grand Rapids: William B. Eerdmans Publishing Co., 1976.

Bach, Marcus. *Major Religions of the World*. New York: Abingdon Press, 1959.

Braden, Charles S. *These Also Believe*. New York: The Macmillan Publishing Co., Inc., 1951.

_____. *The World's Religions*. rev. ed. New York: Abingdon Press, 1954.

Bradley, David G. *A Guide to the World's Religions*. Englewood Cliffs, N.J.: Prentice-Hall, 1963.

Cohen, Daniel. *The New Believers*. New York: M. Evans and Company, 1975.

Davies, Horton. *The Challenge of the Sects*. Philadelphia: Westminster Press, 1961.

Ellwood, Robert S., Jr. *Many Peoples, Many Faiths*. Englewood Cliffs, N.J.: Prentice-Hall, Inc., 1976.

Gerstner, John H. *The Theology of the Major Sects*. Grand Rapids: Baker Book House, 1960.

Heydt, Henry J. *A Comparison of World Religions*. Fort Washington, Pa.: Christian Literature Crusade, 1967.

Hoekema, Anthony. *The Four Major Cults*. Grand Rapids: William B. Eerdmans Publishing Co., 1963.

Martin, Walter R. *The Kingdom of the Cults*. Revised and

expanded edition. Minneapolis: Bethany Fellowship, 1985.

―――――. *The New Cults*. Santa Ana, Calif.: Vision House, 1980.

Mathison, Richard R. *Faiths, Cults, and Sects of America*. Indianapolis: Bobbs-Merrill Co., Inc., 1960.

Needleman, Jacob. *The New Religions*. New York: Doubleday and Co., 1970.

Noss, John B. *Man's Religions*. Fifth edition. New York: The Macmillan Publishing Co., Inc., 1974.

Petersen, William J. *Those Curious New Cults*. New Canaan, Conn.: Keats Publishing, Inc., 1973.

Ringgren, Helmer, and Ström, Åke V. *Religions of Mankind*. Philadelphia: Fortress Press, 1967.

Rosten, Leo. *Religions of America*. New York: Simon and Schuster, Inc., 1975.

Schoeps, Hans-Joachim. *The Religions of Mankind*. Garden City, N.Y.: Doubleday and Co., 1966.

Smith, Huston. *The Religions of Man*. New York: Harper & Row Publishers, Inc., 1958.

Smith, Paul B. *Other Gospels*. London: Marshall, Morgan & Scott, 1970.

Sparks, Jack. *The Mindbenders*. Nashville: Thomas Nelson Publishers, Inc., 1977.

Van Baalen, J.K. *The Chaos of Cults*. Fourth revised edition. Grand Rapids: William B. Eerdmans Publishing Co., 1962.

Vos, Howard F., ed. *Religions in a Changing World*. Chicago: Moody Press, 1959.